Brexit and the Future of Private International Law in English Courts

Brexit and the Future of Private International Law in English Courts

MUKARRUM AHMED

LLB (Hons), LLM (Lond), PhD (Aberd), Barrister (Lincoln's Inn)

Lecturer in Business Law, University of Lancaster

OXFORD
UNIVERSITY PRESS

OXFORD
UNIVERSITY PRESS

Great Clarendon Street, Oxford, OX2 6DP,
United Kingdom

Oxford University Press is a department of the University of Oxford.
It furthers the University's objective of excellence in research, scholarship,
and education by publishing worldwide. Oxford is a registered trade mark of
Oxford University Press in the UK and in certain other countries

First Edition published in 2022

Published in the United States of America by Oxford University Press
198 Madison Avenue, New York, NY 10016, United States of America

British Library Cataloguing in Publication Data

Data available

Library of Congress Control Number: 2022900585

ISBN 978–0–19–284811–6

DOI: 10.1093/oso/9780192848116.001.0001

Foreword

One can but try to muster a wry smile at the antithetical nature of the two defining events for the conflict of laws in the United Kingdom in the past half-century. The significance of the first, the United Kingdom's accession to what was then the European Economic Community in 1973, unfolded over a period of four decades, from early negotiations concerning the UK's accession to the 1968 Brussels Convention (completed in 1978) and possible harmonisation of choice of law rules for contractual and non-contractual obligations (partially achieved by the conclusion in 1980 of the Rome Convention on the law applicable to contractual obligations) to the UK's participation in several legislative initiatives in the sphere of civil justice in the first two decades of the twenty-first century, including the Brussels I (and recast Brussels I), Rome I, and Rome II Regulations. The second, the UK's withdrawal from the European Union, was realised rather more suddenly, from the narrow referendum vote in 2016 and the ensuing political flux, via the Withdrawal Agreement (24 January 2020) and the UK-EU Trade and Co-operation Agreement (30 December 2020), to the end of the transition (implementation) period on 31 December 2020.

It would, however, be misleading to characterise this history as a simple rise and fall of the European Union's influence upon the UK's legal systems. Two underlying truths must also be acknowledged. First, the UK's participation in the common justice area was always equivocal, revealed in early doubts about the choice of law project and more concretely in the opt-out negotiated by the UK and Ireland from measures adopted under what is now Title V of Part Three of the Treaty on the Functioning of the European Union. That opt-out meant that the UK did not participate in some of the more ambitious EU private international law initiatives, and led some of our European partners to perceive us as less than a full partners in the enterprise. Secondly, the UK's private international law landscape has undoubtedly been transformed beyond recognition since 1973. This is true not only of the legislative rulebook, and the body of judicial decisions, but also of the ways in which those who study, practice, and apply the law think about the conflict of laws and the functions which it performs. It is no longer sufficient to think about the subject as enlightened common lawyers, as Dicey and Morris once did. Instead, today's expert must carry a well-stocked legal toolbox, bringing insights (for example) from public and public international law, contract and constitutional law, legal history, and human rights law. As a result, the discipline has been revitalised.

In this book, Dr Mukarrum Ahmed casts his gaze upon the transformative effect that the UK's EU membership, and its abrupt cancellation, have had—and will continue to have—upon the private international law of England and Wales concerning civil and commercial matters. He considers not only the post-Brexit landscape, but also the process of transition from EU to retained EU law, and possible future developments, including possible accession by the UK to the 2007 Lugano Convention (an option which now seems politically remote) and to the 2019 Hague Judgments Convention.

After an opening chapter, which surveys the historical development and key constitutional features of the current legal framework, Dr Ahmed sub-divides his analysis along traditional lines with chapters on jurisdiction, foreign judgments, and the applicable law. In the closing chapter, he reflects on the current state of the law and offers his own perspective as to the most desirable direction of travel. He is critical of what he describes as the 'substantive law paradigm' of English private international law, prioritising the parties' rights and obligations *inter se*, and the court's role in protecting those rights and enforcing those obligations, over the horizontal relationship between legal systems operating under state sovereignty. He sees both the retention of the Rome I and Rome II Regulations ('a new and unique category of law that is neither EU law nor English law *per se*') and broadening treaty networks, in particular under the auspices of the Hague Conference on private international law, as antidotes to the dominance of this paradigm in common law thinking.

The law is constantly moving. Since Dr Ahmed delivered the manuscript for this work, the Supreme Court has (finally) handed down its decision in the second *Brownlie* appeal (*FS Cairo (Nile Plaza) LLc v Brownlie* [2021] UKSC 45, [2021] 3 WLR 1011). Lord Leggatt's powerful judgment, dissenting on the gateway issue, reflects a growing dissatisfaction with the current jurisdictional framework and may—fingers crossed while typing—ultimately prove to be more influential in shaping the law. Separately, the Law Commission has announced a new project on the rules of the conflict of laws as they apply to emerging technology, including smart contracts and digital assets.

These are exciting times for the conflict of laws in England and Wales, and elsewhere in the United Kingdom. Mukarrum Ahmed's new book provides an informative and thought-provoking account of the journey we have all taken, and the one on which we are about to embark. I congratulate him on its publication.

Professor Andrew Dickinson
Oxford
31 December 2021

Preface

> The end of a melody is not its goal; but nonetheless, if the melody had not reached its end it would not have reached its goal either. A parable.[1]

From an initial rebellious deafness on the part of common lawyers to the crescendo of EU private international law in English courts, the tune has now finally come to an end with Brexit, but the goal persists. The goal of a UK private international law regime that is grounded in the common law's ingenuity and is capable of providing strategic leadership in the Hague Conference's international judicial cooperation instruments.

This book is meant to be the first of its kind in the English language. It is intended for practitioners and academics with an interest in private international law. It aims to provide a clear and concise commentary on the principal changes in the post-Brexit private international law regime for civil and commercial matters in England and Wales. The book covers the three classical pillars of private international law: jurisdiction, the recognition and enforcement of judgments, and the applicable law. In the process, some of the main areas of difficulty will be indicated and solutions will be offered. At this juncture, Brexit provides us with a once-in-a-generation opportunity to take stock of and survey our private international law rules with a view to proposing amendments to the law or adjusting its application.

During the course of writing this book it became apparent that the UK's accession to the Lugano II Convention would not materialise. Nonetheless and for the sake of comparison the Lugano II Convention's approach to particular issues has been referred to in the book where appropriate. The substance and form of the Hague Conventions of 2005 and 2019 is emblematic of the future direction of private international law in English courts. A path that is neither well-trodden nor European but one that is forged at the Hague Conference and ushers in a different multilateral relationship between the United Kingdom and the EU in matters of private international law. It is a private international law relationship that is not premised on unilateralism or regionalism but one that is founded in internationalism.

This book was necessarily written within a modest time frame because a longer period could not be afforded. The project grew out of the author's continued research interest in the developments surrounding Brexit and its implications for private international law. Professor Andrew Dickinson of the University of Oxford

[1] Friedrich Nietzsche, *Nietzsche: Human, All Too Human: A Book for Free Spirits* (RJ Hollingdale ed, CUP 1996) 360.

has been an excellent source of guidance from the project's inception to its very culmination. I would like to express my sincere gratitude to him for his interest in the project and for writing the Foreword of this book.

The book benefitted immensely from two research presentations on aspects of the topic at the SLS Conferences 2019 and 2020 at the University of Central Lancashire and the University of Exeter respectively. I have had the opportunity to test many an idea in the lectures and seminars of the Private International Law, International Commercial Litigation, and International Commercial Arbitration modules that I convene at the University of Lancaster. I would like to thank Professor David Milman, Professor Paul Beaumont, Professor Jonathan Harris QC, Professor Jonathan Fitchen, Professor Geert van Calster, and numerous unnamed lest not forgotten colleagues, reviewers, and curious students for their engagement with my work and the occasional modicum of scepticism. I am grateful to Andy Redman, Fay Gibbons, and Ella Capel-Smith at OUP for facilitating this project.

At a personal level, this book could not have been possible without the untiring support and encouragement of my partner, Nau'ma and daughters, Nurayn and Mashal. Further afield, the contributions of my parents and siblings have been instrumental in securing my progress. This book is dedicated to my family. They have been gracious enough to bear with me over a frenzied summer where my pursuits were largely esoteric.

Mukarrum Ahmed
August 2021
University of Lancaster

Contents

Table of Cases

EUROPEAN COURT OF JUSTICE

Chronological list

Alphabetical list

UNITED KINGDOM

NATIONAL CASES

Australia

Bermuda

Canada

France

Germany

Netherlands

Singapore

Spain

Table of Legislation

TABLE OF UK LEGISLATION

Statutes (UK)

Regulations and other Statutory Instruments (UK)

TABLE OF EUROPEAN LEGISLATION

European Union (EU)

DECISIONS

DIRECTIVES

REGULATIONS

Switzerland

Table of Treaties and International Instruments

BILATERAL TREATIES

1

Brexit and Private International Law

An End and a New Beginning

A. Objective and Method

The objective of this book is to provide a clear and concise commentary on the principal changes in the post-Brexit private international law regime for civil and commercial matters in England.[1] In the process, some of the main areas of difficulty will be indicated and solutions will be offered. Equivalent questions arise in relation to Scots law and Northern Irish law but these are outside the scope of this work.[2] The book covers jurisdiction, the recognition and enforcement of judgments and the applicable law in civil and commercial matters which were subject to the Brussels–Lugano regime, the Rome I Regulation, and the Rome II Regulation in the United Kingdom (UK).[3]

This book will examine post-Brexit private international law in English courts in the transition, post-transition, and future phases. Each chapter will consider the architecture of the private international law relationship between the UK and the European Union (EU) during the transition or implementation period, which ended on 31 December 2020.[4] The substantive part of each chapter will analyse the dynamics of the post-transition relationship between the UK and the EU in relation to cross-border judicial cooperation in civil and commercial matters. A roadmap of what lies ahead for private international law in English courts will be canvassed in Chapter 5 of this book.

[1] References to 'England' in this book are to be read as 'England and Wales'. European private international law instruments generally allocated jurisdiction to the courts of the UK which was a Member State. The identification of a court within the UK is generally a matter of domestic law.

[2] This book may refer to developments in Scots and Northern Irish law where considered appropriate.

[3] Council Regulation (EU) 1215/2012 of the European Parliament and of the Council of 12 December 2012 on jurisdiction and the recognition and enforcement of judgments in civil and commercial matters (recast) [2012] OJ L351/1 (hereafter Brussels Ia Regulation); Convention on jurisdiction and the recognition and enforcement of judgments in civil and commercial matters OJ L 339/3, 21.12.2007, OJ 2009, L 147/5 (hereafter Lugano II Convention); Regulation (EC) No 593/2008 of the European Parliament and of the Council of 17 June 2008 on the law applicable to contractual obligations (Rome I) OJ L/2008/177/6 (hereafter Rome I Regulation); Regulation (EC) No 864/2007 of the European Parliament and of the Council on the Law Applicable to Non-Contractual Obligations [2007] OJ L199/40 (hereafter Rome II Regulation).

[4] Article 126 of the Agreement on the withdrawal of the United Kingdom of Great Britain and Northern Ireland from the European Union and the European Atomic Energy Community (2019/C 384 I/01) (hereafter EU Withdrawal Agreement).

Brexit and the Future of Private International Law in English Courts. Mukarrum Ahmed, Oxford University Press.
 DOI: 10.1093/oso/9780192848116.003.0001

This chapter will commence with a summary of the key political developments that occurred from the EU Referendum till the culmination of Brexit. This outline of events will assist us in contextualising the legal developments that unfolded as a result of Brexit. This will be followed by a note on the constitutional nature of EU law and its implications. The apogee and perigee of EU private international law in English courts will be narrated next. In this regard, the mutual interaction of two major systems of international litigation is charted. The European private international instruments that applied in England are introduced summarily. This is followed by the examination of Brexit's principal legislative instruments affecting private international law. These instruments include both primary and secondary legislation on private international law. The new and unique category of retained EU law in the domestic law of the UK is introduced. The post-Brexit status of pre-existing private international law conventions where the UK was a Contracting State by virtue of its membership of the EU is examined. The Hague Convention on Choice of Court Agreements is now applicable via the Private International Law (Implementation of Agreements) Act 2020. The impact of Brexit on international civil and commercial dispute resolution in England is assessed. This includes both international litigation and international arbitration even though the latter is outside the immediate scope of this book. A comparative perspective sheds light on the state of international litigation and arbitration in England. The last section of this introductory chapter narrates the sense of loss experienced by the discipline of comparative private international law at the hands of Brexit.

B. Outline of Political Developments from the EU Referendum to Brexit Day

In the referendum held on 23 June 2016, the majority voted to choose to leave the EU.[5]

On 29 March 2017, in writing to European Council President Donald Tusk, the Prime Minister formally triggered Article 50 and began the two-year countdown to the UK formally leaving the EU (known as 'Brexit' in common parlance).

The UK had long been expected to leave the EU at 11 p.m. on 29 March 2019. However, following a House of Commons vote on 14 March 2019, the government sought permission from the EU to extend Article 50 and agree a later Brexit date.

On 20 March 2019 the Prime Minister wrote to European Council President Donald Tusk, asking to extend Article 50 until 30 June 2019.

[5] Adapted from N Walker, 'Brexit Timeline: Events Leading to the UK's Exit from the European Union' (6 January 2021) House of Commons Library Research Briefing <Brexit timeline: events leading to the UK's exit from the European Union - House of Commons Library (parliament.uk)> accessed 31 August 2021.

Following a European Council meeting the next day, EU27 leaders agreed to grant an extension.

On 2 April 2019, the Prime Minister announced she would seek a further extension to the Article 50 process and offered to meet the Leader of the Opposition to agree a deal that can win the support of Members of Parliament (MPs).

At a meeting of the European Council on 10 April 2019, the UK and the EU27 agreed to extend Article 50 until 31 October 2019.

On 19 October 2019, the Prime Minister's new Brexit deal was lost on amendment in the Commons. In accordance with the European Union (Withdrawal) (No. 2) Act 2019—commonly known as the 'Benn Act'—the Prime Minister wrote to European Council president Donald Tusk, to request an extension to the Brexit process.

On 28 October 2019, EU Ambassadors agreed a further Brexit extension to 31 January 2020.

On 12 December 2019, Boris Johnson won a majority in the UK General Election and reaffirmed his commitment to 'get Brexit done' by 31 January 2020.

On 23 January 2020, the European Union (Withdrawal Agreement) Act 2020 received Royal Assent. This is the legislation that will implement the withdrawal agreement negotiated by the UK and the EU.

At 11 p.m. on 31 January 2020, the UK left the EU and entered a transition period.

At 11 p.m. on 31 December 2020, the transition period ended and the UK left the EU single market and customs union.

C. The Constitutional Nature of EU Law and its Implications for Brexit

This book will examine Brexit and its implications for the future of international civil and commercial litigation before English courts. Brexit created an impasse for cross-border civil and commercial judicial cooperation because the legal framework was based mainly on EU Regulations on jurisdiction, recognition and enforcement of judgments and the applicable law. The continued application of these EU Regulations in the post-Brexit civil judicial relationship between the UK and the EU was not possible because the Regulations derived their legal basis from an EU Treaty.[6]

In this regard, the UK Supreme Court in *R (on the application of Miller and another) v Secretary of State for Exiting the European Union* ('Miller') observed that the European Communities Act 1972 authorised a dynamic process by which EU

[6] Article 288 of the Treaty on the Functioning of the European Union (TFEU).

law became a source of UK law and took precedence over all domestic sources of UK law, including statutes.[7] The European Communities Act 1972 operated as a partial transfer of law-making powers, an assignment of legislative competences, by Parliament to EU institutions, unless and until Parliament decided otherwise.[8] It was not accepted that the rule of recognition (ie the fundamental rule by reference to which all other rules are validated) underlying UK laws was varied by the European Communities Act 1972 or would be varied by its repeal.[9] The majority of the Court said that because withdrawal made a fundamental change to the UK's constitutional arrangements, by cutting off the source of EU law, the UK constitution required such changes to be effected by Parliamentary legislation.[10] According to the terms of the European Union (Withdrawal) Act 2018, on 'Exit Day',[11] the European Communities Act 1972 was repealed.[12] This removes the municipal legal basis which enables or gives effect to a substantial corpus of EU private international law instruments in the UK.

The Supreme Court was also asked to examine the devolution aspect of triggering Article 50, issues which had not been raised before the High Court in the Miller case but had been heard earlier in the Northern Ireland High Court.[13] It was asked to consider whether, given the fact that Brexit will have an impact on devolved matters, the devolved administrations should normally have a say via a consent motion, as the so-called Sewel Convention requires. Further, since the devolved administrations have a statutory obligation not to breach EU law, it was argued that the prerogative could not be used to undermine legislation in such a way. On this point the UK Supreme Court was unanimous—it had no jurisdiction to rule on a Convention: 'Judges are neither the parents nor the guardians of political conventions; they are merely observers.' It continued that while they can 'recognise the operation of a political convention in the context of deciding a legal question', judges cannot 'give legal rulings on its operation or scope, because those matters are determined within the political world'.[14]

[7] *R (on the application of Miller and another) v Secretary of State for Exiting the European Union* [2017] UKSC 5. On appeals from: [2016] EWHC 2768 (Admin) and [2016] NIQB 85. See generally, C Barnard, 'Law and Brexit' (2017) 33 Oxford Review of Economic Policy S4, S5.

[8] [2017] UKSC 5, [67]–[68].

[9] ibid [60]. For discussion on the rule of recognition, see HLA Hart, *The Concept of Law* (2nd edn, OUP 1994) ch 6.

[10] [2017] UKSC 5, [82]. The government had argued that the European Communities Act 1972 was merely a 'conduit' for EU rights. It did not create EU rights but ensured that EU rights could be exercised so long as the UK remained a Member State of the EU. Therefore, since the European Communities Act conferred no rights, Parliament did not need to be involved in the decision to trigger Article 50. cf P Craig, 'Miller: Alternative Syllogisms' (Oxford Human Rights Hub, 23 November 2016) <http://ohrh.law.ox.ac.uk/miller-alternative-syllogisms/> accessed 31 August 2021.

[11] Section 20 of the European Union (Withdrawal) Act 2018.

[12] Section 1 of the European Union (Withdrawal) Act 2018.

[13] *R (McCord) v The Secretary of State for Northern Ireland* [2016] NIQB 85.

[14] [2017] UKSC 5, [146].

It was always likely that the Supreme Court would uphold the High Court's ruling on the main issue of whether an Act of Parliament was needed because the government had not changed its mind on the key concession it had made to the High Court that Article 50, once triggered, is irreversible. The political reason for this concession was clear: if the Article 50 process was reversible, Brexit would no longer mean Brexit. But there is a legal reason, too: if there is uncertainty over whether a decision to trigger Article 50 is reversible, this is a matter for the Court of Justice of the European Union (CJEU) to decide on a 'reference' from the Supreme Court under Article 267 of the Treaty on the Functioning of the European Union (TFEU). The Supreme Court, as the court of last resort in the UK, would be obliged to make a reference, but only if the point was necessary to enable it to give judgment. The delay resulting from any reference, together with the potential of a serious political backlash if 'Europe' was seen to be impeding the Brexit process, made a reference unlikely. The Supreme Court wanted to decide the case itself, with an 8:3 majority in favour of the claimant. An eleven-justice court was a first for the Supreme Court—and necessitated by the need to avoid any perception that, were the usual five judges to hear the case, they had been selected for their pro- or anti-EU sentiments.

The next decade will be a challenging period for the UK judiciary.[15] The courts will be asked to interpret the EU (Withdrawal) Act 2018, and in particular to work out when the courts might decide not to apply pre-Brexit decisions of the CJEU. The courts will also need to interpret and give effect to the 600 or so Statutory Instruments (SI, secondary law) that have been rushed through Parliament to give effect to Brexit.

D. The Rise and Fall of European Private International Law in English Courts

The last quarter of the twentieth century witnessed the parallel development of the European and English systems of international civil and commercial litigation.[16] At the beginning of this period the two systems of international litigation were almost unbeknownst to each other. The furore of legislative and judicial activity following the Treaty of Amsterdam may for posterity represent the high water mark of the UK's engagement with the EU's civil judicial cooperation measures.[17] In *Dicey,*

[15] C Barnard, 'Law and the Courts' in A Menon (ed), *Brexit: What Next?* (*The UK in a Changing Europe*, 13 February 2020) <https://ukandeu.ac.uk/wp-content/uploads/2020/02/Brexit-what-next-report.pdf> accessed 31 August 2021.

[16] R Fentiman, *International Commercial Litigation* (2nd edn, OUP 2015) ch 1; A Briggs, *Agreements on Jurisdiction and Choice of Law* (OUP 2008) Preface vii (hereafter Briggs, *Agreements*); A Briggs, *The Conflict of Laws* (2nd edn, OUP 2008) ch 1, 1–2.

[17] After the entry into force of the Treaty of Amsterdam (1 May 1999), the EU acquired competence to legislate on judicial cooperation in civil and commercial matters. Under Article 65 of the EC Treaty, measures were adopted on cross-border civil judicial cooperation, in so far as they were necessary for the proper functioning of the internal market. These measures did not apply to the UK or Ireland, unless

Morris and Collins on the Conflict of Laws, Lord Collins of Mapesbury remarked that 'Professor Dicey, and even Dr Morris, could not of course have foreseen the huge impact which a supra-national body of law, namely European law, would have on the subject of the conflict of laws' and that '[s]ince the last edition was published in 2006, the EU has demonstrated its intention to legislate for virtually the whole area'.[18] Professor Briggs has gone further by describing the field as 'a European legal structure of private international law, if one with a residuum of common law content'.[19] However, in the shadow of the twilight, Brexit has meant that EU private international law has come full circle in English courts. The two systems of international litigation are once again disengaged from each other.

A hard and abrupt Brexit for a large swathe of private international law is nevertheless a watershed moment for the development of the discipline.[20] The last seismic event of comparable proportions occurred when the Brussels Convention was given effect in UK law by the Civil Jurisdiction and Judgments Act 1982.[21] It then became necessary for English practitioners and academics to learn about a new system of international litigation and its 'language game'[22] relatively quickly.[23] In the words of Kerr LJ:[24] 'there still appears to be considerable ignorance about the consequences which this Convention will soon have for the jurisdiction of our Courts, and … these deserve study and preparation in advance'. At first, some common lawyers were dismayed by the radically different rubric but they soon rose to the challenge to appreciate and develop a deep understanding of European

they elected to participate in the adoption of or to accept the measure in question. Whilst the former Article 61(c) and Article 65 of the EC Treaty required that any measures on civil judicial cooperation had to assist with the proper functioning of the internal market, the Lisbon Treaty modified this requirement. According to Article 81 TFEU, the European Parliament and the Council may adopt measures '*particularly* when necessary for the proper functioning of the internal market' (emphasis added). See G van Calster, *European Private International Law* (3rd edn, Hart Publishing 2021) 10–13 (hereafter van Calster, *EU PIL*).

18 L Collins and others (eds), *Dicey, Morris & Collins The Conflict of Laws* (15th edn, Sweet & Maxwell 2012) xvii.

19 A Briggs, *The Conflict of Laws* (3rd edn, OUP 2013) Preface. Elsewhere, Briggs notes that EU private international law and the common law of conflict of laws flow in 'two separate streams, but while one is in spate, the other is looking rather parched': A Briggs, *Private International Law in English Courts* (OUP 2014) v (hereafter Briggs, *Private International Law*).

20 In this context, Dickinson refers to the UK moving out of its orbit within the European Union's legal system in A Dickinson, 'Realignment of the Planets—Brexit and European Private International Law' [2021] Praxis des Internationalen Privat- und Verfahrensrechts 213, 213.

21 For two excellent introductions to the last comparable watershed moment for private international law in English courts, see, L Collins, *The Civil Jurisdiction and Judgments Act 1982* (Butterworths 1983) and TC Hartley, *Civil Jurisdiction and Judgments: The Application in England of the Convention on Jurisdiction and the Enforcement of Judgments in Civil and Commercial Matters under the Civil Jurisdiction and Judgments Act 1982* (Sweet & Maxwell 1984).

22 See generally, L Wittgenstein, *Philosophical Investigations* (Blackwell 1953).

23 'So far as the new material was concerned, the immediate task was to understand: not only what it said, but also what it meant.': A Briggs, 'Four Decades of Private International Law' Oxford Law Faculty website <https://www.law.ox.ac.uk/content/adrian-briggs-qc-hon> accessed 31 August 2021.

24 *Citadel Insurance Co v Atlantic Union Insurance Co SA* [1982] 2 Lloyd's Rep 543, 549 (Kerr LJ).

private international law.[25] Perhaps, it is now time to unpack a lot of the luggage of European private international law but this book will argue that a conscious unlearning of the central precepts of EU private international law will be to the detriment of the future of private international law in the UK. First, the bridges that lie ahead for private international law in the UK rely in some way or the other on the legal epistemology of European private international law. Eventually, the Hague Judgments Convention (2019) and perhaps even the Lugano II Convention (2007) may be encountered on a path that leads us back to a semblance of the past.[26] However, this reminiscence should not be mistaken for obsolescence as it will fulfil the yearning for a comprehensive legal framework for cross-border civil judicial cooperation. Secondly, the principles of EU private international law will serve as a useful comparator when adjusting or reforming aspects of private international law in England.

E. The Parallel Development of European and English Private International Law

Prior to the phase of concurrent development in the last quarter of the twentieth century, the rules that regulated the civil jurisdiction of an English court could be comprehensively stated in a relatively concise manner. If the defendant was present in England and was served with the writ, the service of process founded the court's jurisdiction.[27] If the court's jurisdiction existed, it would exercise it. If the defendant was not in England, rendering service abroad depended on obtaining leave of the court. The process for obtaining leave of the court was slightly more resource intensive. A single set of rules largely applied to all defendants and to all actions *in personam*.

[25] The EU private international law Regulations in civil and commercial matters may be characterised as 'closed systems' in the sense that every possible eventuality is governed by a limited number of general principles. In contrast, common law systems are 'open' in the sense that new rules may be created or imported for new facts. Advocate General Lagrange in Case 28/62 *Da Costa en Schaake NV, Jacob Meijer NV, Hoechst-Holland NV v Netherlands Inland Revenue Administration* [1963] ECR 00031, 44, urged the CJEU to accept the strict French conception of *res judicata*, according to which a decision of any court cannot have a regulatory effect for anyone who was not a party to the litigation. Whilst a particular line of decisions may be partially constitutive of the law, the court may simply ignore a previous decision of its own whose ruling it now disapproves. In AG Lagrange's opinion it is 'better for a court to interpret the law, the purpose for which it is set up, than to interpret its own decisions'. See generally, W Tetley, 'Mixed Jurisdictions: Common Law v. Civil Law (Codified and Uncodified)' (2000) 60 Louisiana Law Review 677, 706.

[26] On 1 July 2021, Switzerland, which is the depository of the Lugano II Convention 2007, notified the Parties to the Convention of the EU's refusal to give its consent to the UK's accession to the Convention: Swiss Federal Council, 'Communication by the depositary with respect to the application of accession by the United Kingdom of Great Britain and Northern Ireland' 1 July 2021 <2https://www.eda.admin.ch/dam/eda/fr/documents/aussenpolitik/voelkerrecht/autres-conventions/Lugano2/20210701-LUG_en.pdf> accessed 31 August 2021.

[27] *Maharanee of Baroda v Wildenstein* [1972] 2 QB 283.

The UK's membership of the EU heralded a sea change with the arrival of harmonised rules to determine civil jurisdiction and the recognition and enforcement of judgments.[28] A set of rules derived and aligned with the civil jurisdiction and judgments regime of the Member States extended to the European Free Trade Association (EFTA) States.[29] The internal civil jurisdictional law of the UK was amended to reflect, as between England, Scotland, and Northern Ireland, the rules of international civil jurisdiction by which the UK was bound as a Member State.[30] The common law rules of civil jurisdiction and the recognition and enforcement of judgments were now part of the residual national private international law regime.

In some places, these European instruments did not aim to stipulate the precise jurisdictional powers of national courts but directed the application of domestic legal rules. The result is that the traditional jurisdictional rules of the common law served two distinct purposes. In cases which fell right outside the scope of the European instruments they always were the source of the law on jurisdiction. But in cases within the scope of those instruments, into which they are incorporated by reference, they operate as rules of residual jurisdiction.

As stated earlier, the English courts had started to reassess their fundamental understanding of the existence and exercise of common law jurisdiction. Until *The Atlantic Star*[31] it was assumed that a claimant was entitled to decide whether a defendant would be summoned to court, and that a defendant had practically no say in the matter.[32] In *The Atlantic Star* a collision at sea in Belgian waters led to proceedings in Belgium. When proceedings in respect of the same collision were commenced in England the House of Lords stayed them on the ground that the English forum was not that in which such a dispute should be tried. The case involved parallel proceedings but the reasoning used was not confined to such situations.[33]

A series of decisions developing the concept of the 'appropriateness' of an English court to exercise jurisdiction were handed down by the House of Lords.[34] This is an illustration of how a court with inherent jurisdiction may develop its own jurisdictional rules without the need for any legislation.[35] As a matter of common

[28] The Brussels regime collectively refers to the Brussels Convention, the Brussels I Regulation (2001), and the Brussels Ia Regulation (2012).

[29] The Lugano Convention (1988) and the Lugano II Convention (2007).

[30] Section 16 of the Civil Jurisdiction and Judgments Act 1982 and the internal UK jurisdiction provisions in Schedule 4.

[31] *Atlantic Star v Bona Spes (The Atlantic Star)* [1974] AC 436.

[32] The history of the law up to 1974 can be read in the seminal decision in *The Atlantic Star* [1974] AC 436 in the opinions of Lord Wilberforce (who favoured granting a stay) and Lord Morris (who did not favour granting a stay).

[33] For a particular case that might be decided differently today on the basis of the plea of *forum non conveniens*, see *Maharanee of Baroda v Wildenstein* [1972] 2 QB 283.

[34] *The Atlantic Star* [1973] QB 364; *MacShannon v Rockware Glass Ltd* [1978] AC 795; *Amin Rasheed Shipping Corporation v Kuwait Insurance Co* [1984] AC 50; *The Abidin Daver* [1984] AC 398. Lord Goff's speech in *Spiliada Maritime Corporation v Cansulex Limited (The Spiliada)* [1987] AC 460 is the cornerstone of the modern law on *forum non conveniens*.

[35] The common law's disdain for a statutory approach to English private international law has been expressed by Cheshire in that the field 'has been only lightly touched by the paralysing hand

law, it is necessary but not sufficient to serve process on the defendant. Though this service gives rise to the existence of jurisdiction if the defendant disputes it the court must adjudicate on the exercise of jurisdiction. The court may stay proceedings so that the claimant has no alternative but to bring proceedings before the courts of another country.

In order to assess the loss of European private international law in English courts properly, it is necessary to understand the extent of its permeation into English procedural law and conflict of laws. The following section will introduce the principal European private international law instruments in civil and commercial matters that were applied by English courts.

F. European Private International Law in English Courts

An awareness of the relationship between European law and the English common law is essential to an understanding of private international law in English courts. European private international law rules did not operate by amending the indigenous common law rules. Instead, European private international law displaced the English common law rules to the periphery as the residual conflict of laws regime. Implementation by amending the common law rules would risk creating a halfway house between European law and the common law and the changes would be construed as working within an existing system, rather than giving rise to an entirely new set of rules.

Article 293 (formerly Article 220) of the Treaty establishing the European Community (EC) provided that Member States shall enter into negotiations with each other for the purpose of securing for the benefit of their nationals specified advantages including the simplification of formalities governing the reciprocal recognition and enforcement of judgments. Therefore, a new law of civil jurisdiction and the recognition and enforcement of judgments emerged which was interpreted by the CJEU.[36] The most significant legislation was the Brussels Convention and its progeny, the Brussels I Regulation and the Brussels Ia Regulation.[37] The

of the Parliamentary draftsman': GC Cheshire, *Private International Law* (OUP 1935) Preface. Lord Wilberforce has observed, in the context of the proposed replacement of the English common law rules on choice of law in tort by Part III of the Private International Law (Miscellaneous Provisions) Act 1995, that the 'subject of conflict of laws is essentially one which ought to be left to the judges. It has been developed by the judges over the years and, on the whole, the judges have done a very good job. There are very few cases where injustice has been seen to be done. One does not want this part of the law frozen into the lapidary phrases of the Parliamentary draftsmen, however well drafted they may appear to be. It is better to leave it to the judges.': Hansard, HL 6 December 1994, col 840.

36 The Contracting States of the Brussels Convention concluded a Protocol on the interpretation of the Convention by the Court of Justice of the European Communities, 1 June 1971 [1978] OJ L304/97.

37 Brussels Ia Regulation; Council Regulation (EC) 44/2001 on jurisdiction and the recognition and enforcement of judgments in civil and commercial matters (Brussels I) [2001] OJ L12/1 (hereafter Brussels I Regulation); Brussels Convention of 27 September 1968 on jurisdiction and the

Lugano Convention was closely aligned with the Brussels Convention and the Lugano II Convention mirrored the provisions of the Brussels I Regulation.[38] These instruments relied upon harmonised 'direct' rules of jurisdiction which in turn facilitated the free movement of judgments between the Member States and Contracting States.[39] Outside the ambit of civil and commercial matters and the specific exclusions, the Brussels–Lugano regime had no immediate application.

The Rome Convention and the Rome I Regulation governed the applicable law for cross-border contractual obligations in civil and commercial matters. The Rome II Regulation governed the applicable law for cross-border non-contractual obligations in civil and commercial matters.

European private international law made cross-border litigation simpler and more predictable, service out of the jurisdiction was easier, reduced the risk of a race to the courthouse, or of parallel proceedings in different EU Member States leading to irreconcilable decisions. The European rules also ensured that judgments were automatically recognised and enforced in other EU Member States and indeed, that there were assets against which to enforce them.

From 1 January 1987, English courts were increasingly concerned with these rules of European law and to a lesser extent with the residual common law rules. The European rules operated as follows:[40] allocate the English court jurisdiction over the dispute; potentially allocate jurisdiction to the English courts and to the courts of another state; or allocate jurisdiction to the courts of another state and simultaneously deny it to the English courts. In the first case, it would be mandatory for the court to adjudicate on the dispute. In the second case, the court would have jurisdiction and would be bound to adjudicate on the matter if it was the court first seised, but it would have no jurisdiction if the court in the other state was seised first and did not decline proceedings. In the third case, the court cannot adjudicate on the dispute at all.

enforcement of judgments in civil and commercial matters [1972] OJ L 299/32, as amended including by the Convention on the accession of the Kingdom of Denmark, Ireland and the UK of Great Britain and Northern Ireland to the Convention on jurisdiction and the enforcement of judgments in civil and commercial matters and to the Protocol on its interpretation by the Court of Justice (Luxembourg, 9 October 1978) (consolidated version) [1998] OJ C 27/1 (hereafter Brussels Convention).

[38] Lugano II Convention; Convention on jurisdiction and the enforcement of judgments in civil and commercial matters—Done at Lugano on 16 September 1988 OJ L 319, 25.11.1988 (hereafter Lugano Convention). The EU rather than individual Member States had the exclusive competence to conclude the Lugano II Convention. See Opinion 1/03 *Lugano Opinion* [2006] ECR I-1145.

[39] Direct rules of jurisdiction determine whether the courts of a particular Member State have jurisdiction, or do not have jurisdiction, to decide a particular case. Indirect rules of jurisdiction refer to the jurisdictional standards for courts that have issued judgments which the court addressed is asked to recognise and enforce.

[40] A Briggs, *Civil Jurisdiction and Judgments* (7th edn, Informa Law from Routledge 2021) 7 (hereafter Briggs, *Civil Jurisdiction*).

The jurisdiction conferred by this legislation is codified or statutory. The 'great divide'[41] between the English common law and continental civil law on matters of jurisdiction has led to 'mutual incomprehension'[42] on both sides.[43] Indeed, the prevalence of a 'fundamentally'[44] or 'paradigmatically'[45] different jurisdictional regime has been a source of an uneasy friction which has at times surfaced with the principles of the common law conflict of laws being on 'trial' at the CJEU.[46] On the one hand, a 'theory driven'[47] legislative and territorial conception of civil jurisdiction does not empower a judge in one state to rule on the jurisdiction of another state. On the other, a practice-driven conception of civil jurisdiction which accords primacy to the principle of *pacta sunt servanda* will not refrain from enforcing the private law rights and obligations of the litigating parties.[48] It is comprehensible that rules of judicial procedure which apply when a court deals with common law jurisdiction will be different from a court dealing with a case where jurisdiction has been allocated according to mandatory and direct rules of jurisdiction.

[41] A Fiorini, 'The Codification of Private International Law in Europe—Could the Community Learn from the Experience of Mixed Jurisdictions' (2008) 23 Tulane European and Civil Law Forum 89, 100.

[42] Briggs, *Agreements* (n 16) 201.

[43] ibid 8: when referring to the common law conception of choice of court agreements as contracts, Briggs refers to a 'clash of legal cultures' precipitated by the fact that 'the intellectual tradition of private international law has been to be more wary of appeals to plain contractual reasoning, on the footing that the international element in conflicts cases calls for special attention and different sensitivity'.

[44] Briggs, *Civil Jurisdiction* (n 40) 7; J Harris, 'Understanding the English Response to the Europeanisation of Private International Law' (2008) 4 Journal of Private International Law 347, 352–53 (hereafter Harris, 'English Response to Europeanisation'); A Gardella and LG Radicati Di Brozolo, 'Civil Law, Common Law and Market Integration: The EC Approach to Conflicts of Jurisdiction' (2003) 51 American Journal of Comparative Law 611.

[45] R Michaels, 'Two Paradigms of Jurisdiction' (2006) 27 Michigan Journal of International Law 1003.

[46] The triumvirate of decisions in Gasser, Turner, and Owusu have been referred to as 'fifteen months of infamy' in A Briggs, 'The Impact of Recent Judgments of the European Court on English Procedural Law and Practice' (2005) II(124) Zeitschrift fur Schweizerisches Recht 231, 232 (hereafter Briggs, 'Recent Judgments of the European Court').

[47] TC Hartley, 'The European Union and the Systematic Dismantling of the Common Law of Conflict of Laws' (2005) 54 International and Comparative Law Quarterly 813, 814 (hereafter Hartley, 'Dismantling of the Common Law Conflict of Laws').

[48] P Nygh, 'The Preliminary Draft Hague Convention on Jurisdiction and Foreign Judgments in Civil and Commercial Matters' in P Borchers and J Zekoll (eds), *International Conflict of Laws for the Third Millennium* (Transnational Publishers, 2001) 264, notes that traditionally common law judges have been guided by pragmatism and a strong commercial sense and these concerns have been 'placed on a pedestal'; Hartley, 'Dismantling of the Common Law Conflict of Laws' (n 47) 814–15, observes that the civilian systems focus on the structure (and logic) of the law while common law systems are based on the operation (and experience) of the law. He also highlights the existence of a conflict between common law systems and civilian systems in relation to the interests of the parties assuming priority in the former and the interests of the states involved taking priority in the latter; Hartley's understanding of the common law in general reflects the famous aphorism: 'The life of the law has not been logic; it has been experience' in OW Holmes, *The Common Law* (1st edn Macmillan 1882) 1; cf E Coke, *The First Part of the Institutes of the Laws of England, or, A Commentary on Littleton* (first published 1628, F Hargrave and C Butler eds, 19th edn, London 1832) 97b: 'Reason is the life of the law.'

1. The Brussels Conventions

The first of these instruments was the Brussels Convention. The original Brussels Convention was signed on 27 September 1968.[49] The original Contracting States were France, Germany, Italy, Belgium, the Netherlands, and Luxembourg.

When the UK, Ireland, and Denmark joined the EC they acceded to the Brussels Convention.[50] The opportunity was taken to make some amendments to the Convention, and an Accession Convention was entered into on 9 October 1978. The UK became a Contracting State of the Brussels Convention when it took effect in the UK on 1 January 1987.

When Greece joined the EC it acceded to the Brussels Convention. This was done by an Accession Convention, which incorporated Greece and its courts, but which made no other changes to the Convention. It was signed on 25 October 1982 and was published in the Official Journal.[51] The third edition of the Brussels Convention appeared in the Civil Jurisdiction and Judgments Act 1982 (Amendment) Order 1989.[52] It took effect in the UK on 1 October 1989.

When Spain and Portugal joined the EC they acceded to the Brussels Convention. This was done by an Accession Convention, signed on 26 May 1989, which incorporated Spain and Portugal into the scheme but which also made some substantive changes to the text of the existing Brussels Convention. The text was published in the Official Journal,[53] and the fourth edition of the Brussels Convention appeared in the Civil Jurisdiction and Judgments Act 1982 (Amendment) Order 1990.[54] It took effect in the UK on 1 December 1991.

And finally, when Austria, Finland, and Sweden joined the EU, as it had by then become, they acceded to the Brussels Convention. This was done by an Accession Convention signed on 29 November 1996, which incorporated Austria, Finland, and Sweden into the scheme, but which made no other substantive changes to the text of the existing Brussels Convention. The fifth edition of the Brussels Convention was published in the Official Journal,[55] and in the Civil Jurisdiction and Judgments Act 1982 (Amendment) Order 2000.[56] It took effect in the UK on 1 January 2001. This fifth edition of the Brussels Convention was the last one to be produced.

49 [1978] OJ L304/36.
50 [1978] OJ L304/77.
51 [1982] OJ L388/1.
52 SI 1989 No 1346.
53 [1989] OJ L285/1.
54 SI 1990 No 2591.
55 [1997] OJ C15/1.
56 SI 2000 No 1824.

2. The Rome Convention

Following a meeting of experts of the six original Member States in 1968, interim work was carried out from 1970 to June 1972, when the text of a draft 'Convention on the Law Applicable to Contractual and Non-Contractual Obligations' was submitted to the governments of the Member States. In 1975, the group of experts decided to limit their task to a Convention on Contractual Obligations, apparently on the ground that work on the law relating to non-contractual obligations was too complex. The Convention on the Law Applicable to Contractual Obligations was finalised and opened for signature on 19 June 1980.[57] The CJEU acquired jurisdiction to interpret the Rome Convention from 1 August 2004.

3. The Lugano Conventions

A parallel Convention was concluded in 1988 in Lugano, between the then states of the EC and those states party to the EFTA which at that date were not also members of the EC: Norway, Sweden, Finland, Iceland, Austria, and Switzerland. Its substance was largely the same as the fourth edition of the Brussels Convention, but as it was not part of the family of Brussels Conventions, the CJEU had no jurisdiction to interpret it. When Austria, Finland, and Sweden joined the EU they became Member States bound by the Brussels I Regulation. However, in relation to Iceland, Norway, and Switzerland, the Lugano Convention remained the sole jurisdictional text. It was for a short period extended to Poland, though from 1 January 2004, Poland was a Member State of the EU. The 1988 Lugano Convention was published in the Official Journal,[58] and appeared as Schedule 1 to the Civil Jurisdiction and Judgments Act 1991.[59] It came into force in the UK on 1 May 1992.[60]

After 2001, when the Brussels Convention was transformed into a Regulation and changes made to the text, the Lugano II Convention was produced, bringing its substance into line with the Brussels I Regulation 44/2001.[61] The parties to the Lugano II Convention were the EU, which had by then acquired the external

[57] The Rome Convention 1980 on the law applicable to contractual obligations (OJ C 27, 26.1.1998, 36–53) was brought into force in the UK on 1 April 1991 by the Contracts (Applicable Law) Act 1990 (hereafter Rome Convention).

[58] [1988] OJ L319/9.

[59] The 1991 Act amended the 1982 Act by the insertion of a new Section 3A and Schedule 3C, and made other consequential changes. The effect was that the 1982 Act, as amended, was the statutory basis for the Lugano Convention in the UK.

[60] SI 1992 No 745.

[61] Lugano II Convention. See F Pocar, 'The New Lugano Convention on Jurisdiction and the Recognition and Enforcement of Judgments in Civil and Commercial Matters' (2008) 10 Yearbook of Private International Law 1.

competence for the negotiation of such Conventions which the Member States had ceased to have,[62] and the Contracting States of Iceland, Norway, and Switzerland.

The Pocar Report on the Lugano II Convention was also a useful guide to the Brussels I Regulation (2001). The Lugano II Convention took effect in relation to Norway on 1 January 2010, Switzerland on 1 January 2011, and Iceland on 1 May 2011.

4. The Brussels I Regulation

As the EU acquired competence to legislate in the field of private international law, the Council of the EU adopted the Brussels I Regulation which was directly applicable[63] and had direct effect[64] in the Member States of the EU. The term 'Member States', when used in this context, originally excluded Denmark, which chose not to be bound by the Brussels I Regulation until 1 July 2007. It was published in the Official Journal and took effect in all Member States on 1 March 2002.[65] Its practical effect was to supersede the Brussels Convention as between the Member States in relation to proceedings commenced on or after that date.

5. The Rome II Regulation

The European Commission published a preliminary draft proposal for the Rome II Regulation in 2002. In the UK, there was opposition to the Rome II proposal largely on the grounds that it would have deleterious effects on e-commerce and on the international circulation of the press. The UK decided to opt in to the negotiations in accordance with Article 3 of the Protocol on the position of the UK and Ireland. The Rome II Regulation was finally adopted in July 2007.[66]

[62] See 1/03 *Lugano Opinion* [2006] ECR I-1145.

[63] The principle of direct applicability refers to the extent to which EU measures take effect in the legal system of each Member State without the need for further implementation by the Member States themselves. Authority for this interpretation is Article 288 TFEU which states specifically that a Regulation 'shall be binding in its entirety and directly applicable in all Member States'. Therefore, Regulations shall take effect in the legal system of each Member State without the need for any further implementation.

[64] The principle of direct effect can be interpreted as meaning the extent to which EU law can produce legal rights and obligations which can be used in an action before a national court. The CJEU decision in *Van Gend en Loos v Nederlandse Administratie der Belastingen* (26/62) [1963] ECR 1, [1963] CMLR 105 states that '[Union] law has an authority which can be invoked by their nationals before those courts and tribunals'. See P Craig and G De Burca, *EU Law: Text, Cases and Materials* (5th edn, OUP 2011) ch 7 (hereafter Craig and De Burca, *EU Law*).

[65] Brussels I Regulation.

[66] Rome II Regulation.

6. The Rome I Regulation

The European Commission began work on the conversion of the Rome Convention of 1980 on the law applicable to contractual obligations into the Rome I Regulation in 2003.[67] The UK decided not to opt in to negotiations largely because it was dissatisfied with the possibility for courts in Member States to apply the overriding mandatory rules of a third country and also due to its dissatisfaction with the proposed rules on the applicable law for consumer contracts.[68] Nevertheless, the UK ultimately decided to opt in once the Regulation had been adopted in June 2008.[69]

7. The Brussels Ia Regulation

A project to recast the Brussels I Regulation (2001) was commenced five years into its operation. The principal basis underlying the recast Brussels I Regulation was the Heidelberg Report.[70] The broad aims of the Brussels Ia Regulation (2012) were less ambitious than those envisaged by the Heidelberg Report. The four significant areas of reform were: (i) to render the enforcement of judgments faster and simplified; (ii) to accord greater priority to the court chosen in a choice of court agreement; (iii) to disentangle the complications caused by the interface between arbitration and the Regulation; and (iv) to take a step towards the harmonisation of rules for taking jurisdiction over defendants who were not domiciled in any Member State. The Brussels Ia Regulation was published in 2012 and entered into force on 10 January 2015.[71]

8. The Hague Convention on Choice of Court Agreements

Following the conclusion of the Lugano II Convention,[72] which fell entirely within the sphere of exclusive competence of the EU,[73] the Hague Convention on Choice

[67] COM(2002) 654 final.

[68] See the Protocol on the position of the UK and Ireland. By virtue of Article 1, the UK and Ireland do not participate in the adoption of proposed measures pursuant to Title IV EC. However, either of those States may opt in to negotiations within three months of a proposal being tabled (Article 3) or to the instrument adopted (Article 4).

[69] Rome I Regulation.

[70] B Hess, T Pfeiffer, and P Schlosser, 'Report on the Application of Regulation Brussels I in the Member States' (Study JLS/C4/2005/03, September 2007) (hereafter Heidelberg Report).

[71] Denmark agreed to be bound by the Brussels Ia Regulation by separate agreement with the European Union: [2013] OJ L79/4. An amendment to the original text of Regulation 1215/2012, to provide for the Unified Patent Court, was made by Regulation 542/2014, [2014] OJ L163/1.

[72] Lugano II Convention; See Explanatory Report by Professor F Pocar: OJ 2009, C 319/1.

[73] See Opinion 1/03 *Lugano Convention* [2006] ECR I-1145; Opinion 1/13, EU:C:2014:2303 of the CJEU (Grand Chamber) confirms that the exclusive competence of the EU encompasses the acceptance of the accession of a third state to the Hague Convention on the civil aspects of international child abduction concluded on 25 October 1980.

of Court Agreements (Hague Convention) was also concluded by the EU on behalf of the Member States (except Denmark).[74] The fact that the EU is a party has important consequences within the Union. The Hague Convention has the status of EU law within the EU (except Denmark)[75] and the CJEU will have the final word on its interpretation as far as the EU Member States are concerned.[76] The Hague Convention as EU law is directly applicable,[77] would almost certainly fulfil the requirements for direct effect,[78] and would prevail over the law of the Member States in case of conflict.[79] The Hague Convention is accompanied by the Explanatory Report by Professor Hartley and Professor Dogauchi.

9. Expert Reports

These legislative texts were, as the case may be, the primary source of the rules on jurisdiction and the effect of foreign judgments. They were written in all official languages of the EU, and as a matter of European law, all of them were equally authentic.[80]

The Brussels and Lugano Conventions were each supplemented by a Report giving background and explanation to the text. These Reports had significant influence in the interpretation of the Conventions and therefore bear on the construction of corresponding provisions of the Brussels I Regulation.[81] The Brussels Convention was accompanied by the Report signed by Mr Jenard.[82] The Accession Convention for the UK was accompanied by the Report signed by Professor Schlosser.[83] The Accession Convention for Greece was accompanied by the Report of Professors Evrigenis and Kerameus.[84] The Accession Convention for Portugal and Spain was accompanied by the Report of Messrs Almeida Cruz, Desantes Real, and Jenard.[85] The Lugano Convention was accompanied by the Report of Messrs

74 Council Decision 2014/887/EU.

75 TC Hartley, *Choice of Court Agreements under the European and International Instruments* (OUP 2013) ch 1, 22–23 (hereafter Hartley, *Choice of Court*).

76 ibid 23. See Article 267 TFEU; See TC Hartley, *The Foundations of European Union Law* (8th edn, OUP 2010) ch 9 (hereafter Hartley, *European Union Law*).

77 See n 63.

78 See n 64.

79 In *Costa v ENEL* (6/64) [1964] ECR 585 the CJEU espoused the principle of supremacy of EU law and stated that EU law could not 'be overridden by domestic legal provisions, however framed, without being deprived of its character as [Union] law and without the legal basis of the [Union] itself being called into question'. See Hartley, *European Union Law* (n 76) ch 7.

80 After Completion Day, only the English language versions will be authentic. However, if the UK were to accede to the Lugano II Convention as an independent Contracting State, Article 79 of the Lugano II Convention provides that the twenty-five language versions of the Convention are equally authentic.

81 cf C-533/07 *Falco Privatstiftung v Weller-Lindhorst* [2009] ECR I-3327.

82 [1979] OJ C59/1.

83 [1979] OJ C59/71.

84 [1986] OJ C298/1.

85 [1990] OJ C189/35.

Jenard and Möller.[86] The Lugano II Convention was accompanied by the Report signed by Professor Pocar.[87] The Rome Convention was accompanied by the Report by Professors Giuliano and Lagarde.[88]

As far as English law is concerned, the legislation which implemented the relevant Conventions expressly provided that the English courts were entitled to consult the Reports and to attribute significance to them as was appropriate under the circumstances.[89] In practice, the English courts tended to follow the advice provided in the Reports. The CJEU followed the advice in the Reports but there were a few instances where the CJEU departed from the Report.

10. The Preliminary Reference Procedure

In order to establish uniformity in the application and interpretation of EU private international law, the CJEU has jurisdiction to accept references for a preliminary ruling from the national courts of the Member States. Article 267 of the TFEU allows any court which 'considers that a decision on the question is necessary to enable it to give judgment' to make a reference for a preliminary ruling on the interpretation of EU law. A preliminary reference to the CJEU from the highest court of a Member State is mandatory on a question of EU law that is necessary for the outcome of the case and is not clear beyond reasonable doubt without any case law from the CJEU or where the national court cannot decide the answer to the question simply by following the existing case law of the CJEU.[90] No question of reference would arise if the national court were to consider the answer to be *acte claire*.[91] The preliminary reference procedure was the central mechanism for the creation of uniform pan-European characterisations of terms and concepts used in the EU private international law instruments.[92]

[86] [1990] OJ C189/57.

[87] [2009] OJ C319/1.

[88] Report on the Convention on the law applicable to contractual obligations by Mario Giuliano, Professor, University of Milan, and Paul Lagarde, Professor, University of Paris I OJ C 282, 31.10.1980, 1–50.

[89] See, for example, Section 3 of the Civil Jurisdiction and Judgments Act 1982.

[90] See Article 267(3) TFEU; Case C-283/81 *CILFIT Srl and Lanificio di Gavardo SpA v Ministry of Health* [1982] ECR 3415. Craig and De Burca, *EU Law* (n 64) ch 13.

[91] If the CJEU considers that the answer to the national court's question is clear, it may dispose of the matter by making a reasoned order without the need for a hearing: see Article 99 of the Rules of Procedure of the Court.

[92] The decisions of the national courts of the Member States and the commentary of jurists also contributed to the development of EU private international law concepts.

11. Judicial Authority

The CJEU renders authoritative decisions and its rulings are binding on the courts of all EU Member States.[93] In relation to the decisions of the courts of the Member States on EU law it is well to bear in mind that 'the persuasive value of a particular court's decision must depend on its reputation and status, the extent to which its decisions are binding on courts of co-ordinate and inferior jurisdiction in its own country and the coverage of the national law reporting system'.[94]

G. A Broad Outline of Brexit's Implications for Private International Law

The European Union (Withdrawal) Act 2018 ('EUWA 2018') and the European Union (Withdrawal Agreement) Act 2020 ('EUWA 2020') provided the legislative basis for Brexit. At the macro level, the UK's membership of the EU terminated at 11 p.m. on 31 January 2020. According to the Withdrawal Agreement, a transition or implementation period would last until the end of 2020. During the transition period, EU law continued to apply in the UK but its legislative basis was the EUWA 2018 and the EUWA 2020. At the end of the transition period, detailed legislation prescribes, as the default position, that much of EU law and EU derived law as it stands on that date will be retained as the domestic law of the UK.[95] Subsequent EU legislation will be of no effect in the UK but the CJEU's interpretation of EU laws may have persuasive value for English courts.

The EUWA 2018 provided the government a broad statutory power to amend or revoke EU laws, which would otherwise qualify for retention as laws of the UK, where the law liable to be retained would be defective or deficient. That power has been used in relation to the EU law with which this book is concerned. The Rome I Regulation and the Rome II Regulation have been incorporated into domestic law as retained EU law after some consequentialist amendments. The Brussels–Lugano regime has been revoked because a unilateral regime cannot replicate the multilateral jurisdiction and judgments framework premised on reciprocity or mutual recognition between states. In its place and at the risk of oversimplification, the common law jurisdiction of English courts will be wider, the ancillary powers of English courts will be greater, and the effect of English judgments will be less than would be the case if the UK acceded to the Lugano II Convention.

[93] Section 3 of the European Communities Act 1972.

[94] *Fothergill v Monarch Airlines* [1981] AC 251, 284 (Lord Diplock).

[95] EU law: Legislation, CJEU case law, and principles of EU law in particular. EU derived law: Domestic laws made to implement or to complement EU law.

The Private International Law (Implementation of Agreements) Act 2020 provides a statutory basis for the UK to join as an independent Contracting State certain international Conventions which it had been bound by virtue of its EU membership. The 2020 Act applies to the Hague Convention on Choice of Court Agreements (2005).[96]

On 8 April 2020, the UK applied to accede to the Lugano II Convention, which would have replicated the Brussels I Regulation (2001) on civil jurisdiction and the recognition and enforcement of judgments. Accession to the Lugano II Convention is a four-step process:

1. Requesting to join.[97] The UK requested accession on 8 April 2020.[98]
2. Unanimous approval by the current Contracting States: the EU (including Denmark, which is a Contracting State in its own right)[99] and the EFTA states.[100]
3. Depositing the instrument of accession by the UK, as the party requesting to join.[101]
4. Entry into force on the first day of the third month following the deposit of its instrument of accession. During that interval, a Contracting State that previously approved the UK's accession may still object. If a Contracting State objects, the Convention will not enter into force between the UK and that party.[102]

Therefore, for the UK's Lugano II Convention accession to have been seamless and effective on 1 January 2021, the Contracting States, especially the EU, should have given their approval by 1 October 2020 at the very latest. The European Commission has indicated that the Hague Convention on Choice of Court Agreements (2005) and the Hague Judgments Convention (2019) should provide the framework for future cooperation between the EU and the UK in the field of

96 The UK deposited an instrument of ratification in 2018, and several declarations (as the date of Exit Day elapsed) during 2019, and withdrew all of them on 31 January 2020. On that date it also notified an intention to deposit a fresh instrument of accession during 2020, which it did on 28 September 2020. The instrument which purported to incorporate the Convention into English law (Civil Jurisdiction and Judgments (Hague Convention on Choice of Court Agreements 2005) (EU Exit) Regulations 2018, SI 2018 No 1124), has not been revoked, but the Convention was given (or re-given) effect in English law by Private International Law (Implementation of Agreements) Act 2020, which inserted the Hague Convention 2005 into the Civil Jurisdiction and Judgments Act 1982.

97 Article 72(1) of the Lugano II Convention.

98 The Treaty was laid before Parliament in November 2020, see: <https://www.gov.uk/government/publications/convention-on-jurisdiction-and-the-recognition-and-enforcement-of-judgments-in-civil-and-commercial-matters-and-amendments-to-the-convention-of-20112> accessed 31 August 2021.

99 Because of its exclusion from the Treaty basis pursuant to which the Brussels Regulation was concluded.

100 Article 72(3) of the Lugano II Convention.

101 Article 73(4), 72(1) of the Lugano II Convention.

102 Article 72(4) of the Lugano II Convention.

civil judicial cooperation whilst concluding that the EU should not give its consent to the UK's accession to the Lugano II Convention.[103] This leaves the UK necessarily reliant on a more fragmented regional and international framework for private international law at least until the UK and the EU accede to the Hague Judgments Convention. The European Commission has indicated that the EU will conclude the Hague Judgments Convention in the 'near future'.[104] On 1 July 2021, Switzerland, which is the depository of the Lugano II Convention, notified the Parties to the Convention of the EU's refusal to give its consent to the UK's accession to the Convention.[105] It states the EU is not 'in a position to give its consent to invite the UK to accede to the Lugano Convention', quoting the note verbale received by the depository from the EU on 28 June 2021.[106]

H. Brexit's Primary Legislation Relevant to Private International Law

The amendments rendered by Brexit's principal primary legislation to private international law are discussed in this section. The amendments considered precede from general changes that impact upon the entire English legal system to more specific developments that have an impact on either one or more of jurisdiction, recognition, and enforcement of judgments and the applicable law in civil and commercial matters.

1. Provision for Exit Day and the Post-Brexit Transition Period

The European Communities Act 1972 was repealed on Exit Day.[107] Exit Day was the day when the UK ceased to be a Member State of the EU and was stipulated as 11 p.m. on 31 January 2020.[108] The provision for a transition period extends from Exit Day until Completion Day.[109] The Completion Day is stipulated as 11 p.m. on

[103] Communication from the Commission to the European Parliament and the Council, Assessment on the application of the United Kingdom of Great Britain and Northern Ireland to accede to the 2007 Lugano Convention, COM(2021) 222 final, 4 May 2021 <https://eur-lex.europa.eu/legal-content/EN/TXT/PDF/?uri=CELEX:52021DC0222&from=EN> accessed 31 August 2021.

[104] ibid 4.

[105] Swiss Federal Council, 'Communication by the depositary with respect to the application of accession by the United Kingdom of Great Britain and Northern Ireland' 1 July 2021 <https://www.eda.admin.ch/dam/eda/fr/documents/aussenpolitik/voelkerrecht/autres-conventions/Lugano2/20210701-LUG_en.pdf> accessed 31 August 2021.

[106] European Commission, 'Note Verbale concerning the application of the United Kingdom of Great Britain and Northern Ireland to accede to the 2007 Lugano Convention' 28 June 2021 <20210701-LUG-ann-EU.pdf (admin.ch)> accessed 31 August 2021.

[107] Section 1 of the EUWA 2018.

[108] Section 20 of the EUWA 2018 as amended by SI 2019 No 1423.

[109] Section 1A of the EUWA 2018 inserted be Section 1 of the EUWA 2020.

31 December 2020.[110] There is provision for Completion Day to be delayed exclusively by primary legislation.[111] During the transition period, EU law applies in the UK as if the UK had continued to be a Member State of the EU.[112]

2. The Identification and Interpretation of Retained EU Law

To address the void that would result from a complex disengagement of integrated legal frameworks, the EUWA 2018 makes provision for the new and unique category of 'retained' EU law that will continue to be part of the law of the UK.[113] Examples of retained EU law include domestic legislation derived from EU law,[114] EU legislation such as Regulations which were directly effective,[115] and pre-Brexit decisions of the CJEU and the UK courts interpreting retained EU legislation.

The concept of retained EU law is distinct from the liberal system of precedent created by Article 1(1) of Protocol No 2 on the Uniform Interpretation of the Lugano II Convention. The courts of a Contracting State applying the Lugano II Convention shall 'pay due account' to the principles laid down by any relevant decisions on the Lugano Convention (1988), Brussels I Regulation (2001), Brussels Ia Regulation (2012), Brussels Convention (1968), and the Convention between the EU and Denmark applying the Brussels I Regulation to that Member State.[116] It has been argued that Protocol No 2 is an insufficient tool to keep the different procedural cultures of civil law and common law together after Brexit.[117] If and when the Lugano II Convention is applied and interpreted (in the unlikely event that the UK applies again to join the Convention),[118] UK courts will have to 'pay due account' to the decisions not only on the Lugano II Convention itself but also on equivalent provisions of the Brussels regime. On 1 July 2021, Switzerland, which is the depository of the Lugano II Convention, notified the Parties to the Convention of the EU's refusal to give its consent to the UK's accession to the Convention.[119]

[110] Section 39 of the EUWA 2020.

[111] Section 15A of the EUWA 2018 inserted by Section 33 of the EUWA 2020.

[112] Section 3(1) of the EUWA 2018 as amended by Section 25(2)(a) of the EUWA 2020.

[113] Department for Exiting the European Union, *Legislating for the United Kingdom's Withdrawal from the European Union* (White Paper, Cm 9446, 2017).

[114] Section 2 of the EUWA 2018.

[115] Section 3 of the EUWA 2018.

[116] See Hartley, *Choice of Court* (n 75) 15–18.

[117] B Hess, 'The Unsuitability of the Lugano Convention (2007) to Serve as a Bridge between the UK and the EU after Brexit' (2018) Max Planck Institute Luxemburg for Procedural Law Research Paper Series No 2018 (2).

[118] The Lugano II Convention does not limit the number of attempts a state can make to accede to the Convention. This means (theoretically) the UK can apply again in the future.

[119] Swiss Federal Council, 'Communication by the depositary with respect to the application of accession by the United Kingdom of Great Britain and Northern Ireland' 1 July 2021 <271 (admin.ch)> accessed 31 August 2021.

Retained EU law constitutes a new and unique legal category in the domestic law of the UK. It is neither English law nor EU law *per se*. Rather it is a frozen-in-time remnant of EU law as it stood on 31 December 2020.[120] The identification and interpretation of retained EU law will give rise to its own set of challenges. Ultimately, fidelity to EU law will have to be balanced with the ability of UK appellate courts to diverge from retained EU law and develop their own jurisprudence. There is provision for the UK Supreme Court and the Court of Appeal of England and Wales to depart from retained EU law. The post-Brexit CJEU jurisprudence will not be binding on the English courts but it will continue to influence courts when interpreting the same piece of legislation. The basic rules and principles applicable to retained EU law are laid down in the EUWA 2018 and the EUWA 2020. They are summarised below and will be referred to during the course of this book at appropriate junctures.

The driving policy behind the constitutionally significant EUWA 2018 is ensuring continuity and legal certainty. By converting EU law into domestic law and preserving UK laws made to implement EU obligations, the Act ensures that there is continuity and certainty for businesses, individuals, and government. However, the EUWA 2018 does bring radical change to the UK's legal system:[121] it transforms the statute book by repealing the European Communities Act 1972; it creates a new and unique category of domestic law; it gives wide ranging power to ministers; it has given rise to a large volume of delegated legislation; and it amends the devolution statutes. The EUWA 2018 aims to balance the tension between continuity and change.[122]

A significant example of the tension between continuity and change is found in the retention of the principle of supremacy of EU law.[123] The operation of the principle of supremacy of EU law in the courts of EU Member States is controversial and complex.[124] The way in which the duty of consistent interpretation operates in

[120] The Secretary of State for Exiting the European Union described the approach as: '[taking] a snapshot of the body of EU law that currently forms part of the United Kingdom legal system and [ensuring] that it will continue to apply in the United Kingdom after we leave'. (HC Deb 7 September 2017, vol. 628, col. 342)

[121] E Duhs and I Rao, *Retained EU Law: A Practical Guide* (The Law Society 2021) 4–5 (hereafter Duhs and Rao, *Retained EU Law*).

[122] ibid.

[123] The House of Lord Select Committee on the Constitution said it its report to the European Union (Withdrawal) Bill that it considered that it was 'impossible to see in what sense "the principle of the supremacy of EU law", set out in clause 5, could meaningfully apply in the UK once it has left the EU'. (Select Committee on the Constitution, *European Union (Withdrawal) Bill* (HL 2017-09, 69), [88]).

[124] In *Costa v ENEL* (6/64) [1964] ECR 585 the CJEU espoused the principle of supremacy of EU law and stated that EU law could not 'be overridden by domestic legal provisions, however framed, without being deprived of its character as [Union] law and without the legal basis of the [Union] itself being called into question'. See Hartley, *European Union Law* (n 76) ch 7. For the application of the supremacy of EU law in UK courts, see, *R v Secretary of State for Transport Ex Parte Factortame (No 2)* (1991) 1 AC 603 (Lord Bridge); *Benkharbouche v Secretary of State for Foreign and Commonwealth Affairs* [2017] UKSC 62, [78] (Lord Sumption): 'a conflict between EU law and English domestic law must be resolved in favour of the former, and the latter must be disapplied'; *Benkharbouche v Embassy of the Republic of Sudan* [2015] EWCA Civ 33, [76]-[81].

the courts of EU Member States is unpredictable.[125] These subsisting issues will be inherited by retained EU law and its interpretation by the UK courts. The EUWA 2018 retains the principle of supremacy of EU law as a precept for organising and ensuring clarity in the statute book in terms of how different legislation interacts.[126] However, it is difficult to see how the principle of the supremacy of EU law can operate in a domestic law context when its essential characteristics no longer apply. The principle of supremacy of EU law is a means of harmonising the law and it is an acknowledgement that the legal systems of the EU Member States have 'limited their sovereign rights'. These issues will be resolved by the decisions of the UK courts when applying and interpreting the EUWA 2018.

EU law that existed before Completion Day will continue in force and effect in the UK as retained EU law.[127] Retained EU law means EU law (legislation, case law, general principles of European law) that existed before Completion Day which continues to have effect in the UK after Completion Day.[128] Retained EU law has effect as domestic law of the closest equivalent category.[129] Retained case law means principles and decisions of UK courts and the CJEU as they had effect immediately before Completion Day.[130] Retained EU law is to be interpreted in accordance with retained case law and general principles of EU law.[131] General principles of EU law apply as retained EU law after Completion Day only if they had been recognised as such by the CJEU in a decision rendered before Completion Day.[132] Any question requiring the interpretation of retained EU law is a question of law.[133] The principle of the supremacy of EU law applies as part of the interpretation of any law made before Completion Day.[134] The principle of the supremacy of EU law does not apply to any law made after Completion Day.[135] An English court is not bound by any decision of the CJEU given after Completion Day.[136] An English court is permitted to refer to law made and judgments rendered after Completion Day if it is relevant to

[125] The German Federal Constitutional Court has taken the view that EU law cannot operate to override core principles of the German constitution: *Brunner v European Union Treaty* [1994] 1 CMLR 57. In May 2020, the German Federal Constitutional Court held that the European Central Bank's decisions on the Public Sector Purchase Programme and the CJEU's judgment on the legality of those decisions were legally invalid: BVerfG, Judgment of the Second Senate of 5 May 2020 - 2 BvR 859/15 -, paras 1–237.

[126] Duhs and Rao, *Retained EU Law* (n 121) 119.

[127] Section 3(1) of the EUWA 2018 as amended by Section 25(2)(a) of the EUWA 2020.

[128] Section 6(7) of the EUWA 2018 as amended by Section 26(1)(a) of the EUWA 2020.

[129] Section 7(1), (1A) of the EUWA 2018 as amended by Schedule 5, [40] of the EUWA 2020.

[130] Section 6(7), of the EUWA 2018 as amended by Section 26(1)(a) of the EUWA 2020.

[131] Section 6(3) of the EUWA 2018 as amended by Section 26(1)(a) of the EUWA 2020.

[132] Section 5(6), Schedule 1, [2] of the EUWA 2018.

[133] Section 15(2), Schedule 5, para [3] of the EUWA 2018.

[134] Section 5(2) of the EUWA 2018 as amended by Section 25(4)(a) of the EUWA 2020

[135] Section 5(1) of the EUWA 2018 as amended by Section 25(4)(a) of the EUWA 2020.

[136] Section 6(1)(a) of the EUWA 2018 as amended by Section 26(1)(a) of the EUWA 2020. This would apply to decisions of the CJEU given in relation to provisions forming retained EU law.

do so.[137] An English court has no power after Completion Day to make references to the CJEU.[138]

3. Departure from Retained EU Law

The UK Supreme Court is not bound by retained EU law after Completion Day.[139] In deciding whether to depart or diverge from retained EU law the Supreme Court is to use the test which it applies when invited to depart from one of its own decisions.[140] No court is bound by any retained domestic case law that it would not otherwise by bound by.[141] This makes clear that the normal doctrine of precedent which determines whether a domestic court is bound by the judgment of another domestic court applies unchanged. For instance, the Court of Appeal would not be bound by a judgment of the High Court.

Other courts may be permitted, by Regulations made under Section 5A of the 2020 Act, to be not bound by retained EU law.[142] This power has been extended to the English Court of Appeal and equivalent courts in the other UK jurisdictions.[143] Laws which would be retained as EU law may by Regulation be amended or revoked if they would not operate effectively or contain a deficiency.[144] The principle of Parliamentary sovereignty is recognised and nothing in EUWA 2020 derogates from it.[145]

The same test is applied by other courts to which the power to change retained EU law is extended to promote consistency of approach and legal certainty across the different jurisdictions in the UK. Any additional court should apply the test the UK Supreme Court applies in deciding whether to depart from its own case law. The UK Supreme Court test in deciding whether to depart from its own case law is set out in a House of Lords Practice Statement of 26 July 1966:[146]

[137] Section 6(2) of the EUWA 2018 as amended by Section 26(1)(a) of the EUWA 2020. In this regard, Green LJ refers to the 'non-binding persuasive effects' of EU law in *Lipton v BA City Flyers Limited* [2021] EWCA Civ 454, [65].

[138] Section 6(1)(b) of the EUWA 2018 as amended by Section 26(1)(a) of the EUWA 2020. It has the power until that date: Article 86 of the EU Withdrawal Agreement (n 4).

[139] Section 6(4)(a) of the EUWA 2018.

[140] Section 6(5) of the EUWA 2018 as amended by Section 26(1)(c) of the EUWA 2020.

[141] Section 6(4)(c) of the EUWA 2018.

[142] Section 6(4)(ba) of the EUWA 2018 inserted by Section 26(1)(b) of the EUWA 2020.

[143] European Union (Withdrawal) Act 2018 (Relevant Court) (Retained EU Case Law) Regulations 2020, SI 2020 No 1525.

[144] Section 8 of the EUWA 2018.

[145] Section 38 of the EUWA 2020.

[146] The Practice Statement (Judicial Statement) [1966] 3 All ER 77; [1966] 1 WLR 1234; [1966] 2 Lloyd's Rep. 151, was made in the House of Lords by Lord Gardiner LC on 26 July 1966 on behalf of himself and the Lords of Appeal in Ordinary, that they would depart from precedent in the Lords in order to achieve justice. Louis Blom-Cooper has described the change brought about by the Practice Statement as being as if the Lords 'dropped a pebble into the judicial pool that produced not merely a few ripples but also a seismic wave in English juridical thinking . . . the story of that legally historic event displays the carapace of traditional English lawyers' disinclination readily to accept radical change and

> Their Lordships regard the use of precedent as an indispensable foundation upon which to decide what is the law and its application to individual cases. It provides at least some degree of certainty upon which individuals can rely in the conduct of their affairs, as well as a basis for orderly development of legal rules.
>
> Their Lordships nevertheless recognise that too rigid adherence to precedent may lead to injustice in a particular case and also unduly restrict the proper development of the law. They propose therefore to modify their present practice and, while treating former decisions of this House as normally binding, to depart from a previous decision when it appears right to do so.
>
> In this connection they will bear in mind the danger of disturbing retrospectively the basis on which contracts, settlements of property and fiscal arrangements have been entered into and also the especial need for certainty as to the criminal law.
>
> This announcement is not intended to affect the use of precedent elsewhere than in this House.

In summary, the test applied by the UK Supreme Court to depart from its previous case law is 'whether it appears right to do so'. This test will also apply to depart from retained EU case law.[147] In deciding whether to depart from its own case law, the UK Supreme Court will have regard *inter alia* to 'the danger of disturbing retrospectively the basis on which contracts, settlement of property, and fiscal arrangements have been entered into'.[148]

Even outside the immediate context of retained EU law, it has been argued that the Practice Statement should extend to the intermediate appellate court (Court of Appeal) as it cannot sensibly be confined to the judges in the final court of appeal (UK Supreme Court).[149] Lord Halsbury had argued for a strongly consequentialist justification of the ruling that House of Lords precedents ought to bind all courts

to the cautious application of such change, once it is ultimately conceded'. See L Blom-Cooper, '1966 and All That: The Story of the Practice Statement 1' in L Blom-Cooper QC, B Dickson, and G Drewry (eds.), *The Judicial House of Lords: 1876–2009* (OUP 2009) 128–44 (hereafter Blom-Cooper and others, *Judicial House of Lords*).

[147] Duhs and Rao, *Retained EU Law* (n 121) 144–46.

[148] The Practice Statement (Judicial Statement) [1966] 3 All ER 77; [1966] 1 WLR 1234; [1966] 2 Lloyd's Rep 151.

[149] Blom-Cooper and others, *Judicial House of Lords* (n 146); R Cross and JW Harris, *Precedent in English Law* (4th edn, Clarendon Press 1991) 114. cf *Young v Bristol Aeroplane Company Limited* [1944] 1 KB 718 (Lord Greene MR): The Court of Appeal is bound to follow its own decisions and those of courts of coordinate jurisdiction, and the 'full' court is in the same position in this respect as a division of the court consisting of three members. The only exceptions to this rule are: (1) The court is entitled and bound to decide which of two conflicting decisions of its own it will follow; (2) the court is bound to refuse to follow a decision of its own which, though not expressly overruled, cannot, in its opinion, stand with a decision of the House of Lords; (3) the court is not bound to follow a decision of its own if it is satisfied that the decision was given per incuriam, eg, where a statute or a rule having statutory effect which would have affected the decision was not brought to the attention of the earlier court.

and to be reversible only by Parliament.[150] But the consequences of adhering to that ruling have in turn been found sufficiently unsatisfactory for the House of Lords to have reversed itself on that point.[151] The extension of the legal provision to depart from retained EU law to the Court of Appeal has rendered the body of retained EU case law more susceptible to change than ordinary English law precedent. This extension will also mitigate the practical operational impact on the UK Supreme Court and allow the Supreme Court to benefit from prior judicial deliberation on complex issues before adjudication. In terms of a theory of adjudication, the tension between the category of 'fit' exemplified by retained EU case law and the category of 'justification' based on principle or policy in hard cases will result in the indigenous development of the corpus of retained EU law.[152]

Apart from legal provision for the UK Supreme Court and the Court of Appeal not to follow retained EU case law, judges sometimes rely on viable consequentialist arguments and arguments of principle, to apply a very narrowly restricted interpretation of a statutory provision.[153] On occasion and for similar justifications, judges also interpret precedents very restrictively in order to 'distinguish' or 'explain' them from the point in issue in a given case.[154] Therefore, the possibility of distinguishing or explaining a particular statutory provision or precedent of retained EU law will provide UK lawyers and courts the flexibility to work around retained EU law.

The government does not intend to specify a list of considerations that all courts and tribunals with the power to depart should take into account when making such determinations. It is argued that the power to depart from retained case law should not in principle be extended to UK courts and tribunals beyond the UK Supreme Court. The UK Supreme Court is best placed to consider the full implications of any such departures. Any change from this position constitutes a major shift in the administration of justice. This could result in a lack of legal certainty through the emergence of aberrant judgments that are either not binding on other courts or are inconsistent with precedent. Precedent provides some degree of certainty upon which individuals can rely in the conduct of their affairs. If the power to depart is granted more extensively, it should be restricted to the Court of Appeal and

150 N MacCormick, *Legal Reasoning and Legal Theory* (Clarendon Press 1978) 134.

151 ibid.

152 See generally, R Dworkin, *Taking Rights Seriously* (Harvard University Press 1977) ch 4.

153 For example, Section 4(4) of the Foreign Compensation Act 1950 in *Anisminic Ltd v Foreign Compensation Commission* [1969] 2 AC 147, [1969] 2 WLR 163 (HL). A unified 'contextual' approach to statutory interpretation was identified by Rupert Cross which was supported by dicta of the House of Lords. Cross suggested that the English approach involves not so much a choice between alternative rules as a progressive analysis in which the judges first consider the ordinary meaning of the words in the broad general context of the statute. The judges then moves on to consider other possibilities if the ordinary meaning leads to an absurd result. See R Cross, J Bell, and G Engle, *Cross: Statutory Interpretation* (3rd edn, OUP 1995) 49.

154 MacCormick, *Legal Reasoning and Legal Theory* (n 150) 219–24; JW Harris, *Legal Philosophies* (2nd edn, Butterworths 1997) 183.

its equivalents to help to mitigate the erosion of precedent.[155] A balance has to be struck between the policy aim of encouraging timely departure from retained EU case law, where appropriate, and the negative impacts of driving re-litigation, and therefore case volumes, creating uncertainty and reducing confidence in the UK as a forum in which to settle disputes.[156] If the power to change retained EU law is extended to the High Court and equivalent courts and tribunals, it risks creating conflicting precedents within the judicial system and considerable legal uncertainty.

The test that the UK Supreme Court uses to depart from its own rulings has certain benefits in that the test is uncodified and flexible, the bar is necessarily high, and it will have the value of reinforcing legal clarity and certainty. This clarity, coupled with the quality of the judges who apply the case law, has traditionally been seen as a strength when making arguments about the UK as the jurisdiction of choice.

However, it is envisaged the development of the test to depart from retained EU case law may be too wide and additional factors should be for consideration by the courts. The preference is for the courts to outline these factors. The UK Supreme Court could establish the 'schedule of considerations' for this purpose in one of its first judgments, taking account of both existing case law and the need to consider potential departures in this field holistically.

The proposals on the departure from EU retained law could see a significant shift in the administration of justice in England and lead to a lack of legal certainty. Granting the power to depart to lower courts is likely to encourage litigation by parties who hope to overturn an earlier judgment which relied upon EU case law, and subsequently increase the volume of cases. This will inevitably put additional pressure on the courts, which are already facing a significant backlog caused by the COVID-19 pandemic.

Conversely, restricting the power to depart to the highest courts is likely to help prevent frivolous claims. The emergence of differing judicial interpretations to case law, which has been noted to be a probable risk should the power to depart be widely given, is likely to lead to an increase in the volume of cases, due to an increased number of appeals in order to address these inconsistencies. This would be the case both within and across the UK's jurisdictions.

It is reasonable to expect those areas of law which have been shaped more by EU case law and the CJEU to be subject to greater impact. Within the discipline of private international law, the retained Rome I Regulation and retained Rome II Regulation are likely to give rise to challenges to the continued application of

[155] See Ministry of Justice, 'Response to the consultation on the departure from retained EU case law by UK courts and tribunals' (CP 303, October 2020), <https://assets.publishing.service.gov.uk/government/uploads/system/uploads/attachment_data/file/926811/departure-eu-case-law-uk-courts-tribunals-consultation-response.pdf> accessed 31 August 2021. The paper concluded that it was appropriate to allow courts at the level of the Court of Appeal of England and Wales to depart from retained EU case law.

[156] ibid p. 17.

pre-Brexit case law in the English courts. From the perspective of lawyers practising in private international law, the legal uncertainty means that many clients will seek advice and there may be a surge in litigation, at least in the short to medium term.

From 1 January 2021, the continuing effect of EU law is subject to Regulations made under Section 8 of the EUWA 2018. EU law may be amended where this is necessary for its effective operation in the UK. It may also be revoked, for instance, where the legislation is based on the principle of reciprocity or mutual recognition. The most significant effect of Regulations made under Section 8 will be to revoke almost all provisions of EU legislation on civil jurisdiction and recognition and enforcement of judgments.[157] As a result, the case law of the CJEU and Member State courts interpreting the EU legislation on civil jurisdiction and recognition and enforcement of judgments will be redundant.

The Brussels Convention, the Brussels I Regulation (2001), the Brussels Ia Regulation (2012), and the Lugano II Convention, effective in the UK by virtue of EU law, will be revoked as rules of UK law. International conventions and other instruments[158] which applied in the UK immediately before Completion Day by reason of its status as a Member State[159] will cease to be part of English law unless and until the UK acts on its own initiative to adopt them. It will be as though the EU, and the private international law relating to it, ceased to exist.

On the other hand, the Rome I Regulation and the Rome II Regulations on the applicable law in cross-border contractual and non-contractual obligations respectively constitute retained EU law. The case law of the CJEU and the UK courts prior to Completion Day on the Rome I and II Regulations will be retained EU law. An English court is permitted but not bound to follow the law made and judgments rendered by the CJEU on the Rome I and II Regulations after Completion Day. Issues relating to the identification, interpretation, and divergence from retained EU will doubtless arise in the context of the applicable law for cross border contractual and non-contractual obligations and are dealt with in Chapter 4 of this book.

I. Brexit's Delegated Legislation Revoking Private International Law Instruments and Provisions

The revocations rendered by Brexit's delegated legislation to private international law instruments and provisions are considered in this section.

[157] Including English law made to give effect to that EU legislation.

[158] The Charter of Fundamental Rights will have no effect after Completion Day: Section 5(4) of the EUWA 2018 as amended by Section 25(4)(a) of the EUWA 2020.

[159] Taking effect, for example, under Article 216(2) TFEU.

The Brussels Convention, as originally made and amended, is revoked and removed in its entirety from the Civil Jurisdiction and Judgments Act 1982.[160]

The Lugano Convention 1988 is revoked and removed in its entirety from the Civil Jurisdiction and Judgments Act 1982.[161]

Reference to the various Accession Conventions, and to the Expert Reports associated with them, is deleted from the Civil Jurisdiction and Judgments Act 1982.[162]

Rights, powers, etc., derived from the Brussels Convention, Lugano I and II Conventions, the Brussels Accession Conventions, and the EC–Denmark Agreement, cease to be recognised and will not form part of retained EU law.[163]

The provisions of the Civil Jurisdiction and Judgments Act 1982, as amended, which supplement the Conventions are revoked and repealed (in whole or in part, as circumstance requires) to the extent that they performed this function.[164]

The Brussels I Regulation 44/2001 is revoked and will not be part of retained EU law.[165]

The Brussels Ia Regulation 1215/2012 is revoked and will not form part of retained EU law.[166]

The Civil Jurisdiction and Judgments Order 2001, making provision and providing for supplementary rules of English law for the purpose of the Brussels I Regulation is mostly, but not entirely, repealed.[167]

The Service Regulation 1393/2007 is revoked and will not form part of retained EU law.[168]

The Taking of Evidence Regulation 1206/2001 is revoked and will not form part of retained EU law.[169]

The European Enforcement Order Regulation 805/2004 is revoked and will not form part of retained EU law.[170]

160 Civil Jurisdiction and Judgments (Amendment) (EU Exit) Regulations 2019, SI 2019 No 479, Pt 2.

161 Civil Jurisdiction and Judgments (Amendment) (EU Exit) Regulations 2019, SI 2019 No 479, Pt 2.

162 Civil Jurisdiction and Judgments (Amendment) (EU Exit) Regulations 2019, SI 2019 No 479, regs 52–58.

163 Civil Jurisdiction and Judgments (Amendment) (EU Exit) Regulations 2019, SI 2019 No 479, reg 82.

164 Civil Jurisdiction and Judgments (Amendment) (EU Exit) Regulations 2019, SI 2019 No 479, Pt 2.

165 Civil Jurisdiction and Judgments (Amendment) (EU Exit) Regulations 2019, SI 2019 No 479, reg 84.

166 Civil Jurisdiction and Judgments (Amendment) (EU Exit) Regulations 2019, SI 2019 No 479, reg 85.

167 Civil Jurisdiction and Judgments (Amendment) (EU Exit) Regulations 2019, SI 2019 No 479, reg 75.

168 Service of Documents and Taking of Evidence in Civil and Commercial Matters (Revocation and Saving Provisions) (EU Exit) Regulations 2018, SI 2018 No 1257, reg 7.

169 Service of Documents and Taking of Evidence in Civil and Commercial Matters (Revocation and Saving Provisions) (EU Exit) Regulations 2018, SI 2018 No 1257, reg 12.

170 European Enforcement Order, European Order for Payment and European Small Claims Procedure (Amendment etc) (EU Exit) Regulations 2018, SI 2018 No 1311, reg 7.

The European Small Claims Procedure Regulation 861/2007 is revoked and will not form part of retained EU law.[171]

The European Order for Payment Regulation 1896/2006 is revoked and will not form part of retained EU law.[172]

The parts of Civil Procedure Rules (CPR) Part 6 which provide for service of process where the English court has jurisdiction under the Conventions or Regulations are deleted.[173]

The parts of CPR Part 74 which provide for the mechanism for the enforcement of judgments under the Conventions or the Regulations are deleted.[174]

CPR which are made to govern matters to which EU laws apply which are not retained are deleted.

J. Laws that Persist Regardless of the Brexit Legislation

Some of the applicable legal framework has survived unscathed despite the revocations and amendments affected by the Brexit legislation on private international law. The law which remains in force is outlined below.

Section 16 of the Civil Jurisdiction and Judgments Act 1982, and the internal UK jurisdiction provisions in Schedule 4, will, with minor amendment,[175] continue to have effect to determine the allocation of jurisdiction in civil and commercial matters within, and as between the parts of, the UK.

The Civil Jurisdiction and Judgment Act 1982 (Gibraltar) Order 1997,[176] making provision for jurisdiction and the recognition and effect of judgments as between the UK and Gibraltar will remain in force with minor amendment.[177]

The Civil Jurisdiction and Judgments Act 1982 is amended by the insertion of Section 3D and Schedule 3F, which gives effect to the Hague Convention on Choice of Court Agreements (2005), pursuant to Section 1(2) of the Private International Law (Implementation of Agreements) Act 2020.

Sections 15A to 15E of the Civil Jurisdiction and Judgments Act 1982, which provide for jurisdiction in matters relating to local consumers and local employees, will come into effect on Completion Day.[178]

[171] European Enforcement Order, European Order for Payment and European Small Claims Procedure (Amendment etc) (EU Exit) Regulations 2018, SI 2018 No 1311, reg 10.

[172] European Enforcement Order, European Order for Payment and European Small Claims Procedure (Amendment etc) (EU Exit) Regulations 2018, SI 2018 No 1311, reg 9.

[173] Civil Procedure Rules 1998 (Amendment) (EU Exit) Regulations 2019, SI 2019 No 521, reg 4.

[174] Civil Procedure Rules 1998 (Amendment) (EU Exit) Regulations 2019, SI 2019 No 521, reg 15.

[175] Civil Jurisdiction and Judgments (Amendment) (EU Exit) Regulations 2019, SI 2019 No 479, reg 28

[176] SI 1997 No 2602.

[177] Civil Jurisdiction and Judgments (Amendment) (EU Exit) Regulations 2019, SI 2019 No 479, reg 73.

[178] Inserted by Civil Jurisdiction and Judgments (Amendment) (EU Exit) Regulations 2019, SI 2019 No 479, reg 26.

The Civil Jurisdiction and Judgments Act 1982 (Interim Relief) Order 1997, which widened the scope of Section 25 of the Act, remains in force with the deletion of the reference to the Brussels Convention, Lugano Convention, and Brussels I Regulation.[179]

The bilateral treaties between the UK and several Member States made and given effect under the Foreign Judgments (Reciprocal Enforcement) Act 1933, which have been in suspension since the relationship between the UK and the state in question was first governed by the Brussels or Lugano Convention, will revive.

The Rome I Regulation and Rome II Regulation on the law applicable to cross-border civil and commercial contractual and non-contractual obligations respectively constitute retained EU law.[180]

K. Service of Documents to European States after Brexit

When considering the impact of Brexit, it is important to be aware that issues of service are inextricably interlinked with questions of jurisdiction when serving documents outside England. Service of documents out of the jurisdiction requires the permission of the court. Brexit not only affects service of documents to EU Member States but also the service of documents to Contracting States of the Lugano II Convention.

This section considers the implications for UK lawyers seeking to serve process on entities in European states in civil or commercial matters after Completion Day. Before venturing into this discussion, it is useful to remind ourselves of the legal landscape for cross border service of process to Member States prior to Brexit and also consider the law during the Brexit transition period.

1. Cross-border Service in the Civil Procedure Rules

Service of process out of the jurisdiction requires the permission of the court[181] and in cases where no permission is required CPR 6.40 explains how service must be rendered. In principle, a claim that the claim form has not been properly served on technical grounds or an averment that service should be set aside because the court should not have granted permission may be an impediment.[182] English

[179] Redundant, because of an order made under Section 25(3) of the 1982 Act.

[180] The Law Applicable to Contractual Obligations and Non-Contractual Obligations (Amendment etc) (EU Exit) Regulations 2019, SI 2019 No 834. (Only minor corrections were made to the Rome I and II Regulations to adapt to UK law).

[181] CPR 6.36.

[182] *Abela v Baadarani* [2013] UKSC 44, [2013] 1 WLR 2043; see also *Weston v Bates* [2012] EWHC 590 (QB), [2013] 1 WLR 189 (service of copy of claim form).

process must be served in accordance with the rules of English law as these apply to service of English process in the particular country for service to be regular. The claimant must also act in accordance with[183] the law of the place where service is to be made.[184]

The basic principle is that service should be made by any method permitted[185] for the service of English process by the law of the country in which it is to be served,[186] and if it is contrary to the law of the country in which it is made, the service will not be service authorised by the Civil Procedure Rules. No general response can be given to a question about the appropriate method of service in order for the service to be effective. It depends on the law of the country in which service is to be made, and the advice of a local lawyer is recommended.[187]

2. The EU Service Regulation and the Brexit Transition Period

The EU Service Regulation regulates the service of judicial and extrajudicial documents between EU Member States and has applied since 13 November 2008.[188] It provides, *inter alia*, a procedure for the service of documents via designated 'transmitting agencies' and 'receiving agencies' without recourse to consular and

[183] The method of service should not be prohibited by the law of the place where service is to be made. cf This is distinct from not being provided for under the law of that state: *Embassy of Brazil v de Castro Cerqueira* UKEAT/456/13, [2014] 1 WLR 3718.

[184] CPR 6.40(4).

[185] The method of service should not forbidden by the law of the country in which service is to be made: *Habib Bank Ltd v Central Bank of Sudan* [2006] EWHC 1767 (Comm), [2007] 1 WLR 470; *Abela v Baadarani* [2013] UKSC 44, [2013] 1 WLR 2043.

[186] CPR 6.40(3). In *Knauf UK GmbH v British Gypsum Ltd* [2001] EWCA Civ 1570, [2002] 1 Lloyd's Rep 199, the court expressed uncertainty why a claim form to be served in Germany could not be served by first class post. The answer appears to be that English first-class post (CPR 6.3(1)(b)) does not operate outside the UK and service by post is not permitted by German law. For confirmation, see *Burns-Anderson Independent Network v Wheeler* [2005] EWHC 575 (QB), [2005] 1 Lloyd's Rep 580.

[187] CPR Pt 6 PD B, para. 4.2, invites enquiries to the Foreign Process Section, Royal Courts of Justice, Strand, London WC2A 2LL. For an illustration of the potential problems, see *Shiblaq v Sadikoglu* [2004] EWHC 1890 (Comm), [2004] ILPr 826, dealing with service of documents in Turkey in circumstances where Turkish law did not make it easy to understand whether service by notary public (which is valid for service of Turkish documents in Turkey) was valid service for English documents: held no; *Arros Invest Ltd v Nishanov* [2004] EWHC 576 (Ch), [2004] ILPr 366 (service by post inside Russia); *BAS Capital Funding Corp v Medfinco Ltd* [2003] EWHC 1798 (Ch), [2004] 1 Lloyd's Rep 652 (service in Malta before Malta became a Member State).

[188] Regulation (EC) No 1393/2007 of the European Parliament and of the Council of 13 November 2007 on the service in the Member States of judicial and extrajudicial documents in civil or commercial matters (service of documents), and repealing Council Regulation (EC) No 1348/2000 OJ L 324, 10.12.2007, 79–120. Following a review of the EU Service Regulation by the European Commission, Regulation (EU) 2020/1784 on the service in the Member States of judicial and extrajudicial documents in civil or commercial matters (service of documents) (recast) (Recast Service Regulation) was published in the Official Journal (OJ L 405/40) on 2 December 2020. The Recast Service Regulation will apply in Member States from 1 July 2022.

diplomatic channels, and other methods of service. The EU Service Regulation applies to all EU Member States, including Denmark.[189]

Before Brexit, English court proceedings were able to be served on defendants in other EU Member States in accordance with the EU Service Regulation, which was relatively quick and cost effective. It permitted a variety of methods of service including service between designated state central bodies;[190] postal service where proceedings are sent by the EU Member State;[191] and direct service where permitted under the law of the EU Member State,[192] although several EU Member States did not permit direct service. Following Brexit, service in other EU Member States is still possible but it is likely to be slower.

The relevant transitional provisions for service of documents in an EU Member State are set out in Article 68 of the Withdrawal Agreement and are limited to the process of service, that is the application of the Service Regulation. Where the process of service has commenced and one of the criteria set out in Article 68 was met prior to 31 December 2020 at 11 p.m., service can continue after that date under the provisions of the EU Service Regulation. The criterion is that the EU Service Regulation shall apply to judicial and extrajudicial documents which were received for the purposes of service before the end of the transition period by one of the following:

(1) a receiving agency
(2) a central body of the state where the service is to be effected, or
(3) diplomatic or consular agents, postal services or judicial officers, officials or other competent persons of the state addressed, as referred to in Articles 13, 14, and 15 of that Regulation.

The EU Service Regulation applied to the UK during the Brexit transition period but ceased to apply to the UK on a reciprocal basis at the end of the transition period, except as provided for in Part Three of the UK–EU Withdrawal Agreement in relation to procedures pending as at that date.[193]

[189] Denmark notified the EC, by letter of 20 November 2007, of its decision to implement EU Service Regulation (OJ 2008 L331/21) and the Danish Ministry of Justice confirmed that Denmark is bound by the EU Service Regulation by statutory order number 1476 of 12 December 2007.

[190] Article 4 of the EU Service Regulation.

[191] Article 14 of the EU Service Regulation.

[192] Article 15 of the EU Service Regulation.

[193] The Service of Documents and Taking of Evidence in Civil and Commercial Matters (Revocation and Saving Provisions) (EU Exit) Regulations 2018 (SI 2018/1257) reg 9 (as amended by the Civil, Criminal and Family Justice (Amendment) (EU Exit) Regulations 2020 (SI 2020/1493) reg 2(3)) contain transitional provisions which mean that the Regulation will continue to apply to outstanding requests for documents to be served, where those requests were received in the UK before Exit Day. However, nothing in Part 2 of EU Exit Regulation, SI 2018/1257 will affect the application of Article 68(a) of the EU Withdrawal Agreement and that the Service Regulation will continue to have affect for the purposes of that Article. SI 2018/1257, reg 10 set out savings provisions for the application of the Service Regulation under the EU/ Denmark Agreement. However, reg 10(2) was also substituted by SI 2020/1493, reg 2(4) which states that nothing in Part 2 of EU Exit Regulation, SI 2018/1257 will affect

From the end of the transition period, the EU Regulation on the service of judicial and extrajudicial documents in civil or commercial matters (service of documents) is no longer applicable between the UK and the EU Member States.[194] Delegated legislation was needed to prevent the EU Service Regulation, which cannot operate without reciprocity from becoming part of UK law under the EU (Withdrawal) Act 2018. That Act provides that direct EU legislation (including EU Regulations) which is operative immediately before Exit Day forms part of domestic law on and after exit day. Without the statutory instrument, therefore, the Service Regulation would be incorporated into UK law from that point.

The Hague Convention of 15 November 1965 on the Service Abroad of Judicial and Extrajudicial Documents in Civil or Commercial Matters (the Hague Service Convention) has instead become applicable between the UK and those EU Member States which are part of the Convention. The UK acceded to the Convention in 1967 and all twenty-seven EU Member States are signatories. The Convention has regulated the service of documents between the UK and the EFTA member countries (with the exception of Liechtenstein) and Denmark. The Convention is widely applied and the total number of Contracting States is currently seventy-nine.

Numerous aspects of the service procedure are regulated by the Convention. Aside from methods provided for under the Convention, it also permits other methods of service as long as they are sanctioned by the receiving state's internal law.[195] Contracting States of the Convention cannot object to a mode of service as long as it satisfies the terms of the convention, unless the state would deem compliance with the same an infringement of its sovereignty or security.[196]

the application of Article 69(3) of the EU Withdrawal Agreement which relates to the UK–Denmark Agreement.

[194] The Service of Documents and Taking of Evidence in Civil and Commercial Matters (Revocation and Saving Provisions) (EU Exit) Regulations 2018 (SI 2018/1257) reg 7 (as amended by the Civil, Criminal and Family Justice (Amendment) (EU Exit) Regulations 2020 (SI 2020/1493)) revoked the retained EU law version of the EU Service Regulation for most purposes (subject to saving provisions in relation to pending procedures) and amended EU retained law relating to the EU Service Regulation. The regulations also revoked Council Decision (EC) 2005/794 of 20 September 2005, on the signing, on behalf of the Community, of the Agreement between the European Community and the Kingdom of Denmark on the service of judicial and extrajudicial documents in civil or commercial matters and Council Decision (EC) 2006/326 of 27 April 2006, concerning the conclusion of the Agreement between the European Community and the Kingdom of Denmark on the service of judicial and extrajudicial documents in civil or commercial matters. The Civil Procedure Rules 1998 (Amendment) (EU Exit) Regulations 2019 (SI 2019/521) (as amended by the Civil, Criminal and Family Justice (Amendment) (EU Exit) Regulations 2020 (SI 2020/1493)) made changes to the provisions in CPR 6 relating to service outside the jurisdiction, consequential on the revocation of the EU Service Regulation.

[195] Article 19 of the Hague Service Convention.

[196] Article 13 of the Hague Service Convention.

3. Methods of Service under the Hague Convention

The Convention is applicable to all civil and commercial cases and provides for three basic methods of service.[197]

a) Through the central authority

The most formal method is through the central authority.[198] Service through the central authority requires the sender to transmit the summons and complaint, and to complete a service request form and a form summarising the document to be served.[199] Only forms on pages 1 and 4 must be filled in. Having received the appropriate forms, each central authority may effect service in accordance with its country's internal law.

Provided it conforms with internal law, the documents may be served by a method requested by the sender.[200] Article 5 further stipulates that the document may always be served by delivery to an addressee who accepts it voluntarily.

A certificate stating that the document was served is completed by the central authority upon service. This stipulates how and upon whom service was made, and the date and place of such service. The certificate then goes back to the individual who requested service.[201]

b) Through competent persons

The second method allows service to be effected directly through diplomatic or consular agents, judicial officers, officials, or other competent persons.[202]

The receiving state can object to such service and some states have opted to oppose full application of Article 8:

> Each contracting state shall be free to effect service of judicial documents upon persons abroad, without application of any compulsion, directly through its diplomatic or consular agents. Any state may declare that it is opposed to such service within its territory...

c) Through the mail

The least formal method of service is that designated under Article 10(a), which permits judicial documents to be sent directly through the mail, provided the receiving state has not objected.

Article 10 states:

197 Articles 1 and 6–10 of the Hague Service Convention.
198 Article 2 of the Hague Service Convention.
199 Article 3 of the Hague Service Convention.
200 Article 5 of the Hague Service Convention.
201 Article 6 of the Hague Service Convention.
202 Articles 8, 9, 10(b), (c) of the Hague Service Convention.

> Provided the state of destination does not object, the present convention shall not interfere with—(a) the freedom to send judicial documents, by postal channels, directly to persons abroad . . .

d) Designation of central authorities

According to Articles 15 and 16, each state must designate all prescribed central authorities and agencies established by each member nation to receive and serve documents forwarded by other member nations.

In order to identify the appropriate authority to be tasked with effecting service in any particular Member State, one must consult the list of reservations and declarations for that state.

e) National objections

Each signatory has the right to state its opposition, if any, to the service methods provided for under the convention, other than service through the central authority.

Most of the EU Member States have registered the following objections:

> objection to service, as proposed in Article 8 paragraph 1 (service upon persons abroad without application for compulsion and directly through diplomatic or consular agents) unless the document is to be served on a national of the state in which the document originates. You may have to apply for compulsion and serve directly through diplomatic or consular agents if you want to serve on a national of the receiving state
>
> objection to methods of service set out in Article 10 (freedom to serve directly by post; freedom of judicial officers or interested persons to serve through judicial officers, officials or other competent persons in the receiving state).

f) Declarations

According to Articles 2 and 21, signatories can additionally declare any stipulations with respect to the entry of, or relief from, a default judgment.

The main declarations made pursuant to Articles 2 and 21 are in respect of Articles 15 and 16:

> Article 15 paragraph 2—freedom to give judgment even if document has not been served by a method prescribed by internal law; and document delivery cannot be proved (with certificate of service or delivery), as long as:
>
> the document was transmitted by one of the methods provided for in this convention no less than six months have passed since transmission, and
>
> no certificate of any kind has been received although reasonable effort to obtain through competent authorities of the state can be proved.

Article 16 paragraph 3—a judge may give judgment even if no certificate of service or delivery has been received, subject to the three criteria in the point above.

Article 16 paragraph 3—most states have declared that following judgment, an application for relief will not be entertained if it is filed after one year following the date of the judgment.

g) Lingual requirements

Most states require documents to be translated in the official language of the receiving state in order for service to be effected.[203]

h) Declarations and reservations

The general position adopted by the Hague Service Convention has been considered but each of the EU Member States has exercised its right to make declarations and reservations in respect of the full text of the convention. Accordingly, one must consult the list for the specific receiving state to determine the scope of the Convention.

The EU Service Regulation simplified the service of process and enabled quicker timelines. The procedure may be more cumbersome, but it will still be possible to serve proceedings out of the jurisdiction on defendants domiciled in EU Member States and Lugano II Convention Contracting States using the mechanisms for service of process under the Hague Service Convention.

L. Taking of Evidence after Brexit

This section considers the implications for UK lawyers seeking to obtain evidence from entities in EU Member States in civil or commercial matters after the expiry of the Brexit transition period. Before venturing into this discussion, it is useful to remind ourselves of the legal landscape for cross-border taking of evidence in EU Member States prior to Brexit and also consider the law during the Brexit transition period.

1. EU Regime

The Taking of Evidence Regulation has laid down rules for the taking of evidence from a witness in one EU Member State to assist in proceedings before the courts of another EU Member State.[204]

[203] Article 5 of the Hague Service Convention.

[204] Council Regulation (EC) No 1206/2001 of 28 May 2001 on cooperation between the courts of the Member States in the taking of evidence in civil or commercial matters OJ L 174, 27.6.2001, 1–24. (Taking of Evidence Regulation)

2. Transitional Application: Article 68(b) of the Withdrawal Agreement

The relevant transitional provisions for the taking of evidence are set out in Article 68(b) of the Withdrawal Agreement and require that one of the specific criteria for the making of the request is met by 31 December 2020. The criteria are that the request has been received by:

a requested court;

a central body of the State where the taking of evidence is requested; or

a central body or competent authority referred to in Article 17(1) of Regulation (EC) 1206/2001, the Taking of Evidence Regulation;

Where one of these criteria are met, the provisions in the Regulation will continue to apply to the UK after 31 December 2020.

To enable the UK to comply with its obligations under the Withdrawal Agreement, delegated legislation has laid down savings provisions for the application of the Taking of Evidence Regulation which include modifications to the Regulation.[205]

3. Post-Brexit Transition Period

From the end of the transition period, Council Regulation (EC) No 1206/2001 on cooperation between the courts of the Member States in the taking of evidence in civil or commercial matters is no longer applicable between the UK and the EU Member States.[206] From 1 January 2021, where the transitional provisions are not engaged, the Hague Convention of 18 March 1970 on the taking of evidence abroad in civil or commercial matters ('Hague Evidence Convention') has instead become applicable between the UK and those EU Member States that are Contracting States of the Convention.[207]

The exceptions where the Hague Evidence Convention does not apply are Austria, Belgium, and Ireland. Where the Convention is not applicable, letters will have to be sent to the national courts via diplomatic channels.

[205] The Service of Documents and the Taking of Evidence in Civil and Commercial Matters (Revocation and Savings Provisions) (EU Exit) Regulations 2018, SI 2018/1257, reg 13. However, reg 13 has been substituted by The Civil, Criminal and Family Justice (Amendment) (EU Exit) Regulations 2020, SI 2020/1493, reg 2(5) which states that nothing in EU Exit Regulation, SI 2018/1257 will affect the application of Article 68(b) of the EU Withdrawal Agreement and that the Taking of Evidence Regulation will continue to have affect for the purposes of that Article.

[206] The Service of Documents and the Taking of Evidence in Civil and Commercial Matters (Revocation and Savings Provisions) (EU Exit) Regulations 2018, SI 2018/1257, reg 12.

[207] Convention of 18 March 1970 on the Taking of Evidence Abroad in Civil or Commercial Matters.

The UK acceded to the Hague Evidence Convention in 1976. The Hague Evidence Convention establishes methods of cooperation for the taking of evidence abroad in civil or commercial matters, between parties via letters of request,[208] and diplomatic or consular agents and Commissioners.[209]

Under Article 12, the execution of a letter of request can be refused if either:

in the receiving state the execution of the letter does not fall within the functions of the judiciary; or

the state addressed considers that its sovereignty or security would be prejudiced by the execution.

4. Letters of Request

To obtain evidence that is intended for use in judicial proceedings, a letter of request[210] must be sent from a judicial authority of the requesting state to a competent authority of the requested state. A letter of request cannot be used for obtaining evidence that is not intended for use in judicial proceedings, commenced, or contemplated.[211] This letter must be transmitted to the central authority of the requested state, which then will forward it to the competent authority for execution; the law of the requested state will apply to the execution. Each state has a designated central authority,[212] and federal states might have more than one.[213]

In order to expedite and facilitate execution, the Convention provides an option to allow the presence of the parties and/or their representatives at the execution of the letter of request.

The requesting authority may also request the use of a special method or procedure in the execution of the letter of request, provided this is not incompatible with the law of the requested state or impossible to perform.[214]

If the Contracting State has not made a reservation under Article 33, letters in English or French or translated into these languages will be accepted.[215] The translation must be certified as correct, either by a diplomatic officer or consular agent or by a sworn translator or by any other person so authorised in either state.

A letter of request does not need any legalisation or other formality, but it must specify:[216]

208 Articles 1 to 14 of the Hague Evidence Convention.
209 Articles 15 to 22 of the Hague Evidence Convention.
210 ch I of the Hague Evidence Convention.
211 Article 1 of the Hague Evidence Convention.
212 Article 2 of the Hague Evidence Convention.
213 Article 24.2 of the Hague Evidence Convention.
214 Article 9 of the Hague Evidence Convention.
215 Article 4 of the Hague Evidence Convention.
216 Article 3 of the Hague Evidence Convention.

the authority requesting its execution and the authority requested to execute it, if known to the requesting authority;

the names and addresses of the parties to the proceedings and their representatives, if any;

the nature of the proceedings for which the evidence is required, giving all necessary information;

the evidence to be obtained or other judicial act to be performed.

Further information will be necessary depending on what type of evidence is requested, for example:

the names and addresses of the persons to be examined;

the questions to be put to the persons to be examined or a statement of the subject matter about which they are to be examined;

the documents or other property, real or personal, to be inspected;

any requirement that the evidence is to be given on oath or affirmation, and any special form to be used;

any special method or procedure to be followed under Article 9.

The more detailed the letter is, the less likely it will be rejected or questioned.

5. Diplomatic or Consular Agents and Commissioners

If a state has not made reservations under Article 33, evidence can be taken by diplomatic or consular agents and commissioners.[217]

Subject to the relevant permission, the representative or commissioner may:

take evidence, if their proposed actions are compatible with the law of the state of execution, and have power to administer an oath or affirmation.

6. Pre-trial Discovery

Article 23 is particularly relevant for the UK legal systems and common law legal systems in general[218]:

[217] Chapter II of the Hague Evidence Convention.

[218] Article 23 of the Hague Evidence Convention.

> A contracting state may at the time of signature, ratification or accession, declare that it will not execute letters of request issued for the purpose of obtaining pre-trial discovery of documents as known in common law countries.

Due to existing misunderstandings of the nature of pre-trial discovery, there were meetings of the Hague Conference Special Commission in 2003, 2009, and 2014 where the nature and purpose of this procedure was clarified. States that have made a general, non-specific declaration were invited to revisit their declarations. It has been clarified that the Convention permits states to ensure, by way of declaration, that letters of request for the purpose of obtaining pre-trial discovery of documents are sufficiently substantiated so as to avoid requests whereby a party is merely seeking to find out what documents might be in the possession of the other party to the proceedings.

7. Reservations and Declarations

With the exception of Slovenia, all other EU Member States that have acceded to the Convention have made reservations and declarations in respect of the Convention. One must therefore consult the reservations and declarations for the specific state from which evidence is sought to be recovered.

M. Cross-border Processes

1. The Pre-Brexit EU Regime

When dealing with smaller claims there are a number of EU Regulations that provide simplified procedures to progress a claim or enforce a judgment. They are:

> European Enforcement Order Regulation for uncontested claims.[219]
>
> European Small Claims Procedure (ESCP) Regulation as amended by Regulation (EU) 2015/2421 (amending the ESCP regulation), which applies to cross border claims for less than €5000.[220]

[219] Regulation (EC) No 805/2004 of the European Parliament and of the Council of 21 April 2004 creating a European Enforcement Order for uncontested claims OJ L 143, 30.4.2004, 15–39.

[220] Regulation (EU) 2015/2421 of the European Parliament and of the Council of 16 December 2015 amending Regulation (EC) No 861/2007 establishing a European Small Claims Procedure and Regulation (EC) No 1896/2006 creating a European order for payment procedure OJ L 341, 24.12.2015, 1–13.

European order for payment Regulation as updated by Regulation (EU) 2015/2421.[221]

2. Transitional Application: Article 67 of the Withdrawal Agreement

The relevant transitional provisions for the EU Regulations are laid down in Article 67 of the Withdrawal Agreement and require that specific criteria are met by 31 December 2020 at 11 p.m. in order for the applicable process to continue after that date. The criteria are as follows:

> European Enforcement Order for uncontested claims—transitional provisions apply for judgments, as well as court settlements and authentic instruments where:[222]
>
> The judgment has been given in legal proceedings and the certification as a European Enforcement Order has been applied for on or before 31 December 2020.
>
> Court settlements have been approved or concluded and authentic instruments drawn up before 31 December 2020 at 11 pm and the certification as a European Enforcement Order was applied for on or before 31 December 2020 at 11 pm.

European payment orders—the order must have been applied for on or before 31 December 2020 at 11 p.m.[223]

Small claims procedures—the application must have been lodged on or before 31 December 2020 at 11 p.m.[224]

To enable the UK to comply with its obligations under the Withdrawal Agreement, secondary legislation contained savings provisions for the application of the three Regulations.[225] However, these savings provisions are now omitted under The Civil, Criminal and Family Justice (Amendment) (EU Exit) Regulations 2020, SI 2020/1493, regulation 3, which instead replaces regulation 16 as follows:

[221] Regulation (EU) 2015/2421 of the European Parliament and of the Council of 16 December 2015 amending Regulation (EC) No 861/2007 establishing a European Small Claims Procedure and Regulation (EC) No 1896/2006 creating a European order for payment procedure OJ L 341, 24.12.2015, 1–13.

[222] Article 67(2)(d) of the EU Withdrawal Agreement.

[223] Article 67(3)(d) of the EU Withdrawal Agreement.

[224] Article 67(3)(e) of the EU Withdrawal Agreement.

[225] The European Enforcement Order, European Order for Payment and European Small Claims Procedure (Amendment etc) (EU Exit) Regulations 2018, SI 2018/1311, regs 16, 17, and 18.

> Saving: application of Article 67 of the withdrawal agreement—European Enforcement Orders and European Orders for Payment applied for before IP completion day and European Small Claims Procedures commenced before IP completion day
>
> 16. Nothing in these Regulations affects the application of paragraphs 2(d), 3(d) and (e) of Article 67 of the withdrawal agreement and legislation amended or revoked by these Regulations continues to have effect for the purposes of those paragraphs as if the amendments and revocations had not been made.

The European Enforcement Order, European Order for Payment and European Small Claims Procedure (Amendment etc.) (EU Exit) Regulations 2018, SI 2018/1311, revoked each of the EU Regulations at regs 7, 9, 10, and 13 as well as revoking commission regulations and commission-delegated regulations amending annexes to those regulations.

3. Post-Brexit Transition Period

The European Enforcement Order Regulation, European Order for Payment Regulation, and European Small Claims Procedure Regulation are no longer applicable between the UK and the EU Member States.[226]

From 1 January 2021, where the transitional provisions are not engaged, there are no readily available alternatives. This will have implications for lawyers when considering how best to advise clients who are seeking either to recover, or enforce judgments for, small sums of money. The costs of the whole process may well be prohibitive when compared to the small sum in dispute. Consideration will need to be given as to whether the English courts have jurisdiction to determine the dispute. If they do, proceedings can be instigated in the English County Court, with the claim being allocated to the small claims track.[227] Consideration will also need to be given to the time and costs of both service, given that permission will be required to serve the claim form, and of enforcement.

N. The Impact on London as a Centre for International Civil and Commercial Dispute Resolution

Brexit has brought into sharp focus the increased competition in the international litigation market. The reciprocal provision for the recognition and enforcement

[226] The European Enforcement Order, European Order for Payment and European Small Claims Procedure (Amendment etc) (EU Exit) Regulations 2018.

[227] CPR Part 27 Practice Direction 27.

of English court judgments in the EU and vice versa conferred an advantage on London as a leading centre for international litigation. Achieving a close and comprehensive cross-border civil judicial cooperation agreement with the EU would accordingly be helpful for the recognition and enforcement of judgments and legal certainty in general. Some commentators have argued that the uncertainty in the post-Brexit civil jurisdiction and judgments framework of the English courts will benefit the emerging European centres for international litigation.[228] Some of these centres offer English-language court proceedings and can guarantee the free mobility of their judgments across the EU Member States.[229] Other commentators have doubted that the reputation and attractiveness of litigating in the English courts will suffer post Brexit.[230] Indeed, it remains the case that the changes that have taken place do not call into question the many advantages offered by the English courts as a forum of choice to resolve cross-border disputes.[231] The main findings of Portland's annual Commercial Courts Report 2021 highlighted that there has been a 47 per cent increase in judgments handed down compared to the previous year, making the period April 2020 to March 2021 a record year over the past six years.[232]

English choice of forum and choice of law clauses have been historically popular for a range of reasons. English contract law is, for instance, comparatively predictable and as it is derived from the common law will remain largely unchanged by the UK leaving the EU, as should the quality, speed, and integrity of the English

[228] X Kramer and J Sorabji, 'International Business Courts in Europe and Beyond: A Global Competition for Justice?' [2019] Erasmus Law Review 1 (hereafter Kramer and Sorabji, International Business Courts); P Lambrecht and E Peetermans, 'The Brussels International Business Court: Initial Overview and Analysis' [2019] Erasmus Law Review 42.

[229] Kramer and Sorabji, International Business Courts (n 228) 5.

[230] G Vos, 'A View from the Business and Property Courts in London' [2019] Erasmus Law Review 10. This is a speech delivered in the seminar on 'Innovating International Business Courts: A European Outlook' organised by the Erasmus School of law, Rotterdam, 10 July 2018; J Harris, 'Brexit & Cross-Border Dispute Resolution' (2016) 166 New Law Journal newlawjournal.co.uk) <Brexit & cross-border dispute resolution | New Law Journal | The leading weekly legal magazine> accessed 31 August 2021; P Rogerson, 'After BREXIT: Is International Commercial Litigation in London Doomed?' 2016] New Law Journal <https://www.newlawjournal.co.uk/content/litigation-post-brexit-0> accessed 31 August 2021 (hereafter Rogerson, BREXIT). cf In *Amin Rasheed Shipping Corporation v Kuwait Insurance Co* [1984] AC 50, 67, Lord Diplock rejected the opinion of Lord Donaldson MR in the Court of Appeal that the London Commercial Court should be viewed as an 'international commercial court'.

[231] Portland's annual Commercial Courts Report for 2021, notes a decline in the proportion of litigants from EU Member States, which represent 11.5 per cent of total litigants in 2020–2021 in comparison to 13.6 per cent in 2019–2020 and 14.9 per cent in 2017–2018. According to Portland, this decline can be partly explained by the establishment of international commercial courts across the EU and European litigants choosing to settle their disputes closer to home. Further, Portland noted that the decline in EU Member State litigants has been offset by an increase of litigants from non-EU states, for example, the number of US litigants is said to have risen by 75 per cent over the past year. See <https://portland-communications.com/publications/commercial-courts-report-2021/> accessed 31 August 2021.

[232] ibid. Portland's annual Commercial Courts Report for 2021, highlights that 292 judgments were handed down between April 2020 and March 2021 in the London Commercial Courts.

courts.[233] A British Institute of International and Comparative Law survey indicated that commercial parties choose the English courts for their neutrality, commercial experience of judges and lawyers, reasonable speed and the easy enforcement of English judgments against assets in the UK.[234] A considerable proportion of the cases brought before the Commercial Court are between parties from third states and as a result they are unaffected by Brexit. It is not currently apparent that being able to enforce an English judgment in a Member State is an important factor in choice of the English courts either by parties from Member States or from third states. In any event, after Brexit, English judgments will remain enforceable in Member States' courts. Enforcement will not be automatic but dependent on the rules in the Member State concerned for the enforcement of a third state's judgment.[235] It may be more cumbersome but it is unlikely to make substantive (rather than enforcement) proceedings so much more attractive in a Member State other than England.[236]

O. Brexit and International Arbitration

Some predict a rise in recourse to international arbitration in the short term,[237] at least until the uncertainty in international litigation is settled.[238] Parties may choose to enter into arbitration agreements for resolving their complex high-value commercial disputes. Brexit does not have an impact on the enforcement of English arbitral awards in EU Member States and vice versa. Generally, parties seek recognition and enforcement of arbitral awards under the New York Convention.[239]

[233] In *Premium Nafta Products Limited and others v Fili Shipping Company Limited and others* [2007] UKHL 40, [6], Lord Hoffmann described the reasons for choosing England as a dispute resolution forum in terms of 'neutrality, expertise and privacy, the availability of legal services at the seat of the arbitration and the unobtrusive efficiency of its supervisory law. Particularly in the case of international contracts, [parties] want a quick and efficient adjudication and do not want to take the risks of delay and, in too many cases, partiality, in proceedings before a national jurisdiction'.

[234] E Lein and others, 'Factors Influencing International Litigants' Decisions to Bring Commercial Claims to the London Based Courts' Ministry of Justice Analytical Series 2015 <Ministry of Justice Analytical Series 2015 - Factors Influencing International Litigants' Decisions to Bring Commercial Claims to the London Based Courts (publishing.service.gov.uk)> publishing.service.gov.uk accessed 31 August 2021.

[235] Rogerson, BREXIT (n 230).

[236] ibid.

[237] The Thomson Reuters report on the impact of Brexit on dispute resolution indicates that there may be a move away from litigation in the London Commercial Court to arbitration (and often to the London Court of International Arbitration) rather than to similar courts in other countries. See Thomson Reuters, 'The Impact of Brexit on Dispute Resolution Clauses', 23 July 2018 <The impact of Brexit on dispute resolution clauses: revised survey November 2018 | Practical Law (thomsonreuters.com)> accessed 31 August 2021.

[238] This uncertainty could be addressed by accession to the Hague Judgments Convention 2019. In view of recent developments, the Hague Conventions of 2005 and 2019 will represent the future of UK–EU cross border civil judicial cooperation.

[239] Article III of the United Nations Convention on the Recognition and Enforcement of Foreign Arbitral Awards, 10 June 1958, 330 UNTS 4739 (hereafter New York Convention).

There are 168 Contracting States of the New York Convention, including the UK and all twenty-seven EU Member States. Indeed, an obvious advantage of choosing arbitration is the extensive global reach of the New York Convention. The Convention is not contingent on EU membership and the enforcement of English awards in EU Member States under its provisions is unaffected by Brexit.

Historically, the English courts had demonstrated a willingness to act in support of arbitration by issuing anti-suit injunctions to restrain parties who brought court proceedings in breach of an English arbitration agreement.[240] An anti-suit injunction may offer a superior solution to a stay of court proceedings in breach of an English arbitration agreement under Article II(3) of the New York Convention.[241] In exceptional circumstances, an anti-arbitration injunction has been awarded by an English court to restrain a foreign arbitral tribunal.[242] EU civil procedural law severely curtailed the English courts' power to grant anti-suit injunctions where the contrary court proceedings were commenced in an EU Member State.[243] However, the English courts still issued anti-suit injunctions in relation to proceedings before non-EU courts.[244]

[240] Anti-suit injunctions are discussed further in Chapter 2, Section H. *Aggeliki Charis Compania Maritima v Pagnan (The Angelic Grace)* [1995] 1 Lloyd's Rep 87, 96 (CA) (Millett LJ) (The injunction defendant had 'promised not to bring' the foreign proceedings). See also, *Alfred C. Toepfer International GmbH v. Société Cargill France* [1998] 1 Lloyd's Rep 379, 386 (CA). Mandatory dispute resolution invoked by an arbitration agreement is not only the parties' right but also their obligation; see N Blackaby and C Partasides with A Redfern and M Hunter, *Redfern and Hunter on International Arbitration* (5th edn, OUP 2009) 108.

[241] T Raphael QC, *The Anti-Suit Injunction* (2nd edn, OUP 2019) 34 (hereafter Raphael, *Anti-Suit Injunction*).

[242] *Sabbagh v Khoury & Ors* [2019] EWCA Civ 1219 (David Richards LJ); *Albon v Naza Motor Trading Sdn Bhd* [2007] EWCA Civ 1124, [2008] 1 Lloyd's Rep 1 [16]-[18]; *Claxton Engineering Services Limited v Tam Olaj-Es Gazkutato* [2011] EWHC 345 (Comm) [33]-[44] (Hamblen J).

[243] cf The provision excluding arbitration is Article 1(2)(d) construed along with Recital 12 of the Brussels Ia Regulation and Article 73(2) which provides that the Brussels Ia Regulation will not affect the application of the New York Convention. Advocate General Wathelet has radically argued that the second paragraph of Recital 12 attempts to 'exclude from the scope of the regulation any proceedings in which the validity of an arbitration agreement was contested' and supported the conclusion that anti-suit injunctions in relation to arbitration proceedings are allowed by the Brussels Ia Regulation: Case C-536/13 *'Gazprom' OAO v Lietuvos Respublika* EU:C:2014:2414, [125] (Opinion); M Moses, *The Principles and Practice of International Commercial Arbitration* (3rd edn, Cambridge University Press 2017) 110, also argues that under the Brussels Ia Regulation, the CJEU's distinction between court issued and tribunal issued injunctions should not survive. cf The CJEU's decision in Case C-536/13 *'Gazprom' OAO v Lietuvos Respublika* EU:C:2015:316 (Grand Chamber) ignored Advocate General Wathelet's arguments and treated *West Tankers* as good law. This is supported by *Nori Holdings v Bank Otkritie* [2018] EWHC 1343 (Comm), [2018] 2 Lloyd's Rep 80, [99] (Males J): 'I conclude that there is nothing in the Recast Regulation to cast doubt on the continuing validity of the decision in *West Tankers* (Case C-185/07) [2009] AC 1138 which remains an authoritative statement of EU law'; T Hartley, 'Arbitration and the Brussels I Regulation—Before and After Brexit' (2021) 17 Journal of Private International Law 53, 60 (hereafter Hartley, 'Arbitration After Brexit').

[244] In *Enka Insaat Ve Sanayi A.S. v OOO Insurance Company Chubb* [2020] UKSC 38, Lord Hamblen and Lord Leggatt (Lord Kerr concurred) in the majority judgment confirmed that English courts will generally give significant weight to the parties' bargain in considering whether it is appropriate to grant injunctive relief. They affirmed that it makes no difference whether the arbitration agreement is governed by English law or foreign law in granting an anti-suit injunction. cf Lord Burrows (Lord Sales concurred) in his dissenting judgment concluded that Russian law governs the arbitration agreement and they held that they would remit to the Commercial Court the question of whether, applying Russian

The CJEU has long held that intra-EU anti-suit injunctions are incompatible with EU law.[245] This position was laid down in the CJEU's ruling in *Turner v Grovit* which confirmed the prohibition on anti-suit injunctions in relation to EU Member State court proceedings brought in breach of exclusive choice of court agreements.[246] The CJEU's ruling in *Allianz SpA v West Tankers* held that an anti-suit injunction obtained in the English courts against a party who brought court proceedings in Italy in breach of an English arbitration agreement was incompatible with EU law.[247] The Court of Appeal of England and Wales has held that claims for declarations and damages for breach of exclusive choice of court agreements do not breach EU law even though the matter has not been decided by the CJEU nor resolved by EU legislation.[248] It is highly unlikely that the CJEU would favour a contractual remedy for the European conflicts of jurisdiction which has made its way through the back door as an ingenious alternative to the defunct anti-suit injunction.[249] In effect, the damages remedy serves as a quasi anti-suit injunction for all practical purposes. In an appeal under Section 69 of the Arbitration Act 1996, Flaux J held that the arbitrators had been wrong to rule that a remedy of equitable damages for breach of an arbitration agreement was contrary to EU law.[250]

law, there had been a breach justifying the grant of an anti-suit injunction. See also, *Ust-Kamenogorsk Hydropower Plant JSC v AES Ust-Kamenogorsk Hydropower Plant LLP* [2013] UKSC 35, [2013] 1 WLR 1889, [2013] 1 CLC 1069, [21]–[28] (Lord Mance). cf ibid [61]: Although, the UK Supreme Court confirmed the grant of the injunction enforcing the agreement, Lord Mance observed that there will be cases involving the breach of such agreements where 'the appropriate course will be to leave it to the foreign court to recognise and enforce the parties' agreement on forum'.

245 See generally, M Ahmed, *The Nature and Enforcement of Choice of Court Agreements* (Hart Publishing 2017) (hereafter Ahmed, *Choice of Court Agreements*).

246 Case C-159/02 *Turner v Grovit* [2004] ECR I-3565.

247 Case C-185/07 *West Tankers Inc v Allianz SpA* EU:C:2009:69, [2009] 1 AC 1138.

248 *Starlight Shipping Co v Allianz Marine & Others (The Alexandros T)* [2014] EWCA Civ 1010, [15]–[17] (Longmore LJ). On 25 June 2021, the Supreme Court of Greece requested a preliminary ruling of the CJEU on the question of the compatibility of the right to damages for breach of a choice of court agreement with European public policy in the recognition and enforcement of *The Alexandros T* litigation. Longmore LJ's ruling that EU law presents no obstacle to enforcing a cause of action of damages for breach of an exclusive choice of court agreement was explicitly approved by Christopher Clarke LJ in *Marzillier, Dr Meier & Dr Guntner Rechtsanwaltsgesellschaft mbH v AMT Futures Ltd* [2015] EWCA Civ 143, [61]–[62]. In doing so, he emphasised the divide between issues of jurisdiction subject to the Brussels regime and the private law rights and obligations of the parties in relation to the contractual choice of court agreement and ancillary claims in tort for inducing breach of the choice of court agreement. This issue was not addressed in the appeal to the UK Supreme Court in *AMT Futures v Marzillier* [2018] AC 439, [44] (SC). See also, *Barclays Bank PLC v Ente Nazionale di Previdenza ed Assistenza Dei Medici e Degli Odontoiatri* [2016] EWCA Civ 1261, [37] (Moore-Bick LJ).

249 M Ahmed, 'The Enforcement of Settlement and Jurisdiction Agreements and Parallel Proceedings in the European Union: *The Alexandros T* Litigation in the English Courts' (2015) 11 Journal of Private International Law 406, 438 (hereafter Ahmed, *Alexandros T* Litigation).

250 *West Tankers v Allianz* [2012] EWHC 854 (Comm) [78]; *Nori Holdings v Bank Otkritie* [2018] EWHC 1343 (Comm), [2018] 2 Lloyd's Rep 80, [102] (Males J); *CMA CGM SA v Hyundai Mipo Dockyard Co Ltd* [2008] EWHC 2791 (Comm), [2009] 1 Lloyd's Rep 213 [35], [41]–[47] (Burton J); Advocate General Wathelet in his Opinion in Case C-536/13 *Gazprom OAO* EU:C:2014:2414, n 87, regarded an award of damages as compatible with the Brussels I Regulation, although it was not in issue in that case. cf Hartley casts doubt on Flaux J's decision and argues that imposing damages for suing in the 'wrong' court would prevent the party concerned from even trying to sue in the other Member

The CJEU's rulings have given precedence to the principles of mutual trust and effectiveness of EU law (*effet utile*) amongst EU Member States. However, for commercial parties this offers little comfort as, in practice, not all EU Member State courts effectively enforce arbitration agreements, a number still prioritise their own jurisdiction, or the process is prohibitively slow or expensive.[251] Parties with EU related disputes are therefore left with little remedy in the face of a counterparty breach of the dispute resolution clause. Parties in arbitral proceedings could seek an anti-suit injunction from the arbitral tribunal, which they could then seek to have enforced under the New York Convention, but they would be reliant on the foreign court's willingness and ability to enforce that award.[252]

If the UK accedes to the Lugano II Convention at some point in the future, there can be little doubt that English courts will not be able to grant anti-suit injunctions against proceedings in Lugano II Convention Contracting States.[253] The prohibition against anti-suit injunctions is based on an inherent principle of the Brussels regime,[254] that no court is better placed to determine the jurisdiction of a Member State court than the courts of that Member State.[255] The minor differences between the Lugano II Convention and the Brussels Ia Regulation do not have an impact on this fundamental principle.[256] In any case, *West Tankers* was decided under the Brussels I Regulation (2001) and the Lugano II Convention is equivalent to the Brussels I Regulation in this matter. Notwithstanding, it would be difficult to fathom that the EU would permit the UK to join the Lugano II Convention if there was any possibility of anti-suit injunctions being granted in relation to proceedings to which it applies.

After the Brexit transition period, the limitations of the interface between the Brussels–Lugano regime and arbitration no longer apply to English courts as they are not bound by EU civil procedural law. The English courts are once again free to

State: 'Such a ruling would be an antisuit injunction in all but name.' See TC Hartley, 'The Brussels I Regulation and Arbitration' (2014) International and Comparative Law Quarterly 843, 862–64.

[251] A Dickinson, 'A Charter for Tactical Litigation in Europe?' [2004] Lloyd's Maritime and Commercial Law Quarterly 273, 278–80.

[252] In Case C-536/13 *'Gazprom' OAO v Lietuvos Respublika* EU:C:2015:316, the CJEU circumscribed the prohibition on anti-suit injunctions in aid of arbitration agreements to court to court proceedings in the Member States, which grants arbitral tribunals freedom to enforce arbitral autonomy unhindered by the EU rules on civil procedure, mutual trust and the principle of effectiveness (*effet utile*).

[253] Briggs, *Civil Jurisdiction* (n 40) 641; TC Hartley, *Civil Jurisdiction and Judgments in Europe* (OUP 2017) 375 (hereafter Hartley, *Civil Jurisdiction*).

[254] Case C-185/07 *West Tankers Inc v Allianz SpA* EU:C:2009:69, [2009] 1 AC 1138, [35]: 'It is incompatible with [the Brussels I Regulation] ... for a court of a Member State to make an order to restrain a person from commencing or continuing proceedings before the courts of another Member State on the ground that such proceedings would be contrary to an arbitration agreement.'

[255] See Case C-185/07 *West Tankers Inc v Allianz SpA* EU:C:2009:69, [2009] 1 AC 1138, [29]; Case C-159/02 *Turner v Grovit* [2004] ECR I-3565, [26]; Case C-116/02 *Erich Gasser GmbH v MISAT Srl* [2003] ECR I-14693, [48]; Case C-351/89 *Overseas Union Insurance and Others* [1991] ECR I-3317, [23]-[24].

[256] There is no equivalent in the Lugano II Convention to Article 73(2) and Recital 12 of the Brussels Ia Regulation.

grant anti-suit injunctions in respect of court proceedings contrary to an English arbitration agreement commenced before EU Member State courts. There is also no objection to the award of damages for breach of an arbitration agreement where court proceedings have been instituted before EU Member State courts.

The Court of Appeal's ruling in *SAS Institute Inc v World Programming* highlights how arbitration agreements or exclusive choice of court agreements may serve as a shield against claims for extraterritorial enforcement.[257] This is most apparent in how World Programming's customers domiciled in third countries and whose contracts did not contain English arbitration agreements were excluded from the scope of the anti-enforcement injunctions ordered. In *Bank St Petersburg OJSC & Anor v Arkhangelsky & Ors*, the contracting parties had agreed that the substantive dispute between them was to be resolved exclusively in England.[258] The Court of Appeal was prepared to grant an anti-enforcement injunction to prevent the claimants from breaching the relevant choice of court agreement by attempting to enforce Russian judgments concerning the same matters that were now before the English courts.[259] Although the two latter decisions were outside the scope of the Brussels regime, an anti-enforcement injunction would obstruct the cross-border recognition and enforcement of judgments[260] and fall foul of the principles of mutual trust and the effectiveness of EU law (*effet utile*).[261] However, after the Brexit transition period, English courts will be unencumbered from granting an anti-enforcement injunction to resist enforcement of a judgment from a Member State court that is contrary to an English arbitration clause or exclusive choice of court clause.

Indeed, London might gain a competitive advantage as a seat of arbitration because of the availability of anti-suit relief. An anti-suit injunction can be a powerful weapon in the English courts' armoury in international disputes. The English courts' ability and willingness to order such measures might prove attractive to many parties.

The courts of EU Member States remain prohibited from issuing anti-suit injunctions in support of arbitration for other EU court proceedings. They are free, of

257 *SAS Institute Inc v World Programming* [2020] EWCA Civ 599 (Males LJ).

258 *Bank St Petersburg OJSC & Anor v Arkhangelsky & Ors* [2014] EWCA Civ 593, [2014] 1 CLC 670 [28] (Longmore LJ).

259 ibid [29]. See also, *Ellerman Lines Ltd v Read* [1928] 2 KB 144 (CA) (An anti-enforcement injunction was granted where the foreign judgment had been procured by fraud).

260 Case 145/86 *Horst Ludwig Martin Hoffmann v Adelheid Krieg* [1988] ECR -00645; Case 42/76 *Jozef de Wolf v Harry Cox B.V.* [1976] ECR -01759.

261 Raphael, *Anti-Suit Injunction* (n 241) 281. cf There is an argument that an anti-enforcement injunction may be permitted under the Brussels Ia Regulation as it does not interfere with another Member State court's right to determine its own jurisdiction and could be employed to postpone enforcement of a Member State court judgment in breach of an arbitration agreement until a proper determination of the substantive issues in dispute by the arbitral tribunal. SP Camilleri, 'Recital 12 of the Recast Regulation: A New Hope?' (2013) 62 International and Comparative Law Quarterly 899, 906–07, regards anti-enforcement injunctions as compatible with the CJEU's reasoning in *West Tankers* but considers such injunctive relief as a 'remedy without any teeth'.

course, to grant anti-suit injunctions or damages to restrain a party from pursuing a claim before the English courts. However, the courts of a number of EU Member States either do not grant anti-suit injunctions or award damages (irrespective of the EU law position) or they appear reluctant to do so.[262]

Recently, French and German courts have begun granting anti-anti-suit injunctions in relation to proceedings in courts outside the EU.[263] In December 2019, the Munich Court of Appeal (*Oberlandesgericht*) upheld an injunction ordering a party who had obtained an anti-suit injunction in the United States to have it rescinded.[264] In March 2020, the Cour d'Appel de Paris held that French courts have the power to grant similar orders.[265] The French Cour de Cassation has previously upheld the enforcement in France of an American anti-suit injunction to enforce an exclusive choice of court agreement and rejected arguments that anti-suit injunctions were an infringement of French judicial sovereignty or an interference with a party's right of access to a court.[266] Anti-anti-suit injunctions are usually enforced by a fine, possibly a penalty of a specified amount per diem until the anti-suit injunction is lifted. It is submitted that such a penalty would be enforceable in other EU Member States under the Brussels Ia Regulation, provided that the substantive claim to which the anti-suit injunction applied came within the scope of the Brussels Ia Regulation. This would be so even if the penalty was payable to (and enforceable by) the state or an emanation of the state. This follows from the EU law rule that in deciding whether an ancillary order falls within the scope of the Regulation, one must consider, not the nature of the order itself, but the nature of the rights it is intended to protect.[267] In *Realchemie Nederland v Bayer CropScience*, the CJEU applied this rule and held that the fine could be enforced in the Netherlands under the Regulation, even though it was payable to the German state, not to the claimant. The final ruling of the CJEU stated that the Regulation applies to 'the recognition and enforcement of a decision of a court or tribunal that contains an order to pay a fine in order to ensure compliance with a judgment given in a civil and commercial matter'.[268] As a consequence, a party who obtains

[262] cf The German Federal Court of Justice has recently granted the remedy of damages for breach of a choice of court agreement. The legal reasoning of the *Bundesgerichtshof* extends to arbitration agreements: BGH, III ZR 42/19, 17.10.2019; J Antomo, 'Anmerkung zu BGH III ZR 42/19' [2020] Europäische Zeitschrift für Wirtschaftsrecht 143. See also, *Sogo USA Inc v Angel Jesus*, STS (Sala de lo Civil, Sección 1a), 12 January 2009, *Repertorio de Jurisprudencia* 2009/544; STS (Civil) 23 February 2007, *Repertorio de Jurisprudencia* 2007/2118; SA Gonzalez, 'The Spanish Tribunal Supremo Grants Damages for Breach of a Choice of Court Agreement' [2009] Praxis des Internationalen Privat- und Verfahrensrechts 529.

[263] Hartley, Arbitration After Brexit (n 243) 61.

[264] Oberlandesgericht München, 12 December 2019.

[265] Cour d'Appel de Paris, 3 March 2020.

[266] *In Zone Brands International Inc v In Beverage International* [2010] ILPr 30. cf *Vivendi c Gerard*, Cour d'Appel de Paris (28 April 2010) No 10/01643.

[267] Case C-406/09 *Realchemie Nederland v Bayer CropScience* EU:C:2011:668, [40].

[268] ibid.

an anti-suit injunction from an English court could find that its assets in an EU Member State are in jeopardy.

In *Van Uden v DecoLine*,[269] the CJEU held that a Dutch interim payment order was not outside the scope of the Brussels regime as a result of the arbitration exclusion. Recital 12 of the Brussels Ia Regulation does not cover interim measures of protection. A Dutch interim payment order is similar to an English freezing order, but there is an important difference: under the Dutch system the court can, after a summary hearing, order the defendant to pay a sum of money to the claimant. This sum may be all or part of the sum claimed. If there is subsequently a full hearing and the defendant wins, the money must be repaid. However, if neither party requests a full hearing, the claimant can keep the money.

In *Van Uden*, a Dutch party had a claim against a German party. The claim was subject to arbitration. The Dutch party asked the Dutch court for an interim payment order. This appears to be possible under Dutch law even if the substantive claim is subject to arbitration. The CJEU was asked whether the proceedings for the interim payment order were covered by the Brussels Convention. The CJEU held that they were. The reason was that the interim payment order was really intended to secure payment of the claim, rather than to support any particular procedure for enforcing it. This makes sense in view of the fact that the claimant often just takes what he is given in the proceedings and does not proceed to litigation or arbitration.[270] This does not mean that an order of this kind cannot be obtained where the claim is subject to arbitration. The CJEU said that a claim subject to arbitration should be regarded as being in the same position as a claim subject to the jurisdiction of the courts of another Member State. In this latter case, Article 24 of the Brussels Convention (equivalent to Article 35 of the Brussels Ia Regulation and Article 31 of the Lugano II Convention) provides that application may be made to the courts of a Member State for such provisional and protective measures as may be available under the law of that Member State, even if the courts of another Member State have jurisdiction as to the substance. This, the CJEU held, may also be used where the claim is subject to arbitration.

The significance of this ruling is that the limits on the measures ordered that apply under Article 24 of the Brussels Convention (Article 35 of the Brussels Ia Regulation) cannot be avoided just because the substance is subject to arbitration. The most important limit, which was laid down by the CJEU in *Van Uden*, is that the interim order can apply only to assets located within the territory of the court making the order. This necessarily excludes worldwide freezing orders. After the expiration of the Brexit transition period, there will be no such impediment to an

[269] Case C-391/95 *Van Uden v DecoLine* EU:C:1998:543, [1998] ECR I-7091. See van Calster, *EU PIL* (n 17) 238.

[270] In reaching its conclusion, the CJEU quoted from the Schlosser Report, which in part formed the basis for Recital 12.

English court granting a worldwide freezing injunction in aid of arbitral proceedings. It remains to be seen whether an EU Member State court will enforce the English court order.

P. A Loss for Comparative Private International Law

The chances of cross-fertilisation of legal concepts from one legal tradition to another in the form of methodological pluralism (eclecticism) or as a catalyst for the synthesisation or integration of legal concepts multiplied manifold due to the interface created between the EU's harmonised private international law rules and an ever resilient English common law tradition with its own sophisticated and indigenous conflict of laws regime.[271] Indeed, it would be trite to comment that the EU private international law Regulations that emanate from Brussels interact with the procedural, substantive, and choice of law rules of the legal systems of Member States and thus provide a unique example of private international law as comparative law in action.[272]

The absence of the UK from the EU's legislative and judicial institutions will affect the future development of private international law within the EU by tilting even further the balance of legal traditions among the EU's legal systems. The UK and those trained within its legal systems have made significant contributions to the development of the EU's *acquis communautaire*. In the case of the Rome I Regulation the UK's efforts were regardless of the fact that the UK might not participate in the instrument finally adopted.[273] The UK's general approach to the discipline has synthesised the need for certainty (particularly in commercial transactions) with the flexibility needed to deliver justice in the individual instance. The UK's approach was influential, *inter alia*, in shaping the rules on third country mandatory rules in the Rome I Regulation,[274] the choice of law rules for tort in the Rome II Regulation,[275] the reverse *lis pendens* rule,[276] and the international *lis pendens* rules in the Brussels Ia Regulation.[277] The impact of the UK's departure will be difficult to quantify in precise terms. It seems likely, in any event, that the UK's practitioners and academics will continue to engage with EU private international law and with their counterparts in the EU Member States. It is hoped that these

[271] See generally, R Michaels, 'The Functional Method of Comparative Law' in M Reimann and R Zimmermann (eds), *The Oxford Handbook of Comparative Law* (OUP 2006) 339.

[272] See M Reimann, 'Comparative Law and Private International Law' in ibid 1363; R Michaels, 'Comparative Law and Private International Law' in J Basedow and others (eds), *Elgar Encyclopedia of Private International Law* (Edward Elgar 2017).

[273] Recital 45 of the Rome I Regulation; Commission Decision 2009/26/EC [2009] OJ L10/22.

[274] Article 9(3) of the Rome I Regulation; *Foster v Driscoll* [1929] 1 KB 470; *Regazzoni v KC Sethia* [1958] AC 301; *Ralli Bros v Cia Naviera Sota y Aznar* [1920] 2 KB 287.

[275] Article 4 of the Rome II Regulation read with Recitals 14 and 16.

[276] Article 31(2) of the Brussels Ia Regulation read with Recital 22.

[277] Articles 33 and 34 of the Brussels Ia Regulation.

links will endure the test of time and the lessons learnt from multilateral civil judicial cooperation will not be easily forgotten.

Brexit will result in the cultural loss of the influence of common law concepts in jurisdiction, enforcement of choice of court agreements, the management of parallel proceedings, recognition and enforcement of judgments and the applicable law in the EU. In similar vein, developments in the harmonised EU private international law sphere will no longer directly affect the course of international civil and commercial litigation before the English courts. From the perspective of the development of a more reconciled and integrated paradigm of jurisdiction and party autonomy, Brexit only serves to exacerbate the process by excluding the common law jurisdictional regime from contributing to and from being influenced by a diverse melting pot of legal traditions.[278]

The CJEU's successful efforts in developing harmonised and autonomous EU characterisations for concepts applied under the Brussels Ia Regulation, the Rome I Regulation and the Rome II Regulations will suffer as a result of the UK's departure. The preliminary reference procedure under Article 267 TFEU provided the CJEU with the opportunity to interpret and develop generalised pan-EU concepts without regard to the idiosyncrasies of the national law of Member States. Ireland is now the only remaining Member State with a pure common law legal system, though both Cyprus and Malta have elements of the common law. The CJEU's efforts have taken shape in the form of a piecemeal process of harmonisation of civil procedural[279] and private law[280] concepts applied under the troika of EU Regulations on civil and commercial matters.

Following the Treaty of Amsterdam (1999), the successive waves of EU private international law Regulations coupled with the CJEU's judicial pronouncements have had a profound impact on English procedural law and practice.[281] The need to respond to these changes has compelled private international law academics, practitioners, and the English judiciary to think and innovate.[282] The mobilisation of the damages remedy for breach of choice of court agreements was a response

[278] See Ahmed, *Choice of Court Agreements* (n 245) ch 2, for a discussion of the *substantive law* and *internationalist* paradigms of party autonomy as dialectically opposite categories converging into a new and more reconciled *transnationalist* paradigm of party autonomy. In brief, the English common law jurisdiction regime adopts a *substantive law* paradigm by focusing on the rights and obligations *inter partes* whereas the Brussels regime's reliance on *lis pendens* places it within the *internationalist* paradigm. The Brussels Ia Regulation's Article 31(2) reverse *lis pendens* rule is emblematic of the internationalist paradigm incorporating the concerns of the substantive law paradigm and thus leading to a more reconciled transnationalist paradigm of party autonomy.

[279] For example, the autonomous meaning of 'same cause of action' under Article 29 of the Brussels Ia Regulation discussed in Ahmed, *Alexandros T* litigation (n 249) 419–25.

[280] For example, the autonomous meaning of 'matters relating to contract' and 'matters relating to tort' under Articles 7(1) and 7(2) of the Brussels Ia Regulation respectively. See Hartley, *Civil Jurisdiction* (n 253) 108–14 and 125–26.

[281] Briggs, 'Recent Judgments of the European Court' (n 46) 231–62; Hartley, 'Dismantling of the Common Law Conflict of Laws' (n 47) 813.

[282] Harris, 'English Response to Europeanisation' (n 44).

to the CJEU's decision in *Turner v Grovit*.[283] It was well deployed as an alternative to the then defunct anti-suit injunction in the run up to the CJEU's decision in *West Tankers*.[284] The English common law's latter-day reincarnation of Georges AL Droz's doctrine of reflective effect[285] of the Brussels regime was a response to the wider implications of the CJEU's ruling in *Owusu v Jackson*.[286] These are significant examples of private international law as applied comparative law that will be all but lost in translation with the departure of the UK from the EU's private international law regime.

Brexit's silver lining could be the EU and the UK adopting a truly internationalist perspective in the Hague Conference on Private International Law in order genuinely to enhance cross-border civil judicial cooperation throughout the world.[287] The UK can be one of the leaders of the common law world by using its decades of experience in European civil judicial cooperation to build bridges to the civil law countries in Europe, Asia, Africa, and Latin America.[288] The European Commission has indicated that the Hague Conventions of 2005 and 2019 should provide the framework for future cooperation between the EU and the UK in the field of civil judicial cooperation whilst concluding that the EU should not give its consent to the UK's accession to the Lugano II Convention (2007).[289] The European Commission has indicated that the EU will conclude the Hague Judgments Convention in the 'near future'.[290] The UK should take a lead in making the Hague

[283] Case C-159/02 *Turner v Grovit* [2004] ECR I-3565.

[284] See Briggs, *Agreements* (n 16); Case C-185/07 *West Tankers Inc v Allianz SpA* EU:C:2009:69, [2009] 1 AC 1138.

[285] G Droz, *Compétence judiciaire et effets des jugements dans le marché commun* (Dalloz 1972) [164]–[169] (reflexive effect in relation to paramount jurisdiction regardless of domicile), [204] (reflexive effect in relation to choice of court agreements).

[286] Case C-281/02 *Owusu v Jackson* [2005] ECR I-1383.

[287] M Ahmed and P Beaumont, 'I Thought We Were Exclusive? Some Issues with The Hague Convention on Choice of Court, Brussels Ia and Brexit' (*Conflict of Laws*, 24 September 2017) Conflictoflaws.net <I thought we were exclusive? Some issues with the Hague Convention on Choice of Court, Brussels Ia and Brexit – Conflict of Laws>accessed 31 August 2021 (hereafter Ahmed and Beaumont, 'Hague Convention, Brussels Ia and Brexit').

[288] P Beaumont, 'Some Reflections on The Way Ahead for UK Private International Law after Brexit' (2021) 17 Journal of Private International Law 1 (hereafter Beaumont, 'Private International Law After Brexit'); R Mortensen, 'Brexit and Private International Law in the Commonwealth' (2021) 17 Journal of Private International Law 18, 28–35, discusses the continuing lead that English adjudication has given to private international law in the Commonwealth but also the greater fragmentation of Commonwealth law whilst the UK was in the EU; Ahmed and Beaumont, 'Hague Convention, Brussels Ia and Brexit' (n 287).

[289] Communication from the Commission to the European Parliament and the Council, Assessment on the application of the United Kingdom of Great Britain and Northern Ireland to accede to the 2007 Lugano Convention, COM(2021) 222 final, 4 May 2021. <https://eur-lex.europa.eu/legal content/EN/TXT/PDF/?uri=CELEX:52021DC0222&from=EN> accessed 31 August 2021. The CJEU has previously observed that the conclusion of the Lugano II Convention (2007) falls within the Community's exclusive competence: See Opinion of the Court (Full Court) of 7 February 2006 on 'Competence of the Community to conclude the new Lugano Convention on jurisdiction and the recognition and enforcement of judgments in civil and commercial matters', Opinion 1/03, [2006] ECR I-01145, EU:C:2006:81.

[290] Assessment on the application of the United Kingdom (n 289) 4.

Judgments Convention of 2 July 2019 effective by becoming a Contracting State as soon as possible.[291]

Over the years, the EU has increasingly gained exclusive external competence in matters of private international law.[292] The UK's public role at the Hague Conference on Private International Law was gradually diminishing whilst the UK was an EU Member State. The UK will now be able to play a larger role in developing the future of private international law in The Hague. This would include the current legislative project on jurisdiction, reviewing all the existing Hague Conventions through Guides to Good Practice and Conclusions and Recommendations of Special Commissions called to review Conventions. Indeed, the UK can be at the forefront of developing and promoting ideas for new work at The Hague.

[291] Beaumont, *Private International Law after Brexit* (n 288) 4.

[292] For an analysis of EU external competence constraints in the context of private international law, see, P Franzina (ed), *The External Action of the EU in the Field of Private International Law after Opinion 1/13* (Intersentia 2016). Following the conclusion of the Lugano II Convention, which fell entirely within the sphere of exclusive competence of the EU (see Lugano Convention Opinion 1/03, [2006] ECR I-1145), the Hague Choice of Court Convention was also concluded by the EU on behalf of the Member States (except Denmark). Opinion 1/13, ECLI:EU:C:2014:2303 of the CJEU (Grand Chamber) confirms that the exclusive competence of the EU encompasses the acceptance of the accession of a third state to the Hague Convention on the civil aspects of international child abduction concluded on 25 October 1980.

2
Jurisdiction

A. Introduction

The ideal solution for UK–EU cross border judicial cooperation would be based on reciprocity between the UK and the EU in the adjudication of international civil and commercial matters.[1] The advantages of a 'double convention'[2] framework regulating jurisdiction and recognition and enforcement of judgments cannot be achieved through a unilateral regime. In a double convention, harmonised direct rules of jurisdiction facilitate the free movement of judgments.[3] The UK could have sought an agreement with the EU on the application of the Brussels I Regulation modelled on the agreement entered into by the EU with Denmark.[4] However, the UK's red line as to the Court of Justice of the European Union's ('CJEU') jurisdiction[5] and the supposed internal market rationale for such a deal where the UK has exited the single market presented insurmountable obstacles. Notwithstanding, an elementary objection to such a bespoke deal is that Denmark's example may not be appropriate at all as Denmark is a Member State of the EU. A lack of ambition in the civil justice field, with the limited exception of family law, has been reflected in successive European Council Mandates and in the non-binding Political Declaration setting out the Framework for the Future Relationship, which merely states that '[t]he Parties will explore options for judicial cooperation in matrimonial, parental responsibility and other related matters'.[6]

[1] The Bar Council of England and Wales originally sought a separate EU–UK agreement for civil judicial cooperation in which much of the existing EU civil justice *acquis* would be preserved on a reciprocal basis. <barofenglandandwalesbrexitjudicialcooperationproposaljuly2018.pdf>> accessed 31 August 2021.

[2] 'Conventions that regulate jurisdiction both at the decision stage and at the recognition stage': R Michaels, 'Some Fundamental Jurisdictional Conceptions as Applied in Judgment Conventions' in E Gottschalk and others (eds), *Conflict of Laws in a Globalized World* (Cambridge University Press 2007) 29–30.

[3] Direct rules of jurisdiction determine whether the courts of a particular Member State have jurisdiction, or do not have jurisdiction, to decide a particular case. Indirect rules of jurisdiction refer to the jurisdictional standards for courts that have issued judgments which the court addressed is asked to recognise and enforce.

[4] Agreement between the European Community and the Kingdom of Denmark on jurisdiction and the recognition and enforcement of judgments in civil and commercial matters ([2009] OJ L149/80), as amended.

[5] The CJEU will have jurisdiction via the preliminary reference procedure under Article 267 (previously Article 234 TEC) of the Consolidated version of the Treaty on the Functioning of the European Union, OJ 115, 09/05/2008, 0164–0164.

[6] Political Declaration setting out the framework for the future relationship between the European Union and the United Kingdom: Presented to Parliament pursuant to Section 1 of the European Union

Brexit and the Future of Private International Law in English Courts. Mukarrum Ahmed, Oxford University Press.
 DOI: 10.1093/oso/9780192848116.003.0002

The specific architecture of the post-Brexit jurisdiction and recognition and enforcement of judgments relationship between the UK and the EU is still unsettled. In the wake of the EU referendum, there was consensus among academic commentators that it is politically unlikely that the UK will apply either the Brussels Ia Regulation or the Brussels or Lugano Conventions after Brexit.[7]

The Lugano II Convention may be disadvantageous because it is too heavily influenced by the jurisprudence of the CJEU,[8] it is parallel with the 2001 Brussels I Regulation[9] and it provides for a strict race to the courthouse through the *lis pendens* rule.[10] It seems unlikely that the mutual trust constraints imposed by a European civil procedural regime will appeal to a newly 'liberated' UK. A post-Brexit UK is likely to want to keep its indigenous rules of jurisdiction (at least in England and Wales) with a discretionary system for declining jurisdiction through the doctrine of *forum non conveniens*.[11] However, Scotland will continue to rely on Schedule 8 of the Civil Jurisdiction and Judgments Act 1982 (CJJA) after Brexit even if it cannot remain a party to the Regulation or the Brussels or Lugano Conventions and hence Scottish

(Withdrawal) Act (No 2) 2019 and Section 13 of the European Union (Withdrawal) Act 2018, 19 October 2019, [56] <Political_Declaration_setting_out_the_framework_for_the_future_relationship_between_the_European_Union_and_the_United_Kingdom.pdf> accessed 31 August 2021.

[7] M Ahmed, *The Nature and Enforcement of Choice of Court Agreements* (Hart Publishing 2017) ch 11 (hereafter Ahmed, *Choice of Court Agreements*); A Dickinson, 'Back to the Future: The UK' s EU Exit and the Conflict of Laws' (2016) 12 Journal of Private International Law 195, 201–07, 210; P Beaumont, 'Respecting Reverse Subsidiarity is an Excellent Strategy for the European Union at The Hague Conference on Private International Law: Currently being Well Deployed in the Judgments Project' (2016) 2 Centre for Private International Law Aberdeen Working Paper Series, Working Paper No 2016/3, 4, <www.abdn.ac.uk/law/documents/CPIL_Working_paper_2016_3_revised.pdf> accessed 9 December 2021; B Hess, 'Back to the Past: BREXIT und das europäische internationale Privat- und Verfahrensrecht' (2016) 36 Praxis des Internationalen Privat- und Verfahrensrechts (IPRax) 409; J Basedow, 'Brexit und das Privat- und Wirtschaftsrecht' (2016) 24 Zeitschrift für EuropäischesPrivatrecht (ZEuP) 567–72, notes that the UK is not entitled to join the Lugano II Convention as it is not an EFTA Member State (nor an EEA Member) (Article 70).

[8] Article 1(1) of Protocol 2 on the Uniform Interpretation of the Lugano II Convention; the courts of a Contracting State applying the Lugano II Convention shall 'pay due account' to the principles laid down by any relevant decisions on the Lugano Convention (1988), Brussels I Regulation (2001), Brussels Ia Regulation (2012), Brussels Convention (1968) and the Convention between the EU and Denmark applying the Brussels I Regulation to that Member State. See TC Hartley, *Choice of Court Agreements under the European and International Instruments* (OUP 2013) 15–18 (hereafter Hartley, *Choice of Court Agreements*). cf B Hess, 'The Unsuitability of the Lugano Convention (2007) to Serve as a Bridge between the UK and the EU after Brexit' (2018) Max Planck Institute Luxemburg for Procedural Law Research Paper Series No 2018 (2).

[9] Council Regulation (EC) 44/2001 on jurisdiction and the recognition and enforcement of judgments in civil and commercial matters (Brussels I) [2001] OJ L12/1 (hereafter Brussels I Regulation).

[10] Article 27 of Convention on jurisdiction and the recognition and enforcement of judgments in civil and commercial matters OJ L 339/3, 21.12.2007, OJ 2009, L 147/5 (hereafter Lugano II Convention).

[11] *Forum non conveniens* was developed in Scotland and brought into English law in the last quarter of the twentieth century; see RA Brand, 'Comparative Forum Non Conveniens and the Hague Convention on Jurisdiction and Judgments' (2002) 37 Texas International Law Journal 467, 469–471.

courts may respect the CJEU ban on anti-suit injunctions in cases involving EU Member States.[12] Significantly, unless the Lugano II Convention is re-negotiated it does not contain an optimal solution to the conflicts of jurisdiction for exclusive choice of court agreements because the Convention has not been amended to reflect Article 31(2) of the Brussels Ia Regulation.[13] Therefore, the Lugano II Convention still gives priority to the non-chosen court when it is seised first and the exclusively chosen court is seised second as per with the CJEU's commercially inept decision in *Gasser*.[14] Secondly, the arbitration exclusion in the Lugano II Convention is less clear than the Brussels Ia Regulation.[15] Another defect is that the Lugano II Convention makes no provision for a stay of proceedings in the face of prior parallel litigation in a non-Contracting State. This Eurocentric stance is avoided to an extent by Articles 33 and 34 of the Brussels Ia Regulation. The Lugano II Convention is also not equivalent to the Brussels Ia Regulation as it still requires *exequatur* proceedings. In light of these shortcomings, the book will recommend revision of the Lugano II Convention at the earliest possible opportunity to incorporate the state-of-the-art provisions.

The UK government had applied to remain part of the Lugano II Convention but the unanimous consent of all the Contracting States to the Lugano II Convention is required. The European Commission has indicated that the Hague Conventions of 2005 and 2019 should provide the framework for future cooperation between the EU and the UK in the field of civil judicial cooperation whilst concluding that the EU should not give its consent to the UK's accession to the Lugano II Convention.[16]

[12] Anti-suit injunctions are called 'interdicts of foreign actions' in Scotland; see PR Beaumont and PE McEleavy, *Anton's Private International Law* (3rd edn, SULI/W Green 2011) 367–71 (hereafter Beaumont and McEleavy, *Anton*).

[13] The ruling in *Mastermelt Limited v Siegfried Evionnaz SA* [2020] EWHC 927 (QB), [30] (Waksman J) is clear that the Lugano II Convention remains subject to Case C-116/02 *Erich Gasser Gmbh v MISAT Srl* [2003] ECR I-14693. A court in Zurich interpreted Article 27 of the Lugano II Convention as though it had been amended to reflect Article 31(2) of Council Regulation (EU) 1215/2012 of the European Parliament and of the Council of 12 December 2012 on jurisdiction and the recognition and enforcement of judgments in civil and commercial matters (recast) [2012] OJ L351/1 (hereafter Brussels Ia Regulation). However, Waksman J disagreed that *Gasser* is obsolete in the context of the Lugano II Convention. See I Bergson, 'The Death of the Torpedo Action?' (2015) 11 Journal of Private International Law 1, 29.

[14] Case C-116/02 *Erich Gasser Gmbh v MISAT Srl* [2003] ECR I-14693; cf Articles 31(2)–(4) and Recital 22 of the Brussels Ia Regulation.

[15] There is no equivalent in the Lugano II Convention to Article 73(2) and Recital 12 of the Brussels Ia Regulation.

[16] Communication from the Commission to the European Parliament and the Council, Assessment on the application of the United Kingdom of Great Britain and Northern Ireland to accede to the 2007 Lugano Convention, COM(2021) 222 final, 4 May 2021. <1_en_act_en.pdf> accessed 31 August 2021. The CJEU has previously observed that the conclusion of the Lugano II Convention (2007) falls within the Community's exclusive competence: See Opinion of the Court (Full Court) of 7 February 2006 on 'Competence of the Community to conclude the new Lugano Convention on jurisdiction and the recognition and enforcement of judgments in civil and commercial matters', Opinion 1/03, [2006] ECR I-01145, EU:C:2006:81.

This leaves the UK reliant on a more fragmented and less integrated regional and international framework for private international law at least until the UK and the EU ratify the Hague Judgments Convention. The European Commission has indicated that the EU will conclude the Hague Judgments Convention in the 'near future'.[17] It is recommended that the UK should take a lead in making the Hague Judgments Convention of 2 July 2019 effective by becoming a Contracting State as soon as possible.[18] On 1 July 2021, Switzerland, which is the depository of the Lugano II Convention 2007, notified the Parties to the Convention of the EU's refusal to give its consent to the UK's accession to the Convention.[19] It states the EU is not 'in a position to give its consent to invite the United Kingdom to accede to the Lugano Convention', quoting the note verbale received by the depository from the EU on 28 June 2021.[20]

This chapter deals with the practical jurisdictional implications of EU private international law coming to an end in English courts. As the foundations and edifice of the Brussels–Lugano regime is replaced by the common law jurisdictional regime and the Hague Convention on Choice of Court Agreements ('Hague Convention'), it is essential to highlight the principal jurisdictional changes and to reorient ourselves with the framework of jurisdictional law after Brexit. The Hague Choice of Court Convention will apply to proceedings between two Contracting States including all the EU Member States in matters within its scope and the common law jurisdictional regime will apply in all other cases. The variable geometry of the vertically multi-layered international civil and commercial litigation sphere in the English courts will be simplified because the regional EU rules on jurisdiction and judgments will be replaced by the common law rules and the Hague Convention.

This chapter will commence by providing a summary of the pre-existing jurisdictional regime in civil and commercial matters. This will be followed by a description of the jurisdictional rules during the Brexit transition period. The substantive focus of this chapter will be on the central changes to the law of jurisdiction in the post-exit legal landscape. In the process, some of the main areas of difficulty will be highlighted and solutions will be offered.

17 Assessment on the application of the UK (n 16) 4.

18 P Beaumont, 'Some Reflections on The Way Ahead for UK Private International Law after Brexit' (2021) 17 Journal of Private International Law 1, 4 (hereafter Beaumont, 'Private International Law after Brexit').

19 Swiss Federal Council, 'Communication by the depositary with respect to the application of accession by the United Kingdom of Great Britain and Northern Ireland' 1 July 2021 <https://www.eda.admin.ch/dam/eda/fr/documents/aussenpolitik/voelkerrecht/autres-conventions/Lugano2/20210701-LUG_en.pdf> accessed 31 August 2021.

20 European Commission, 'Note Verbale concerning the application of the United Kingdom of Great Britain and Northern Ireland to accede to the 2007 Lugano Convention' 28 June 2021 <20210701-LUG-ann-EU.pdf> accessed 31 August 2021.

B. Pre-Exit Jurisdictional Regime: Basic Structure of the European and Common Law Rules of Jurisdiction

The Brussels Ia Regulation allocated jurisdiction using detailed and fixed rules of jurisdiction.[21] The material scope of the Regulation encompassed civil and commercial matters but it did not extend to revenue, customs, or administrative matters.[22] The phrase 'civil and commercial matters' covered 'legal actions for compensation for disturbance of ownership and property rights, contractual performance and damages'.[23] Various matters were excluded from the Brussels Ia Regulation's scope.[24]

At the heart of the Brussels Ia Regulation was the defendant domicile rule.[25] A defendant who is domiciled in a Member State would normally be sued in the courts of that state. Special protection was provided to insured parties,[26] consumers,[27] and employees.[28] The regime conferred very little discretion upon judges as to whether to assume jurisdiction.[29] The Brussels Ia Regulation favoured legal certainty over flexibility. One of the central objectives of the Regulation was to enable a claimant to identify easily the court in which to sue and the defendant reasonably to foresee before which court he may be sued.[30] The principle of mutual trust whereby the courts of each Member State are equally competent to interpret the Regulation animates the Brussels Ia Regulation.[31]

In contrast, the English common law rules of jurisdiction, onto which the Brussels Ia Regulation was superimposed, are of a diametrically opposite nature. The inherent jurisdiction of the courts is wide, open, and premised on the service of process at common law. The common law rules are characterised by the existence of relatively few detailed provisions on jurisdiction and still fewer rules of an inflexible nature. There are no specific rules to protect consumers, insured parties, or employees. At the crux of the English common law of jurisdiction is the doctrine of *forum conveniens*, which enables a court to stay proceedings commenced as of right at the behest of the defendant who can demonstrate that the natural forum for the litigation is abroad.[32] Even where more detailed provisions on jurisdiction exist

21 A Briggs, *Civil Jurisdiction and Judgments* (7th edn, Informa Law from Routledge 2021) 52 (hereafter Briggs, *Civil Jurisdiction*).
22 Article 1(1) of the Brussels Ia Regulation.
23 Joined Cases C-226/13, C-245/13, C-247/13, and C-578/13 *Fahnenbrock v Greek Republic* [2016] ILPr 4, [59].
24 Article 1(2) of the Brussels Ia Regulation.
25 Article 4 of the Brussels Ia Regulation.
26 Section 3 of the Brussels Ia Regulation.
27 Section 4 of the Brussels Ia Regulation.
28 Section 5 of the Brussels Ia Regulation.
29 See, in particular, Articles 30, 33, and 34 of the Brussels Ia Regulation.
30 Recital 16 of the Brussels Ia Regulation.
31 Recital 26 of the Brussels Ia Regulation.
32 *Spiliada Maritime Corp v Cansulex Ltd* [1987] AC 460.

for service of the claim form on a defendant outside the jurisdiction,[33] the claimant must still demonstrate that England is the 'proper place' for trial[34] and the judge has discretion whether to permit service out.[35] The English system aims to ensure that litigation takes place in the most appropriate forum even if that flexibility can lead to uncertainty, inefficiency, and litigation about where to litigate.[36]

Significantly, English courts start from the premise that where parties have contractually agreed as to the forum for litigation, no breach of that clause should, in the absence of strong reason, be tolerated.[37] The armoury of the court should be available to prevent a claimant from committing a breach of contract by litigating abroad.[38] English lawyers tend to think that something has gone wrong if a regime of jurisdiction is applied so rigidly as to deprive the litigating parties of those rights. The judicially enforceable private law rights that relate to the jurisdiction of courts is fundamentally at odds with the view that jurisdiction is a matter of public law.[39]

With two different regimes of jurisdiction coexisting in English law it was perhaps unsurprising that the underlying contradictions surfaced occasionally. English lawyers yearned for the discretion to determine whether to exercise jurisdiction when faced with the mandatory rules of direct jurisdiction of the Brussels Ia Regulation.

C. Jurisdictional Rules during the Transition Period

During the Brexit transition period, Articles 66 to 69 of the Agreement on the withdrawal of the United Kingdom of Great Britain and Northern Ireland from the European Union and the European Atomic Energy Community, 19 October 2019,[40] contain provisions on jurisdiction, recognition and enforcement of judgments and the applicable law. Article 67(1)(a) of the EU Withdrawal Agreement stipulates that jurisdiction will be governed by the Brussels Ia Regulation where proceedings are commenced prior to the end of the transition period.[41] Therefore,

[33] CPR 6.36 and PD 6B para 3.1.

[34] CPR Part 6.37(3).

[35] *Seaconsar (Far East) Ltd v Bank Markazi Jomhouri Islami Iran* [1994] 1 AC 438.

[36] *Spiliada Maritime Corporation v Cansulex Ltd (The Spiliada)* [1987] 1 AC 460, 464G-H (HL) (Lord Templeman); *Research in Motion UK Ltd v Visto Corp* [2008] EWCA Civ 153, [2008] Bus LR D141, [3]: 'Too often one finds parties litigating as much about where and when disputes should be heard and decided as about the real underlying dispute.'

[37] Where there is a foreign exclusive choice of court clause, this will usually lead to English proceedings being stayed: *The Eleftheria* [1970] P 94; *The El Amria* [1981] 2 Lloyd's Rep 119; *The Sennar (No 2)* [1985] 1 WLR 490.

[38] The court will usually be willing to issue an anti-suit injunction where proceedings have been commenced in breach of an English exclusive choice of court clause: *British Airways Board v Laker Airways Ltd* [1985] AC 58; *Sohio Supply Co v Gatoil (USA) Inc* [1989] 1 Lloyd's Rep 588; *The Angelic Grace* [1995] 1 Lloyd's Rep 87; *Donohue v Armco Inc* [2001] UKHL 64, [2002] 1 Lloyd's Rep 425.

[39] Ahmed, *Choice of Court Agreements* (n 7) 76–82.

[40] EU Withdrawal Agreement.

[41] The Brexit transition period ended on 31 December 2020.

English courts will continue to render judgments where jurisdiction is governed by the Brussels Ia Regulation for the foreseeable future.

It is not entirely clear what an English court will do if proceedings are commenced in a Member State before Completion Day, and related proceedings are commenced in England after Completion Day. Article 67(1) of the Withdrawal Agreement is quite clear that as long as proceedings have commenced in the UK or the EU Member States before Completion Day, proceedings which are related to those proceedings are subject to the *lis pendens* rules of the Regulation.[42] As Article 67(1) only makes sense if the second set of proceedings is commenced after Completion Day,[43] the second seised English court after Completion Day would be required to apply the *lis pendens* provisions of the Regulation. If the second seised English court after Completion Day is the chosen forum in an exclusive choice of court agreement, the first seised EU Member State court would be required to apply the reverse *lis pendens* rule pursuant to Article 31(2) of the Regulation. The case of UK–EU parallel proceedings straddling on either side of Brexit Completion Day was not expressly addressed by legislation, but an English court may find its answer in the text of the Withdrawal Agreement itself.

D. The Post-exit Jurisdictional Landscape: The Common Law Jurisdictional Regime

The central tenet of Brexit's legislative overhaul is that in proceedings commenced after 1 January 2021, UK courts will in most cases determine questions of jurisdiction over defendants domiciled in EU Member States with reference to the residual national jurisdictional rules that formerly were applied only to non-EU domiciled defendants.[44] These residual national jurisdictional rules have been brought from the periphery to the fore by Brexit. These rules are collectively referred to as the English common law jurisdictional regime.

The Article 5(2) prohibition on the application of the 'exorbitant' rules of jurisdiction formerly listed in Annex I to the Brussels I Regulation (2001) has been lifted. English defendants will no longer be protected from the exorbitant jurisdictional rules of the EU Member States. The Member States will apply their rules of long arm jurisdiction to English defendants, who will lose the basic privilege of being sued at home. However, the exorbitant jurisdictional rules of the common law and Civil Procedure

[42] Article 67(1) of the EU Withdrawal Agreement explicitly refers to the transitional applicability of Articles 29, 30, and 31 of the Brussels Ia Regulation. Bundesgerichtshof (BGH), 15 June 2021, II ZB 35/20 (*Air Berlin*), [40] et seq.

[43] For the approach to be taken when a court is seised before Completion Day but it has not been possible to transmit the document in accordance with Regulation 1393/2007, see Civil Jurisdiction and Judgments (Amendment) (EU Exit) Regulations 2019, SI 2019 No 479, ref 93(3).

[44] Article 6 of the Brussels Ia Regulation.

Rules will equally be applied to those domiciled in EU Member States. As a consequence of the UK's withdrawal from the EU, UK parties are obliged under Section 110 ZPO to provide security for costs in German courts, if the other party so requests.[45]

Under the English common law jurisdictional regime, the adjudicatory jurisdiction of the courts of England and Wales over non-appearing defendants will usually depend on the service of the claim form on the defendant,[46] either within the court's territorial jurisdiction or outside the jurisdiction with the court's permission.[47] The Scottish courts will, by contrast, apply the rules of jurisdiction contained in Schedule 8 CJJA.[48] The rules that apply in Scotland are modelled on the Brussels Convention.[49] On the other hand, the rules that apply in England and Northern Ireland, which can be traced back to the mid-nineteenth century, bear little resemblance to the mandatory direct rules of jurisdiction of the Brussels–Lugano regime,[50] and provide a wide and discretionary basis for asserting jurisdiction.[51] However, the retention of the power of the UK courts to decline jurisdiction on the ground that there in another more appropriate forum (including EU Member State and Lugano II Convention Contracting State courts) has a narrowing effect on the wide and open basis on which an English court asserts its inherent jurisdiction.[52]

Brexit might provide an opportunity for English law to take stock of and adjust its jurisdictional rules. If it is decided that the rules for service out of the jurisdiction are not in the state they should be in they can be amended.[53] It has been argued

45 Bundesgerichtshof (BGH), 1 March 2021, X ZR 54/19–Security for costs also applies to cases initiated before 1 January 2021. See B Hess 'Reforming the Brussels Ibis Regulation: Perspectives and Prospects' (2021) MPILux Research Paper Series 2021 (4) <http://www.mpi.lu/fileadmin/user_upload/MPILux_WP_2021_4__Reforming_Brussels_1bis_BH.pdf> accessed 31 August 2021.

46 The civil jurisdiction of the Northern Irish courts is also determined by service of process. The claim form is referred to as the 'writ'.

47 Civil Procedure Rules (SI 1998/3132, as amended), Part 6 and PD6B; The Rules of the Court of Judicature (Northern Ireland) (SR 1980/346, as amended), Order 10, Order 11.

48 Civil Jurisdiction and Judgments Act 1982, Part III.

49 Beaumont and McEleavy, *Anton* (n 12) 217.

50 The tort jurisdictional gateway was recast along the lines of what is now Article 7(2) of the Brussels Ia Regulation. Recent English case law has, however, interpreted the tort jurisdictional gateway more broadly. The discussion of *FS Cairo (Nile Plaza) LLC v Brownlie* [2020] EWCA Civ 996, later in this chapter illustrates the arguments for and against a broad interpretation of the gateway.

51 CPR, PD6B, para 3.1, jurisdictional gateways (2), (3), (4A), (6)–(7), (9), (11), (16), (20). In contract cases, jurisdiction may be established not only by a breach of contract within the jurisdiction (gateway (7)) but also on the basis of the place of formation of a contract, the location of the defendant's contracting agent or a choice of law agreement (gateway (6)). Gateway (4A) also enables the adding on claims that arise out of the same or closely connected facts as a claim that fits within one of the other grounds. cf Article 7(1) of the Brussels Ia Regulation; The negative definition of a 'matter relating to tort' in Case 189/97 *Kalfelis v Bankhaus Schrçder, Mnchmeyer, Hengst and Co* [1988] ECR I-5565 is the basis for the rule that Articles 7(1) and 7(2) of the Brussels Ia Regulation are comprehensive and mutually exclusive.

52 *Spiliada Maritime Corp v Cansulex Ltd* [1987] AC 460 (*forum non conveniens*). In the service-based regime applicable in England and Wales and Northern Ireland, the burden of proof for service lies on the defendant for service within the jurisdiction and on the claimant for service outside the jurisdiction: see CPR 6.37(3), requiring the claimant to establish that England is the 'proper place' to bring the claim.

53 The rules can be amended by the CPR Committee.

that the jurisdictional gateways should be removed from the Practice Direction (PD) and replaced with a rule that service may be made outside jurisdiction where England is the 'proper place' to sue.[54] If the condition of the natural forum is satisfied, the function served by the jurisdictional gateways may be questioned.[55]

This flexible approach has been deemed contrary to principle.[56] The jurisdictional gateways and the discretion as to *forum conveniens* serve different purposes. The gateways identify relevant connections with England, which define the maximum extent of the jurisdiction which the English court is permitted to exercise. Their ambit is a question of law. The discretion as to *forum conveniens* authorises the court to decline a jurisdiction which it possesses as a matter of law because the dispute, although sufficiently connected with England to permit the exercise of jurisdiction, could be more appropriately resolved elsewhere. The main determining factor in the exercise of the discretion on *forum conveniens* grounds is not the relationship between the cause of action and England but the practicalities of litigation. The purpose of the discretion is to limit the exercise of the court's jurisdiction, not to enlarge it and certainly not to displace the criteria in the gateways. English law has never in the past and does not now accept jurisdiction simply on the basis that the English courts are an appropriate forum if the subject-matter has no relevant jurisdictional connection with England.

Repealing the jurisdictional gateways and making service-out applications conditional on England being the natural forum would lead to an unreasonable augmentation of the jurisdiction of the English courts. It is possible for applications for service outside jurisdiction being successful under the interests of justice limb of the *Spiliada* test where claimants allege that they would face severe delays if they sued the defendants in the most appropriate forum.[57] It is also possible for applications being successful under the interests of justice limb of *Spiliada* where it is argued that the most appropriate forum would be not be prepared to adjudicate on the dispute due to a lack of resources or experience.[58] As a consequence, it is

[54] Apparently, the law in Singapore is moving in that direction. See Briggs, *Civil Jurisdiction* (n 21) 23; A Briggs, *The Conflict of Laws* (4th edn, OUP 2019) 110 (hereafter Briggs, *Conflict of Laws*); A Briggs, 'Service Out in a Shrinking World' [2013] Lloyd's Maritime and Commercial Law Quarterly 415. See also, J Walker, 'The Distant Shore: Discretion and the Extent of Judicial Jurisdiction' in A Dickinson and E Peel (eds), *A Conflict of Laws Companion: Essays in Honour of Adrian Briggs* (OUP 2021) ch 3.

[55] *Abela v Baadarani* [2013] UKSC 44, [2013] 1 WLR 2403, [53] (Lord Sumption). cf *Brownlie v Four Seasons Holdings Inc* [2017] UKSC 80, [2018] 1 WLR 192, [31] (Lord Sumption): 'In *Abela v Baaderani*, I protested against the importation of an artificial presumption against service out as being inherently "exorbitant", into what ought to be a neutral question of construction or discretion. I had not proposed to substitute an alternative, and equally objectionable, presumption in favour of the widest possible interpretation of the gateways simply because jurisdiction thus conferred by law could be declined as a matter of discretion.'

[56] *Brownlie v Four Seasons Holdings Inc* [2017] UKSC 80, [2018] 1 WLR 192, [31] (Lord Sumption).

[57] In *The Vishva Ajay* [1989] 2 Lloyd's Rep 558, the inordinate delay in the natural forum prompted the English court to adjudicate that the dispute will not be justly disposed of in that forum.

[58] In *Connelly v RTZ Corp Plc (No 2)* [1998] AC 854 and *Lubbe v Cape Plc* [2000] 1 WLR 1545, the disputes were closely connected with Namibia and South Africa but the lack of legal aid provisions and insufficient experience in handling mass tort litigation in the natural fora prompted the English courts to not stay proceedings.

argued that the way forward would be to maintain the gateway precondition in the approach to deciding service out applications. Otherwise, there would be a real risk that defendants are summoned to appear in litigation with an even more tenuous connection with England than is allowed at present.

On the other hand, an entirely new set of jurisdictional rules replacing the mid-nineteenth-century service-based model could be devised.[59] The structure of the law on service outside jurisdiction has evolved without any overarching plan and has been subject to significant ad hoc extensions.[60] The new rules should demand a significant connection between the parties or the subject matter of the claim and the forum that warrants the exercise of jurisdiction. In this regard, the Brussels–Lugano regime provides a more suitable point of departure than the grounds currently set out in the PD.[61]

Taking this step would enable the cumbersome requirement to obtain permission to serve a claim form outside England to be abolished, and with it the complex and costly requirement that the claimant show that England and Wales is the 'proper place' for the trial of the action.[62] Instead, the claimant would need to certify that the court has jurisdiction under the new set of rules and the defendant would need to make an application under Civil Procedure Rules (CPR), Part 11 if it considers that the English court does not have or should not exercise jurisdiction.[63] The claimant would bear the burden of establishing jurisdiction but the defendant would bear the burden of persuading the court that it should not be exercised.

Proactive judicial or legislative control of the costly and inefficient *forum conveniens* model is required. Over the years, the senior judiciary has observed that the *Spiliada* test encourages protracted litigation about where to litigate.[64] In many ways, the test is itself to blame for the extensive evaluative enquiry which may equate to a disproportionate mini-trial. Shifting the onus to the defendant in all cases and the requirement that another forum be 'manifestly more appropriate' or that England is the 'clearly inappropriate forum' would be useful to curb the tide along with better case management through strict costs capping, a limit to the amount of evidence and pleadings and a greater willingness to require the losing party to pay costs on an indemnity basis. The proposed stricter variants of the *forum non conveniens* test will help structure the judge's evaluative process and

[59] A Dickinson, 'Walking Solo—A New Path for the Conflict of Laws in England' Conflictoflaws.net, 4 January 2021 <https://conflictoflaws.net/2021/walking-solo-a-new-path-for-the-conflict-of-laws-in-england/> accessed 31 August 2021 (hereafter Dickinson, 'Walking Solo').

[60] CPR 1998, rules 6.36-6.37 (CPR) to be read with PD 6B.

[61] Schedule 8 CJJA.

[62] Dickinson, 'Walking Solo' (n 59).

[63] As had been the practice when the jurisdictional rules of the Brussels–Lugano regime applied.

[64] *Spiliada Maritime Corporation v Cansulex Ltd (The Spiliada)* [1987] 1 AC 460, 464G-H (HL) (Lord Templeman); *Voth v Manildra Flour Mills Pty Ltd* (1990) 171 CLR 538, 565, 571 (HC); *Vedanta v Lungowe* [2019] UKSC 20, [6]-[14] (Lord Briggs); *Okpabi v Shell* [2021] UKSC 3, [107] (Lord Hamblen). See M Davies, '*Forum Non Conveniens*: Now We Are Much More Than Ten' in Dickinson and Peel (eds), *A Conflict of Laws Companion* (n 54) ch 2, 49.

allocation of time and resources in hard cases where there may be no easy answers as to the natural forum especially at the interim stage of proceedings. *Forum non conveniens* is discussed further in this chapter under the Section H.

Under English civil procedural law, personal jurisdiction is founded on the actual or deemed service of the claim form on the defendant. There are two types of cases. First, service within England and Wales may be effected as of right and without the need for permission of the court.[65] Secondly, service outside England and Wales could previously be effected as of right without the court's permission.[66] In recent decades, the latter has included nearly all cases in which the English court's jurisdiction was founded on the Brussels–Lugano regime as well as most cases where service is to be effected in Scotland or Northern Ireland, and a small number of cases where jurisdiction was founded as of right, usually under the terms of an international convention. This class of case has been drastically narrowed by Brexit but will still extend to cases where jurisdiction is founded on choice of court agreements, employment contracts and consumer contracts.[67] Post Brexit, the provisions in the Civil Procedure Rules for permission to serve claims out of the jurisdiction have assumed a greater significance in cross-border litigation.

In all other cases where service is to be effected outside England and Wales, the court's permission is required. There are three hurdles, and the claimant must overcome all three. First, the case must fall within one or more of the classes of case in which permission is required.[68] These are extensive and are now set out in the twenty-two sub-paragraphs of PD 6B to the Civil Procedure Rules. They are commonly referred to as jurisdictional gateways. They include cases which concern:

- A contract made in England, or through an agent trading in England, or governed by English law, or in respect of a breach of contract in England—gateways (6) and (7);
- A tort where the wrongful event or damage occurred in England—gateway (9);
- A claim for an injunction to do or refrain from doing an act in England—gateway (2);
- A defendant who is a necessary or proper party to a claim against another ('anchor') defendant—gateway (3);
- A further claim arising out of the same or closely related facts—gateway (4A);

[65] As regards permissible methods of service, see, CPR 6.9; *Maharanee of Baroda v Wildenstein* [1972] 2 QB 283.

[66] CPR 6.33(1), which previously permitted service of claim forms out of the jurisdiction without permission in EU and EFTA states, has been deleted.

[67] The CJJA Regulations re-enact the EU rules in respect of consumer and employment contracts by inserting new provisions (Sections 15A–E) in the CJJA. CPR 6.33 has been amended by the CPR 1998 (Amendment) (EU Exit) Regulations 2019 so that the claimant may serve a claim form outside the jurisdiction where the claim made against the defendant can be determined under Sections 15A–15E CJJA.

[68] Civil Procedure Rules, Rule 6.37(1)(a).

- A claim for an interim remedy in the absence of jurisdiction on the merits—gateway (5).

The second hurdle in an application for service outside jurisdiction is that the claimant must demonstrate that the claim involves a 'serious issue to be tried'.[69] This is not the civil standard of proof of the balance of probabilities.[70] Lord Goff endorsed Lord Simmonds' earlier formulation as applied to the jurisdictional gateways.[71] Lord Goff held that the existence of a reasonable prospect of success fell to be determined according to a lesser standard, namely that there should be a 'serious issue to be tried'.[72] This has been held to correspond to the test for resisting an application for summary judgment.[73] The requirement is fulfilled if the claimant can provide evidence that the dispute involves allegations that are not fanciful. In *Brownlie v Four Seasons Holdings Inc*, Lord Sumption reformulated the effect of 'the better of the argument' test in *Canada Trust Co v Stolzenberg (No 2)*[74] as follows:[75]

> (i) that the claimant must supply a plausible evidential basis for the application of a relevant jurisdictional gateway; (ii) that if there is an issue of fact about it, or some other reason for doubting whether it applies, the court must take a view on the material available if it can reliably do so; but (iii) the nature of the issue and the limitations of the material available at the interlocutory stage may be such that no reliable assessment can be made, in which case there is a good arguable case for the application of the gateway if there is a plausible (albeit contested) evidential basis for it.

The third hurdle in an application for service outside jurisdiction is that the claimant must show that England is the 'proper place' to bring the claim.[76] This is the *forum conveniens* test and is the counterpart of the power to stay proceedings on the grounds of *forum non conveniens*. Although this is termed a discretionary test, it is not so much an exercise in discretion as an exercise of evaluation of the evidence in order to decide whether England, or some other forum, is the more appropriate forum for the trial of the dispute.[77] The onus is on the claimant to prove

[69] Civil Procedure Rules, Rule 6.37(1)(b).
[70] *Vitkovice Horni a Hutni Tezirstvo v Korner* [1951] AC 869, 880 (HL) (Lord Simmonds).
[71] *Seaconsar Far East Ltd v Bank Markazi Jomhouri Islami Iran* [1994] 1 AC 438 (Lord Goff).
[72] ibid.
[73] ibid.
[74] [1998] 1 WLR 547, 555–57 (Waller LJ).
[75] [2018] 1 WLR 192, [7]. *Goldman Sachs International v Novo Banco SA* [2018] UKSC 34, [9] (Lord Sumption). See also, *Altimo Holdings and Investment Ltd v Kyrgyz Mobil Tel Ltd* [2011] UKPC 7, [71] (Lord Collins); *Bols Distilleries BV v Superior Yacht Services* [2006] UKPC 45, [2007] 1 WLR 12, [26]–[28].
[76] CPR 6.37(3).
[77] See *Vedanta v Lungowe* [2019] UKSC 20, [6]–[14] and *Okpabi v Shell* [2021] UKSC 3, [107]. The need to overhaul the costly and time-consuming Goffian *forum conveniens* model in the post-Brexit legal environment has been suggested in Dickinson, 'Walking Solo' (n 59). Dickinson suggests that the

that England is 'the forum in which the case can suitably be tried for the interests of all the parties and the interests of justice'.[78] To discharge this burden, the English court has to find that England is the dispute's centre of gravity. Claimants point towards a preponderance of connecting factors that link England with the claim. These connecting factors include choice of law, the location of evidence and witnesses, and the existence of parallel proceedings. Even if England is not the dispute's centre of gravity, the court may yet hold that it is *forum conveniens* if it concludes that the claim cannot be tried justly in the more closely connected foreign forum.[79] A defendant who disputes the court's jurisdiction or the validity of service may make an application challenging those matters, without thereby submitting to the English court's jurisdiction over the substance. Post Brexit, there will be greater opportunity for defendants to contest service out and jurisdiction, on the basis of *forum non conveniens*.

It will be useful to highlight the characteristics of some of the jurisdictional gateways including the need for reform so that the future application of the gateways becomes more certain, predictable, and reduces the risk of lengthy and costly jurisdictional disputes.

In a cross-border contractual dispute under gateway 6(a), a claimant can seek to initiate proceedings against a defendant outside England if the contract was made in England. According to English contract law, a contract in which the offeree accepts the offer through the post, the contract is made in England, provided that the letter of acceptance is posted in England.[80] Where the offeree utilises an instantaneous means of communication to accept the offer then the contract is made in England, so long as the acceptance is received there.[81] Notwithstanding, the application of gateway 6(a) has been criticised for its 'artificial nature'.[82] This criticism is due to how the provision has been phrased. Lord Sumption highlights why the gateway and its scope are problematic:[83]

> [The rules for determining when a contract is formed under English law] were adopted for reasons of pragmatic convenience, and provide a perfectly serviceable test for determining whether a contract has been concluded at all. However, their deployment for the purpose of determining when or where a contract was

wide-ranging evaluative enquiry can be reined in by shifting the burden of proof in its entirety to the defendant and requiring a clearly more appropriate forum than England for a stay of proceedings.

[78] [1987] AC 460, 476 (Lord Goff).

[79] Eg, *Oppenheimer v Louis Rosenthal & Co AG* [1937] 1 All ER 23; *Roneleigh Ltd v MII Exports Inc* [1989] 1 WLR 619; *Altimo Holdings and Investment Ltd v Kyrgyz Mobil Tel Ltd* [2011] UKPC 7; [2012] 1 WLR 1804, [71], [81], and [88] (Lord Collins).

[80] *Adams v Lindsell* (1818) 1 B & Ald 681.

[81] *Entores Ltd v Miles Far East Corp* [1955] 2 QB 327; *Brinkibon v Stahag Stahlund Stahlwarenhandels GmbH* [1983] 2 AC 34.

[82] *Brownlie v Four Seasons Holdings Inc* [2017] UKSC 80; [2018] 1 WLR 192, [16] (Lord Sumption).

[83] ibid. cf *Brownlie v Four Seasons Holdings Inc* [2017] UKSC 80; [2018] 1 WLR 192, [34] (Lady Hale).

> made is not at all satisfactory. It depends on assumptions about the point at which an offer is accepted or deemed to be accepted, which are particularly arbitrary when the mode of communication used is instantaneous (or practically so). It also gives rise to serious practical difficulties. The analysis of an informal conversation in terms of invitation to treat, offer and acceptance will often be impossible without a recording or a total recall of the sequence of exchanges and the exact words used at each stage, in order to establish points which are unlikely to have been of any importance to either party at the time. This may be unavoidable under the current wording of gateway 6(a). But the whole question could profitably be re-examined by the Rules Committee.

The current gateway 6(a) has the potential of making it difficult to identify the place where the contract is made. The increased reliance on modern technology to conduct cross border contract negotiations means that it is ever more complex to determine whether a case falls under gateway 6(a).

Gateway 6(a) could be reformed by allowing service outside jurisdiction if the contract 'was concluded in person in England at the residence or place of business of one of the parties'.[84] In similar vein, gateway 6(b) could be applicable if the court finds that the contract 'was concluded in person in England at the residence or place of business of the agent'.[85] Adjusting the jurisdictional gateway will make its application clear and unambiguous. It will also ensure that disputes have a greater and objective territorial connection with the forum.

The tort jurisdictional gateway is wider than the test under Article 7(2) of the Brussels Ia Regulation because it may include cases based on indirect damage.[86] The Court of Appeal of England and Wales in *FS Cairo (Nile Plaza) LLC v Christine Brownlie* has held that direct damage in the jurisdiction is not required in order for a claim to come within the tort jurisdictional gateway.[87] In doing so it followed the observations made by the majority of the UK Supreme Court in an earlier judgment in the same case.[88] Lady Hale, Lord Wilson, and Lord Clarke had held that the ordinary and natural meaning of gateway 9(a)[89] included 'all the detriment,

[84] A Dickinson, 'Faulty Powers: One-Star Service in the English Courts' [2018] Lloyd's Maritime and Commercial Law Quarterly 189, 194.

[85] For an example of how weak the connection with the forum under the existing gateway 6(a) can be, see *Cherney v Deripaska* [2008] EWHC 1530 (Comm); [2009] 1 All ER (Comm) 333. Affirmed by the Court of Appeal [2009] EWCA Civ 849; [2009] 2 CLC 408.

[86] L Collins and others, *Dicey, Morris & Collins The Conflict of Laws* (15th edn, Sweet & Maxwell 2012) [11.142] (hereafter Collins, *Dicey, Morris & Collins*).

[87] *FS Cairo (Nile Plaza) LLC v Christine Brownlie* [2020] EWCA Civ 996. An appeal from this decision has been heard by the UK Supreme Court and is currently awaiting judgment.

[88] *Brownlie v Four Seasons Holdings Inc* [2018] 1 WLR 192. For first instance decisions interpreting that indirect and direct damages sustained by the victim (or their family members) in England fall within the scope of subparagraph 9(a), see *Booth v Phillips* [2004] EWHC 1437 (Comm), [2004] 1 WLR 3292; *Cooley v Ramsey* [2008] ILPr 27 (Tugendhat J); *Wink v Croatia Osiguranje DD* [2013] EWHC 1118 (QB) (Haddon-Cave J); *Stylianou v Toyoshima* [2013] EWHC 2188 (QB); *Pike v Indian Hotels Co Ltd* [2013] EWHC 4096 (QB).

[89] 'damage was sustained or will be sustained within the jurisdiction'.

physical, financial and social, which the plaintiff suffers as a result of the tortious conduct of the defendant'.[90]

The test under the common law is, therefore, different from the test under Article 7(2) of the Brussels Ia Regulation (and the Lugano II Convention) where direct damage in the jurisdiction is a requirement. Given the divergent views expressed on this issue by a number of appellate court judges, the matter remains ripe for further consideration by the UK Supreme Court. Whilst arguments that the common law gateway does or should mirror the test in the Brussels Ia Regulation may diminish post-Brexit, the underlying issue of what amounts to a sufficient connection with the forum to justify tort proceedings in England against a foreign defendant persists.

McCombe LJ observed that the appeal in the case went precisely to the point considered by the UK Supreme Court in very full *obiter dicta* and (like the judge at first instance) he would feel strongly inclined to follow the majority conclusion unless there was another binding authority or he was clearly persuaded not to do so.

After analysing the various arguments raised, he reached the conclusion that the views of the majority were correct. The proper question to ask was whether a claimant had suffered 'significant damage' in the jurisdiction.[91] There was no need to import the legalistic niceties inherent in the concepts of direct and indirect damage.[92] The court rules which applied to common law cases were amended in 1987 so as to apply where damage from a tort was suffered in the jurisdiction, as well as when the acts giving rise to the tort were committed in England.[93] Without the change to the court rules, the tort gateway in common law cases would have been much narrower than the tort provision in the Brussels Ia Regulation. That change, effected by entirely different language to that used in the Brussels Ia Regulation, did not mean the subsequent narrow interpretation of 'damage' adopted in CJEU decisions on the Brussels Ia Regulation also applied to interpret the English common law gateway. It was clear from the decision in *Metall und Rohstoff AG v Donaldson Lufkin & Jenrette Inc* that there were differences between the EU rules and the common law gateway.[94] Under EU rules, if damage is sustained where the causal act took place, there is no jurisdiction in a second state, even if significant further damage is suffered there. That is not the case in England in light of the *Metall und Rohstoff* decision where it was held that at least 'some significant damage' must

[90] *Brownlie v Four Seasons Holdings Inc* [2018] 1 WLR 192, [52] Lady Hale citing *Flaherty v Girgis* (1985) 63 ALR 466, 482 (Kirby P and Samuels JA)

[91] *FS Cairo (Nile Plaza) LLC v Christine Brownlie* [2020] EWCA Civ 996, [53]. See Briggs, *Conflict of Laws* (n 54) 113.

[92] ibid.

[93] That change was made in light of the CJEU's decision in Case 21/76 *Handelswerkerij GJ Bier BV v Mines de Patasse d'Alsace CA* [1978] QB 708. *Bier* had interpreted the phrase 'where the harmful event occurred' in the Brussels regime as meaning either where the damage was sustained or where the act took place that gave rise to the damage.

[94] *Metall und Rohstoff AG v Donaldson Lufkin & Jenrette Inc.* [1990] 1 QB 391.

have been suffered in England.[95] The function of the EU and common law rules is different. The EU rule is not subject to a *forum conveniens* residual discretion. Article 7(2) is in an exceptional rule that is given a construction no wider than is necessary to achieve its purpose. Interpretation of 'damage' in the gateway could not be assisted by looking at the Rome II Regulation on the law applicable to non-contractual obligations.

Arnold LJ took the view that the court should make up its own mind as to the correct answer, given that the UK Supreme Court's views were *obiter*, there was only a bare majority in favour of the broader interpretation and two of the majority acknowledged the need for caution in relying upon the view they expressed.

Arnold LJ's starting point was that the word 'damage' in the gateway was capable of being interpreted broadly or narrowly so it was important to have regard to the context and purpose of the rule, which applied to all tort claims, not just personal injury claims. He concluded that what must be shown is that direct damage was suffered in the jurisdiction and indirect damage is insufficient.[96] Lord Sumption had argued that gateway 9(a) should be understood more restrictively as referring to direct damage.[97] In a personal injury case such as *Brownlie* that meant that the personal injury needed to have occurred in England. Only this would represent a sufficient connection with this jurisdiction to justify the English court asserting jurisdiction over a foreign defendant. Otherwise it would not only confer on the courts what Lord Sumption had described as 'universal jurisdiction to entertain claims by English residents for the more serious personal injuries suffered anywhere in the world'[98] but an equally broad jurisdiction over torts causing pure economic loss.[99]

The amendment of the court rules in 1987 supported the conclusion that the gateway should be interpreted at least as broadly as the tort provision in the Brussels Ia Regulation but did not go further and meant it should not be interpreted more broadly.[100] To that extent he agreed with Lord Wilson's comments in the UK Supreme Court. He was unimpressed however with the argument that the

[95] ibid 437.

[96] Arnold LJ's opinion is supported by the minority in *Brownlie v Four Seasons Holdings Inc* [2017] UKSC 80, [2018] 1 WLR 192.

[97] *Brownlie v Four Seasons Holdings Inc* [2017] UKSC 80, [2018] 1 WLR 192, [23] (Lord Sumption).

[98] ibid.

[99] Recent CJEU decisions demonstrate the difficulties in localising the place of pure economic loss. Several Advocate Generals have invited the CJEU to take up jurisdiction at the place of damage in such cases: Opinion of AG Sánchez Bordona in Case C-343/19 *VKI./.Volkswagen* EU:C:2020:253 [46]–[47], and Opinion of AG Sánchez Bordona in Case C-709/19 *VEB* EU:C:2020:1056, [40] et seq. referring to the Opinion of AG Szpunar in Case C-12/15 *Universal Music* EU:C:2016:161, [38]. According to the case law of the CJEU, pure economic loss occurring at a bank account does not create any 'Erfolgsort' under Article 7(2) of the Brussels Ia Regulation unless additional criteria are present.

[100] *FS Cairo (Nile Plaza) LLC v Christine Brownlie* [2020] EWCA Civ 996, [71] (Arnold LJ): 'The gateways represent the considered judgment of the Civil Procedure Rule Committee as to the classes of case in which it may (but not necessarily will) be appropriate to bring a foreign defendant before the courts of England and Wales.'

CJEU's decisions on the meaning of 'damage' post-dated the amendment in 1987. Where domestic legislation is adopted to be consistent with European legislation, it should be interpreted consistently with how it is interpreted from time to time by the CJEU.

The power to refuse jurisdiction on the basis of *forum non conveniens* was a factor favouring a broader rather than narrow construction of gateways but it was important not to place too much weight on this. Disputes about the determination of the appropriate forum are costly and uncertain. Adopting a wide interpretation of the gateway which left most of the work in identifying appropriate cases for determination in England to the *forum conveniens* rules would encourage litigation about where to litigate.[101]

The decision in *Metall und Rohstoff* was only authority for the proposition that if most of the damage has been sustained in the jurisdiction, it is immaterial that a small amount has been suffered outside. The decision in *ABCI v Banque Franco-Tunisienne* on the other hand was strongly persuasive of the need for direct damage in the jurisdiction.[102]

The UK Supreme Court had unanimously agreed that the Rome II Regulation on the law applicable to non-contractual obligations was not directly relevant when interpreting gateways as jurisdiction and applicable law are distinct concepts.[103] However, Arnold LJ observed that the reasoning in *Lazar v Allianz SpA* was persuasive when it came to identifying the relevant connecting factors for the purposes of jurisdiction.[104]

So far as the damages claimed were concerned, Arnold LJ's view was that damages for bereavement and loss of dependency were indirect consequences of the death of Sir Ian Brownlie in Egypt and Lady Brownlie's claims for pain, suffering, and loss of amenity were the direct consequences of the tort which took place in Egypt. There was therefore no good arguable case that the claims fell within the tort gateway.

Underhill LJ took the view that the approach which accorded proper weight to a fully considered but *obiter* view of a majority of the Supreme Court should be the same as that which a first instance court takes to a decision of a court of coordinate jurisdiction, namely it should follow the decision unless it was clearly wrong. Applying that test, he was not persuaded that the view of the majority in the UK

[101] *Brownlie v Four Seasons Holdings Inc* [2017] UKSC 80, [2018] 1 WLR 192, [51], [54] (Lady Hale). cf *Spiliada Maritime Corporation v Cansulex Ltd (The Spiliada)* [1987] 1 AC 460, 464G-H (HL) (Lord Templeman); *Voth v Manildra Flour Mills Pty Ltd* (1990) 171 CLR 538, 565, 571 (HC); *Vedanta v Lungowe* [2019] UKSC 20, [6]-[14] (Lord Briggs); *Okpabi v Shell* [2021] UKSC 3, [107] (Lord Hamblen).

[102] [2003] 2 Lloyds Rep 146 (Mance LJ).

[103] cf EB Crawford and JM Carruthers, 'Connection and Coherence Between and among European Instruments in the Private International Law of Obligations' (2014) 63 International and Comparative Law Quarterly 1.

[104] *FS Cairo (Nile Plaza) LLC v Christine Brownlie* [2020] EWCA Civ 996, [87]. Case C-350/14 *Florin Lazar v Allianz SpA* EU:C:2015:802, [30], confirms that it is only the place where the direct victim suffers direct damage that is relevant for the purposes of Article 4(1) of the Rome II Regulation.

Supreme Court was wrong. He therefore agreed as to the outcome with McCombe LJ. However in his view there were powerful arguments to be made on both sides and he did not think there was any value in his contributing to the debate about which of the two approaches would be preferable or more in accordance with the case law.

The interpretation of the tort gateway is clearly controversial. In this decision of the Court of Appeal alone, there are only two reasoned judgments on this question and they reach opposite conclusions. Further guidance from the UK Supreme Court would therefore be welcome.

It may be thought that the argument that the common law gateway does or should reflect the tort rules in the Brussels Ia Regulation diminishes with Brexit. However, there is a more fundamental issue at stake here: what is or should be a sufficient connecting factor to justify the English court taking jurisdiction in a tort claim over a foreign defendant. Resolving that issue includes deciding whether gateways should be widely interpreted, given the court's discretion to refuse jurisdiction where England is not the *forum conveniens*, or whether a more narrow interpretation, which accords greater legal certainty to the parties and reduces the likelihood of protracted and costly jurisdictional challenges, should be adopted. It is argued that the latter principled approach is preferable to the exorbitant pragmatism of the former. The place of direct damage as the localising element reflects the objective requirements of jurisdictional connection, comity, and conflicts justice. It is better for the rational and rules-based development of the law on service outside jurisdiction and private international law in general.

In tort disputes, it is recommended that gateway 9(a) should be rephrased so that it would be engaged where 'direct damage was sustained, or will be sustained, within England'. Adjusting the jurisdictional gateway will make it clear and unambiguous. It will also ensure that disputes have an augmented and objective territorial connection with England. It is argued that fine tuning the law will help address the deficiencies in the law on service out of the jurisdiction by rendering it more accessible, certain, and predictable in conferring jurisdiction on English courts.

The English CPR provide that a claim against an English defendant can 'anchor' the case by allowing the courts to exercise jurisdiction over another 'necessary or proper party' to the claim, so long as there is a real issue which is reasonable for the court to try between the claimant and the anchor defendant.[105] The 'necessary or proper party' gateway is wider than Article 8(1) of the Brussels Ia Regulation. Indeed, Article 8(1) may be criticised for being too narrow to comprehensively

[105] CPR 6.36 and PD 6B para 3.1(3). cf Third parties, such as those who might be called upon to contribute or indemnify the defendant, can be joined to a dispute in England using Civil Procedure Rules Part 20 which also covers counterclaims by the defendant. It is possible to obtain jurisdiction over third parties who are out of the territorial jurisdiction so long as the third party is a necessary and proper party: CPR PD 6B para 3.1(4).

achieve the pragmatic objective of facilitating the sound administration of justice. The necessary or proper party jurisdictional gateway is said to be 'extraordinarily wide' as it does not require any connection between the parties, in particular the foreign defendant and England.[106] A single set of proceedings leading to one judgment on all the issues has obvious advantages of efficiency and convenience. The court has a responsibility to ensure that the 'necessary or proper party' gateway is not abused[107] because it allows a claimant to serve a defendant outside jurisdiction on the basis of an associated jurisdictional liability.[108] Therefore, the court should be satisfied that the claim against the 'anchor' defendant is about a real triable issue.[109] If there is no serious issue to be tried in the proceedings against the anchor defendant (or it is bound to fail)[110] then the 'necessary or proper party' ground of jurisdiction is not available against the defendant to be joined. However, so long as there is a good arguable case against the anchor defendant, the claimant's motive is merely a factor in the exercise of the discretion to serve out.

1. The Moçambique Rule is Revived in Cases Involving Immovable Property or Intellectual Property Rights Situated in an EU Member State or Lugano II Convention Contracting State

Let us suppose that a claimant commences litigation in the English courts and the defunct Article 24 of the Brussels Ia Regulation would have conferred exclusive jurisdiction on a Member State Court regardless of the domicile of the parties. Article 24 allocates exclusive jurisdiction *inter alia* on a Member State court in

[106] P Rogerson, *Collier's Conflict of Laws* (4th edn, Cambridge University Press 2013) 150. cf Under Article 8(1) of the Brussels Ia Regulation, the fact that recovery against one defendant may have a direct effect on the measure of recovery against another defendant is not enough to give rise to a risk of irreconcilable judgments: C-311/13 *Profit Investment Sim SpA (in liq) v Ossi* EU:C:2016:282, [2016] 1 WLR 3832, [67].

[107] *The Brabo* [1949] AC 326, 338. In *Vedanta Resources Plc and Another v Lungowe and Others* [2019] UKSC 20 (Lord Briggs) the appeal focused on the claim that the commencement of proceedings against *Vedanta* in order to force *Konkola* to defend itself in English courts was an abuse of EU law. The UK Supreme Court recognised it would be an abuse of this rule to allow the respondents to sue an English domiciled 'anchor' defendant solely to pursue a foreign co-defendant in the English courts but that this exception should be applied strictly. Both the lower courts found on the facts that the respondents had a bona fide claim and a genuine intention to seek a remedy in damages against *Vedanta* even though establishing jurisdiction over *Konkola* was also a key factor in their decision to litigate in England. The UK Supreme Court concluded that there was no abuse of EU law.

[108] A Arzandeh, '"Gateways" within the Civil Procedure Rules and The Future of Service-out Jurisdiction in England' (2019) 15 Journal of Private International Law 516, 539, argues that the concept of 'related actions' under Article 30 of the Brussels Ia Regulation can provide the impetus for reining in the current 'necessary or proper party' jurisdictional gateway.

[109] *Erste Group Bank AG (London) v JSC (VMZ Red October)* [2015] EWCA Civ 379.

[110] The case against the anchor defendant was bound to fail in *Multinational Gas v Multinational Gas Services* [1983] Ch. 258 (CA).

proceedings which have as their object rights *in rem* in immovable property,[111] the validity of the corporation's decisions,[112] and the registration or validity of patents, trademarks, designs, or other similar rights.[113] In the hierarchy of jurisdictional rules and *lis pendens* rules, Article 24 of the Brussels Ia Regulation is paramount. The priority conferred on Article 24 is made apparent by the express provision for non-recognition of a judgment that conflicts with Article 24.[114]

At common law, under the rule in *British South Africa Co v Companhia de Moçambique*,[115] the English court will not adjudicate on questions relating to the title to, or the right to the possession of, foreign immovable property.[116] The jurisdiction of any court in England and Wales to entertain proceedings for trespass to, or any other tort affecting, immovable property shall extend to cases in which the property in question is situated outside that part of the UK 'unless the proceedings are principally concerned with a question of the title to, or the right to possession of' the property.[117]

In *Lucasfilm v Ainsworth*, the UK Supreme Court ruled that an unregistered foreign copyright claim is justiciable providing that there is *in personam* jurisdiction over the defendant.[118] On this issue, the decision was distinguished from *British South Africa Co v Companhia de Moçambique* which expressed the general principle that English courts have no jurisdiction to entertain an action to determine title, where claims applied to foreign intellectual property rights.[119]

As part of their conclusions on the justiciability question, Lord Walker and Lord Collins stated:[120]

> We have come to the firm conclusion that, in the case of a claim for infringement of copyright of the present kind, the claim is one over which the English court has jurisdiction, provided that there is a basis for in personam jurisdiction over

[111] Case C-115/88 *Reichert v Dresdner Bank* [1990] ECR I-27; C-294/92 *Webb v Webb* [1994] ECR I-1717; C-292/93 *Liebr v Gobel* [1994] ECR I-2535; C-343/04 *Land Oberosterreich v CEZ* [2006] ECR I-4557; Case C-605/14 *Virpi Komu v Pekka Komu* EU:C:2015:833; Case C-438/12 *Weber v Weber* EU:C:2014:212, [55]–[56] (Priority of Articles 22(1) over 27(1) of the Brussels I Regulation. The judgment of the court first seised cannot be recognised in the Member State in which the court second seised is situated).

[112] Case C-144/10 *Berliner Verkehrsbetriebe (BVG) v JP Morgan Chase Bank NA* [2011] ECR I-3961.

[113] Case C-4/03 *Gesellschaft für Antriebstechnik mbH & Co KG v Lamellen und Kupplungsbau Beteiligungs KG (GAT v LuK)* [2006] ECR I-6509.

[114] Article 45(1)(e)(ii) of the Brussels Ia Regulation.

[115] *British South Africa Co v Companhia de Moçambique* [1893] AC 602 (Lord Herschell LC); J Hill and M Ní Shúilleabháin, *Clarkson & Hill's Conflict of Laws* (5th edn, OUP 2016) 141–44 (hereafter Hill and Shúilleabháin, *Clarkson & Hill*).

[116] The limits on the subject matter jurisdiction of the Scottish courts are prescribed by Rule 5 of Schedule 8 to the CJJA. These correspond to the rules of exclusive jurisdiction laid down in Article 16 of the Brussels Convention (1968). See Beaumont and McEleavy, *Anton* (n 12) 222–37.

[117] Section 30(1) CJJA. See *Polly Peck International Plc v The Marangos Hotel Company Ltd and Others* [1998] EWCA Civ 789, [1998] 3 All ER 812, [1998] 2 BCLC 185.

[118] *Lucasfilm v Ainsworth* [2011] UKSC 39, [2012] 1 AC 208 (Lord Walker and Lord Collins).

[119] *British South Africa Co v Companhia de Moçambique* [1893] AC 602.

[120] *Lucasfilm v Ainsworth* [2011] UKSC 39, [2012] 1 AC 208 [106] and [107].

the defendant, or, to put it differently, the claim is justiciable. It is clear that much of the underpinning of the *Moçambique* rule and the decision in *Potter v Broken Hill Pty Co Ltd* has been eroded. All that is left of the *Moçambique* rule (except to the extent that it is modified by the Brussels I Regulation) is that there is no jurisdiction in proceedings for infringement of rights in foreign land where the proceedings are "principally concerned with a question of the title, or the right to possession, of that property." So also article 22(1) of the Brussels I Regulation does not apply to actions for damages for infringement of rights in land.

The basis for what remains of the rule was said by the House of Lords in the *Moçambique* case to be that controversies should be decided in the country of the situs of the property because the right of granting it was vested in 'the ruler of the country' and in the *Hesperides* case to be the maintenance of comity and the avoidance of conflict with foreign jurisdictions. It is possible to see how the rationale of the *Moçambique* rule can be applied to patents, at any rate where questions of validity are involved. For example the claims might touch on the validity of patents in sensitive areas, such as armaments, and that no doubt is part of the rationale for article 22(4) of the Brussels I Regulation. But it is very difficult to see how it could apply to copyright.

2. The Jurisdictional Rule in Section 9 of the Defamation Act 2013 Applies to a Defendant Domiciled Outside the UK

Defamation is an oral or written communication that has caused or is likely to cause serious harm to the reputation of the claimant.[121] In *Thornton v Telegraph Media Group Ltd* the decision of the House of Lords in *Sim v Stretch* was identified as authority for the existence of a 'threshold of seriousness' in what is defamatory:[122] 'would the words tends to lower the plaintiff in the estimation of right-thinking members of society generally?'.[123] In *Jameel v Dow Jones & Co* it was established that there needs to be a real and substantial tort.[124] Under the English law of libel is it not, however, necessary for the claimant to prove that this has actually happened: it is presumed. It is also unnecessary to prove any financial loss.

Prior to 1 January 2021, the special jurisdictional rule for torts in Article 7(2) of the Brussels Ia Regulation applied to cross border defamation claims:[125]

[121] See, for instance, *Berezovsky v Michaels* [2000] 1 WLR 1004; *King v Lewis* [2004] EWCA Civ 1329, [2005] ILPr 185; *Richardson v Schwarzenegger* [2004] EWHC 2422. (QB), affirmed [2005] EWCA Civ 25.

[122] *Thornton v Telegraph Media Group Ltd* [2010] EWHC 1414; *Sim v Stretch* [1936] 2 All ER 1237.

[123] *Sim v Stretch* [1936] 2 All ER 1237 (Lord Atkin).

[124] *Jameel v Dow Jones & Co* [2005] EWCA Civ 75.

[125] Article 7(2) of the Brussels Ia Regulation.

> in matters relating to tort, delict or quasi-delict, in the courts for the place where the harmful event occurred or may occur.

In *Shevill v Presse Alliance SA*,[126] which concerned alleged defamation in a newspaper, the CJEU held that the distinction laid down in *Bier v Mines de Potasse d'Alsace* between the place where the damage occurs and the place of the event giving rise to it applies equally where there is no physical or pure economic loss or damage pursuant to Article 7(2) of the Brussels Ia Regulation.[127] It held that, in the case of defamation in a hard copy publication, the place where the damage occurs is the place or places where the publication is distributed, provided that the victim is known in that place or those places. Thus, the courts of each Member State in which the defamatory publication is distributed, and in which the victim claims to have suffered injury to their reputation, have jurisdiction to rule on the injury caused in that state to the victim's reputation.[128]

The leading decisions on online publication are two joined cases, *eDate Advertising v X* and *Martinez v MGN Limited*.[129] These were cases on privacy, but the principles are the same as for defamation. In its judgment, the CJEU held that the two grounds of jurisdiction established in *Shevill* continue to apply in Internet cases, the place of the harm being the place where the online content is or has been accessible,[130] and the place of the causal act being the place where the publisher of the content is established.[131]

The claimant's centre of interests was introduced as a new ground of jurisdiction. Where the court has jurisdiction on this basis, the claimant can obtain compensation for the totality of their loss, wherever occurring.[132] Although it is used as a connecting factor in insolvency law, the centre of the claimant's interests has not been used before in the context of the Brussels Ia Regulation. In *eDate*, the CJEU elucidated it as follows:[133]

> The place where a person has the centre of his interests corresponds in general to his habitual residence. However, a person may also have the centre of his interests in a Member State in which he does not habitually reside, in so far as other factors, such as the pursuit of a professional activity, may establish the existence of a particularly close link with that State.

126 Case C-68/93 *Shevill v Presse Alliance SA* [1995] ECR I-415.
127 ibid [23].
128 ibid [29]–[30].
129 *eDate Advertising v X* and *Martinez v MGN Limited*, Joined Cases C-509/09 and C-161/10, [2011] ECR I-10269.
130 ibid [52].
131 ibid.
132 ibid.
133 ibid [49].

In the case of a legal person, the centre of main interests is located where the latter carries out its main economic activities.[134] In *Mittelbayerischer Verlag*, the CJEU restricted the scope of Article 7(2) in defamation cases by requiring the application of the main centre of interest only if the allegedly libellous content 'contains objective and verifiable elements which make it possible to identify, directly or indirectly, that person as an individual'.[135]

Actions for defamation and invasion of privacy involve balancing two important substantive rights which often conflict. These are the claimant's right to reputation (and privacy) and the defendant's right to freedom of speech. It would be unfair for the claimant to have an unfettered choice of forum and then to be able to sue in one forum for harm caused anywhere in the world.[136]

Section 9 of the Defamation Act 2013 applied to cases where the defendant to the claim was not domiciled either in the UK or in an EU Member State or a Contracting State of the Lugano II Convention. However, Section 9 has now been amended.[137] Section 9 now applies to all cases where the defendant to the claim is not domiciled in the UK. Hence, the scope of Section 9 has widened to include defendants in EU Member States and Lugano II Convention Contracting States.[138]

The English court's jurisdiction over a defamation action against a person not domiciled in the UK is prescribed by:[139]

> A court does not have jurisdiction to hear and determine an action to which this section applies unless the court is satisfied that, of all the places in which the statement complained of has been published, England and Wales is *clearly the most appropriate place* in which to bring an action in respect of the statement.

The Defamation and Malicious Publication (Scotland) Act 2021 contains a similarly phrased provision.[140] The references in Section 9 of the Defamation Act 2013 to the statement complained of include references to any statement which conveys the same, or substantially the same, imputation as the statement complained of.[141] Section 9 of the 2013 Act may be conceptualised as setting forth a special rule for *forum conveniens* in libel actions only.[142] It replaces the classic *forum conveniens*

[134] Case C-194/16 *Bolagsupplysningen* EU:C:2017:766.
[135] Case C-800/19 *Mittelbayerischer Verlag* EU:C:2021:489, [47].
[136] See TC Hartley, 'Jurisdiction in Tort Claims for Non-Physical Harm under Brussels 2012, Article 7(2)' (2018) 67 International and Comparative Law Quarterly 987, 1000.
[137] Civil Jurisdiction and Judgments (Amendment)(EU Exit) Regulations 2019/479, reg 69.
[138] *Craig Wright v Roger Ver* [2020] EWCA Civ 672, [2020] 1 WLR 3913, [56] (Dingemans LJ).
[139] Section 9(2) of the Defamation Act 2013 (emphasis added).
[140] Section 19 the Defamation and Malicious Publication (Scotland) Act 2021.
[141] Section 9(3) of the Defamation Act 2013.
[142] *Walter Tzvi Soriano v Forensic News LLC and others* [2021] EWHC 56 (QB), [41] (Jay J).

rule that England and Wales should be the 'proper place'[143] in which to bring the claim in the context of a libel action.[144]

The purpose of Section 9 of the Defamation Act 2013 is to avoid libel tourism in cases where there is a tenuous connection with England and Wales.[145] In *Craig Wright v Roger Ver*, the Court of Appeal considered a number of factors that were relevant in determining whether England was clearly the most appropriate jurisdiction in which to bring an action for defamation.[146] These factors included:[147] the best evidence available to show all the places where the relevant statement has been published; the number of times in which the statement has been published in each jurisdiction; the amount of damage to the claimant's reputation in England and Wales, compared with elsewhere; the availability of fair judicial processes in the other jurisdictions in which the statement has been published; the available remedies in other jurisdictions; the costs of pursuing proceedings in other possible jurisdictions; language barriers; and the location of likely witnesses. Based on these factors and the evidence before it, the Court of Appeal concluded that England and Wales was not clearly the most appropriate jurisdiction to bring the claim.[148]

The Court of Appeal decision in *Craig Wright v Roger Ver* is particularly relevant to individuals who have global reputations. It is not enough for a claimant to claim an insubstantial or weak link to England and Wales. It is for precisely this reason that Section 9 was enacted. What is clear from the decision is that evidence at this early stage is essential. Claimants will have to consider carefully whether they can prove a clear and definite link with England and Wales by taking the factors above into consideration and showing that it is clearly the most appropriate jurisdiction. This is an important strategic question, but also one that is highly fact-specific.

In particular, a potential claimant should consider whether a statement has been more impactful inside England and Wales, or elsewhere. Evidence of the

[143] CPR 6.37(3). The leading authority for classic *forum conveniens* is *Spiliada Maritime Corporation v Cansulex Limited (The Spiliada)* [1987] AC 460, in particular the opinion of Lord Goff between 478E and 482A.

[144] *Walter Tzvi Soriano v Forensic News LLC and others* [2021] EWHC 56 (QB), [113] (Jay J).

[145] *Ahuja v Politika Novine I Magazini DOO and others* [2015] EWHC 3380 (QB), [2016] 1 WLR 1414, [31]–[32] (Tugendhat J).

[146] *Craig Wright v Roger Ver* [2020] EWCA Civ 672, [2020] 1 WLR 3913 (Dingemans LJ). See also, *Ahuja v Politika Novine I Magazini DOO and others* [2015] EWHC 3380 (QB), [2016] 1 WLR 1414; *Huda v Wells* [2017] EWHC 2553 (QB), [2018] EMLR 7; *Sadik v Sadik* [2019] EWHC 2717 (QB). In *Sadik v Sadik* [2019] EWHC 2717 (QB), [55], Knowles J held that a failure by a defendant to follow the procedure in CPR Part 11 for contesting jurisdiction under Section 9 does not mean that the right to make a jurisdictional challenge has been waived because Section 9(2) is mandatory. Jurisdiction under Section 9 cannot be conferred by waiver, submission, or consent. It is concerned with the subject matter of the suit and not with personal jurisdiction over the defendant.

[147] *Craig Wright v Roger Ver* [2020] EWCA Civ 672, [2020] 1 WLR 3913, [72]–[79].

[148] ibid [71].

statement's impact in England and Wales will be critical to the Court's assessment. The geographical reach and readership of the publication, social media reactions, witness statements, and media publications are all types of evidence that a claimant ought to collate when preparing their case.

Section 9 has been criticised because it requires the English court to dismiss the proceedings, so that if the foreign court which it has in mind does not agree to adjudicate, the claimant will, if he wishes to try again in England, need to start fresh proceedings and will risk running afoul of the limitation period.[149]

E. Intra-UK Jurisdiction

Schedule 4 to the CJJA (a slightly modified version of the Brussels Convention) applies when the defendant is domiciled in the UK and the proceedings are within the material scope of the Brussels Ia Regulation.[150] The purpose of Schedule 4 is to allocate jurisdiction based on domicile among the three legal systems of the UK. Schedule 4 operates in two main ways.

First, it supplements the Brussels Ia Regulation in those cases where its rules allocate jurisdiction to the UK but without specifying any particular legal system of the UK.[151] For instance, the effect of Article 4 of the Brussels Ia Regulation is simply that a person domiciled in the UK may be sued in the UK. Rule 1 of Schedule 4 identifies the particular part or parts of the UK in which proceedings may be brought by providing that a person domiciled in a part of the UK may be sued in that part.

Secondly, Schedule 4 allocates jurisdiction in cases which are internal to the UK but which have connections with more than one part of it. The effect, so far as the English court is concerned, is that Scotland and Northern Ireland are treated as if they were Member States. If the defendant is domiciled in another part of the UK the English court will have jurisdiction only if it would have had jurisdiction had the defendant been domiciled in another Member State. The effect of Schedule 4 is that, as regards disputes that fall within the material scope of the Brussels Ia Regulation, the English court cannot assume jurisdiction on the basis of the traditional rules if the defendant is domiciled in another part of the UK.

The rules in Schedule 4 represent a notable legacy of the Brussels regime in the UK.

149 Briggs, *Civil Jurisdiction* (n 21) 403.

150 Section 16 CJJA.

151 Where the Brussels Ia Regulation allocates jurisdiction to a place rather than to a Member State, Schedule 4 CJJA does not have to be invoked.

F. Jurisdiction in Consumer Contracts and Employment Contracts

In the context of weaker party contracts, a simple reversion to the undiscerning approach of the common law jurisdictional regime to asymmetrical contracts[152] was deemed retrograde.[153] Although the EU rules on jurisdiction will cease to apply on Completion Day,[154] a noteworthy and considered choice has been made to re-enact into domestic law some limited EU jurisdictional rules[155] by superimposing them onto the default common law regime that would otherwise apply.[156] The CJJA Regulations re-enact the EU rules in respect of consumer and employment contracts by inserting new provisions (Sections 15A–E) in the CJJA. The objective of the new statutory rules can be gleaned from the Brussels Ia Regulation itself:[157] 'the weaker party should be protected by rules of jurisdiction more favourable to its interests than the general rules'. It is submitted that legal certainty as to where to sue and where to be sued will be carried forward at least for consumer and employment contracts. If the rule allocating jurisdiction is satisfied the court has jurisdiction and proceedings can be served on the defendant inside or outside the jurisdiction without permission.[158]

Domicile is employed as a personal connecting factor in the new provisions on consumer and employment contracts.[159] The common law's wide basis for assuming jurisdiction where the defendant is merely present in England will not suffice for the purposes of domicile. Jurisdiction under Sections 15A to E will be mandatory as opposed to being discretionary.[160] If jurisdiction over the defendant

[152] See generally, J Hill, *Cross-Border Consumer Contracts* (OUP 2008); L Merrett, *Employment Contracts in Private International Law* (OUP 2011); U Grusic, *The European Private International Law of Employment* (CUP 2015).

[153] Briggs, *Conflict of Laws* (n 54) 43; J Harris, 'Understanding the English Response to the Europeanisation of Private International Law' (2008) 4 Journal of Private International Law 347, 353 (hereafter Harris, 'English Response to Europeanisation'); L Collins, *The Civil Jurisdiction and Judgments Act 1982* (Butterworths 1983) 74, observed that special provision was made in favour of consumers because there was special protection for them in the law of the original Contracting States of the 1968 Brussels Convention.

[154] Civil Jurisdiction and Judgments (Amendment) (EU Exit) Regulations 2019, SI 2019 No 479.

[155] Sections 4 and 5 of Chapter II of the Brussels Ia Regulation. G Ruhl, 'The Protection of Weaker Parties in the Private International Law of the European Union: A Portrait of Inconsistency and Conceptual Truancy' (2014) 10 Journal of Private International Law 335.

[156] Added by Civil Jurisdiction and Judgments (Amendment) (EU Exit) Regulations 2019/479 Pt 2 reg 26.

[157] Recital 18 of the Brussels Ia Regulation.

[158] CPR 6.33 has been amended by the Civil Procedure Rules 1998 (Amendment) (EU Exit) Regulations 2019 so that the claimant may serve a claim form outside the jurisdiction where the claim made against the defendant can be determined under Sections 15A to 15E CJJA.

[159] Articles 62 and 63 of the Brussels Ia Regulation. cf It should be noted that Articles 62 and 63 are part of the general provisions in Chapter V of the Brussels Ia Regulation. Section 15E(2)(a) refers only to any relevant principles and decisions laid down before exit day by the CJEU in connection with Title II of the 1968 Convention or Chapter II of the Regulation when determining the meaning or effect of any provision of that Title or Chapter.

[160] Case C-281/02 *Owusu v Jackson* [2005] ECR I-1383; [2005] QB 801, [37]. See also, Report by Professor Schlosser on the Convention of 9 October 1978 on the Accession of the Kingdom of

is taken on the basis of Article 4 of the Brussels Ia Regulation, even though the courts of another Member State would be the natural forum for the trial,[161] the court has no power to stay its proceedings.[162] The need to apply the jurisdictional corrective of *forum non conveniens* is arguably less likely to arise in the case of a direct rule of jurisdiction that relies on a stable personal connecting factor rather than jurisdiction based on mere presence.

It is argued that these protective provisions have been extracted from the Brussels Ia Regulation without full regard to the wider systemic implications of applying the rules outside the immediate context of the Regulation. At the outset, it should be noted that the Brussels Ia Regulation is a multilateral jurisdiction and judgments instrument, where the hierarchy of rules on jurisdiction resemble public law rules allocating adjudicatory authority, as opposed to giving rise to private law rights and obligations *inter partes*. These protective jurisdictional provisions will also not exist in complete isolation or as if they are hermetically sealed from the common law jurisdictional regime.

It should still be possible to obtain a stay of court proceedings on the basis of a flexible interpretation of the doctrine of reflexive effect.[163] The national private international law approach is posited upon the idea that the Regulation has no application at all where a non-Member State is the alternative forum in circumstances approximate to those of Articles 24, 25, 29, and 30 of the Brussels Ia Regulation. Accordingly, national private international law rules are applied to determine jurisdiction. The doctrine of *forum non conveniens* may be applicable, depending on the circumstances.

Inside the Regulation, the provisions on consumer and employment contracts exist as part of a hierarchy of jurisdictional rules. As provision for *lis pendens* is not possible due to a lack of international reciprocity and the doctrine of *forum non conveniens* cannot be applied, the mandatory rules of jurisdiction might prove to be inflexible. A stay of proceedings on the basis of the principle of reflexive effect may offer the flexibility needed to operate the protective jurisdiction rules outside the Brussels regime.[164] The principle of reflexive effect applies certain provisions of

Denmark, Ireland and the United Kingdom of Great Britain and Northern Ireland to the Convention on Jurisdiction and the enforcement of judgments in Civil and Commercial matters and to the Protocol on its interpretation by the Court of Justice, OJ 1979 C 59, 71, [77]–[78].

[161] Lord Goff in *Spiliada Maritime Corpn v Cansulex Ltd (The Spiliada)* [1987] AC 460, 478A, adopted the expression 'natural forum' from Lord Keith in *The Abidin Daver* [1984] AC 398, 415, who referred to it as 'that with which the action had the most real and substantial connection'.

[162] C-282/92 *Custom Made Commercial Ltd v Stawa Metallbau GmbH* [1994] ECR I-2923, [18].

[163] P De Verneuil Smith, B Lasserson, and R Rymkiewicz, 'Reflections on *Owusu*: The Radical Decision in *Ferrexpo*' (2012) 8 Journal of Private International Law 389, 398; R Fentiman, *International Commercial Litigation* (2nd edn, OUP 2015) 102 (hereafter Fentiman, *International Commercial Litigation*); A Briggs, *Private International Law in English Courts* (OUP 2014) 308 (hereafter Briggs, *Private International Law*).

[164] Case C-387/98 *Coreck Maritime GmbH v Handelsveem BV* [2000] ECR I-09337, [19], citing the Schlosser Report [176]; *PJSC Commercial Bank Privatbank v Kolomoisky* [2019] EWCA Civ 1708, [177]; *Huawei Technologies Co Ltd v Conversant Wireless Licensing Sarl* [2019] EWCA Civ 38; *Masri*

the Brussels Ia Regulation by analogy to third states. Significantly, the legal basis of the principle of reflexive effect is more thoroughly grounded in the unilateral jurisdictional context of the provisions than the Brussels Ia Regulation itself. It has been argued that Articles 33 and 34 have codified the reflexive effect of the Brussels Ia Regulation and it no longer possible in principle to stay proceedings on any other basis.[165] However, the present state of English law is represented by the Court of Appeal decisions in *Huawei Technologies Co Ltd v Conversant Wireless Licensing Sarl*[166] and *PJSC Commercial Bank Privatbank v Kolomoisky*[167] which approve of the principle of reflexive effect.[168] Over time, the English courts may depart from the case law of the CJEU under Chapter II of the Brussels Ia Regulation by permitting a freer and more dynamic interchange between the European jurisdictional concepts in Sections 15A to E and the common law jurisdictional regime.

English courts have held that a 'right' not to be sued outside England could arise in employment contracts under the current Article 22(1) of the Brussels Ia Regulation.[169] However, in Hohfeldian terms, a consumer or employee domiciled

v. Consolidated Contractors International Co SAL [2008] EWCA Civ 303; [2008] 2 Lloyd's Rep 128, [125] (Lawrence Collins LJ); *Plaza BV v The Law Debenture Trust Corporation* [2015] EWHC 43 (Ch) (Proudman J); *Ferrexpo AG v Gilson Investments Limited and ors* [2012] EWHC 721 (Comm) (Andrew Smith J); *Winnetka Trading Corporation v Julius Baer International Limited* [2008] EWHC 3146 (Ch); *Konkola Copper Mines Plc v Coramin Limited* [2005] EWHC 898 (Comm). cf In *Catalyst Investment Group v Lewinsohn* [2009] EWHC 1964 (Ch), [2010] Ch. 218, Barling J interpreted Case C-281/02 *Owusu v Jackson* [2005] ECR I-1383 and decided that the English courts have no power to decline jurisdiction, properly founded on one of the Brussels I grounds of jurisdiction, in favour of a court outside the EU even if it was seised first of an action. See A Layton, 'Shadows and Illusions in European Private International Law: Reflections on Reflexive Effect' in G Barrett and others (eds), *The Future of Legal Europe: Will We Trust in It?* (Springer 2021); L Collins and others (eds), *Dicey Morris & Collins on the Conflict of Laws* (14th edn, Sweet & Maxwell 2006) [12-021].

165 In *Gulf International Bank BSC v Aldwood* [2019] EWHC 1666 (QB), it was held that there is no power under the Brussels Ia Regulation to stay English proceedings in favour of proceedings in a non-EU court commenced pursuant to an exclusive choice of court agreement and the powers to stay proceedings under Articles 33 and 34 are exhaustive. See to similar effect, *UCP Plc v Nectrus Ltd* [2018] EWHC 380 (Comm). cf In *PJSC Commercial Bank Privatbank v Kolomoisky* [2019] EWCA Civ 1708, [180], the Court of Appeal said that nothing could be read into the fact of the amendments to Articles 33 and 34 of the Brussels Ia Regulation. Briggs has observed that the decision in *Gulf International Bank BSC v Aldwood* is 'wrong' in Briggs, *Civil Jurisdiction* (n 21) 360.

166 [2019] EWCA Civ 38. In *Unwired Planet International Ltd v Huawei Technologies (UK) Co Ltd* [2020] UKSC 37, [98], which included an appeal against the decision of the Court of Appeal in *Huawei Technologies Co Ltd v Conversant Wireless Licensing Sarl*, the UK Supreme Court declined to deal with this issue which, on the conclusions which it had otherwise reached, did not arise for determination.

167 [2019] EWCA Civ 1708, [2020] Ch 783, expressly approving *Ferrexpo AG v Gilson Investments Ltd* [2012] EWHC 721 (Comm), [2012] 1 Lloyd's Rep 588.

168 The term 'reflective effect' was preferred by the UK Supreme Court in *Unwired Planet International Ltd v Huawei Technologies (UK) Co Ltd* [2020] UKSC 37, [98].

169 *Petter v EMC Europe Ltd* [2015] EWCA Civ 828; [2015] CP Rep 47; *Samengo-Turner v J&H Marsh & McLennan (Services) Ltd* [2007] EWCA Civ 723; [2008] IRLR 237. cf *Gray v Hurley* [2019] EWCA Civ 2222: An anti-suit injunction to enforce a general 'right to be sued' under Article 4 would render Articles 33 and 34 of the Brussels Ia Regulation obsolete. In essence, a multilateral solution would be encroached upon by a chimerical remedy based on a fictitious right. See M Ahmed, 'A Dangerous Chimera: Anti-Suit Injunctions Based on a "Right to be Sued" at the place of Domicile under the Brussels Ia Regulation?' (2020) 136 Law Quarterly Review 379. A preliminary reference was sent to the CJEU in C-946/19 *MG v HH*, EU:C:2020:788, but it was withdrawn.

in the UK has a jurisdictional privilege to sue in the UK and a jurisdictional immunity against being sued in a part of the UK in which he is not domiciled.[170] The opinion of Advocate General Jääskinen in *Hydrogen Peroxide SA v Akzo Nobel NV* emphasised the subsidiary nature of EU procedural law and suggested that it did not impose rights and obligations on parties.[171] It has been argued that an anti-suit injunction ordering a party not to rely on the choice of court clause nominating a non-EU court in *Samengo-Turner v J&H Marsh & McLennan (Services) Ltd* has cast doubt on the principle of reflexive effect.[172] It is possible that the aberrant decisions in *Samengo-Turner* and *Petter v EMC Europe Ltd* will be applied to the new provisions within the CJJA concerning consumer and employment cases. It will enable UK-based employees and consumers to enforce the 'right' not to be sued abroad by seeking to restrain proceedings commenced by an employer or merchant in a non-UK court including an EU Member State court. The legal basis of an anti-suit injunction is admittedly sounder in the unilateral jurisdictional context in which these protective jurisdictional provisions operate.

If and when the UK becomes a Contracting State of the Lugano II Convention, an English court should apply the provisions in Articles 22, 23, 27, and 28 of the Lugano II Convention as though they had reflexive effect.[173] The decision whether to stay proceedings will be determined in accordance with the principles of English conflict of laws as these apply to cases with a relevant foreign element.

Sections 4 and 5 of the Brussels Ia Regulation create self-contained and exclusive codes in relation to matters within their scope. There are two significant aspects of the protective jurisdictional rules in Sections 4 and 5. As a general rule, the weaker party is able to ensure that litigation occurs in its home forum. Secondly, a choice of court agreement in a consumer contract or an employment contract may be enforced against the weaker party only in limited circumstances.

These provisions are designed to retain the jurisdictional protections and advantages for UK-based consumers and employees. They follow closely the jurisdictional protections of Sections 4 and 5 of Chapter II of the Brussels Ia Regulation. These changes to the 1982 Act were prepared on the basis that the UK would not be

[170] See generally, WN Hohfeld, 'Some Fundamental Legal Conceptions as Applied in Judicial Reasoning' (1913) 23 Yale LJ 16.

[171] Case C-352/13 *Hydrogen Peroxide SA v Akzo Nobel NV* EU:C:2014:2443.

[172] Briggs, *Civil Jurisdiction* (n 21) 361, notes that the decision in *Samengo-Turner v J&H Marsh & McLennan (Services) Ltd* [2007] EWCA Civ 723; [2008] IRLR 237, is 'not reliable; it is wrong'. For trenchant criticism by other commentators, see, A Dickinson, 'Resurgence of the Anti-Suit Injunction: The Brussels I Regulation as a Source of Civil Obligations?' (2008) 57 International and Comparative Law Quarterly 465, 470–71; T Raphael, 'Do As You Would Be Done By? System-transcendent Justification and Anti-Suit Injunctions' [2016] Lloyd's Maritime and Commercial Law Quarterly 256, 266; Harris, *English Response to Europeanisation* (n 153) 386–88.

[173] Briggs, *Civil Jurisdiction* (n 21) 369; cf T Hartley, *Civil Jurisdiction and Judgments in Europe* (OUP 2017) 374 (hereafter Hartley, *Civil Jurisdiction*), adheres to a literal interpretation of Case C-281/02 *Owusu v Jackson* [2005] ECR I-1383.

bound by the Brussels–Lugano regime after the Brexit transition period.[174] If and when the UK accedes to the Lugano II Convention, the provisions discussed herein will apply only if jurisdiction is determined in accordance with Article 4 of the Lugano II Convention[175] or when the claim falls outside the scope of the Lugano II Convention.[176]

Section 15A prescribes the scope of Sections 15B to 15E. Sections 15B and 15C will apply only if the subject-matter of the proceedings and the nature of the proceedings are within the scope of the Brussels Ia Regulation as determined by Article 1 of the Regulation.[177] The Brussels Ia Regulation applies in civil and commercial matters and does not extend to revenue, customs or administrative matters or to the liability of the State for acts and omissions in the exercise of State authority.[178] Sections 15B to 15E do not apply to proceedings listed in Schedule 5 or to proceedings in Scotland.[179]

A consumer, in a consumer contract, means a person who concludes the contract for a purpose which can be regarded as being outside the person's trade or profession.[180] A consumer contract means:

> (a) a contract for the sale of goods on instalment credit terms,
> (b) a contract for a loan repayable by instalments, or for any other form of credit, made to finance the sale of goods, or
> (c) a contract which has been concluded with a person who—
>   (i) pursues commercial or professional activities in the part of the United Kingdom in which the consumer is domiciled, or
>   (ii) by any means, directs such activities to that part or to other parts of the United Kingdom including that part,[181]
>
> and which falls within the scope of such activities, but it does not include a contract of transport other than a contract which, for an inclusive price, provides for a combination of travel and accommodation or a contract of insurance.[182]

174 Civil Jurisdiction and Judgments (Amendment) (EU Exit) Regulations 2019, SI 2019 No 479, Pts 4 and 5.
175 The defendant is not domiciled in a Lugano II Convention Contracting State.
176 Either the proceedings are not on a civil and commercial matter or lack a foreign element.
177 Section 15A(2) CJJA.
178 Article 1 of the Brussels Ia Regulation.
179 Section 15A(3) CJJA.
180 Section 15E(1) CJJA.
181 According to the European Commission, the purpose of Article 17(1)(c) is to ensure that consumer contracts concluded via a website accessible in the state of the consumer's domicile are covered by the protective provisions: European Commission, Brussels I Proposal, COM (1999) 348 final, 16. For the application of the corresponding provision in Article 17(1)(c) of the Brussels Ia Regulation to electronic commerce, see Case C-585/08 *Pammer v Reederei Karl Schluter* & Case C-144/09 *Hotel Alpenhof v Heller* [2010] ECR I-12527 [81]–[83].
182 This provision goes beyond the corresponding provision in Article 17(3) of the Brussels Ia Regulation. Article 17(3) includes contracts for 'package travel' which combine travel and

According to Section 15B, applicable to matters relating to a consumer contract,[183] a UK-domiciled consumer may bring proceedings against the other party to the consumer contract in the courts of any part of the UK where either is domiciled[184] (or, in the case of a non-consumer, deemed to be domiciled[185]). The consumer's ability to sue in the courts of the part of the UK in which it is domiciled applies whether or not the non-consumer is domiciled in the UK. The section, in turn, provides for the consumer to be sued by the non-consumer (wherever domiciled) only in the courts of its domicile.[186] This is without prejudice to the right to bring a counterclaim, or the operation of any rule of law which allows a person not domiciled in the UK to be sued in the UK.

Restrictions are placed on choice of court agreements in consumer contracts.[187] Choice of court agreements will be effective if entered into after the dispute has arisen. They will also be effective if they allow the consumer to bring proceedings in another court, or if they are entered into by the consumer and the other party to the contract, both of whom are at the time of conclusion of the contract domiciled or habitually resident in the UK and in the same part of the UK, and confer jurisdiction on the courts of that part of the UK, provided that the agreement is not contrary to the law of that part of the UK. A consumer who appears before the court confers jurisdiction on the court by his appearance, though the consumer must be informed by the court of his right to object to the jurisdiction if it does not otherwise accord with these provisions.[188]

Section 15C applies when the subject matter of the proceedings is a matter relating to an individual contract of employment. According to Section 15C, an employer may be sued by its employee in the part of the UK where it is domiciled or deemed to be domiciled[189] or (regardless of its domicile) where the employee habitually carries out his or her work or last did so or, if the employee does not habitually carry on work in any country, where the business engaging the employer was

accommodation for an inclusive price (see Case C-585/08 *Pammer v Reederei Karl Schluter* & Case C-144/09 *Hotel Alpenhof v Heller* [2010] ECR I-12527) but excludes other contracts of transport. Section 15E(1)(c)(ii) extends to combinations of travel and a contract of insurance which should bring more travel contracts within the protective jurisdictional regime for consumers pursuant to Section 15B of the CJJA 1982. The CJEU held in the Pammer decision that the exception in what is now Article 17(3) of the Brussels Ia Regulation should be interpreted as covering the same ground as the term 'package travel' in EU Directive 90/314.

[183] Section 15B(1) CJJA. A consumer contract is defined in terms corresponding to those in Article 17(1) of the Brussels Ia Regulation.

[184] Section 15B(2) CJJA.

[185] Section 15B(7) CJJA corresponding to Art 17(2) of the Brussels Ia Regulation.

[186] Section 15B(3) CJJA. The following sub-sections (4) and (5) preserve the 'exclusive' jurisdiction regime in Schedule 4 and provide for supplemental grounds of jurisdiction that overlap but do not exactly correspond with those listed in Articles 15(1) and 18(3) of the Brussels Ia Regulation.

[187] Section 15B(6) CJJA.

[188] Section 15D(2)–(4) CJJA.

[189] Section 15C(7) CJJA.

situated.[190] The section, in turn, provides that an employee domiciled in the UK may be sued by the employer (wherever domiciled) only in the courts of the part of the UK where the employee is domiciled.[191] This is without prejudice to the right to bring a counterclaim, or the operation of any rule of law which allows a person not domiciled in the UK to be sued in the UK.

Choice of court agreements between employee and employer are effective if entered into after the dispute has arisen, or if they allow the employee to bring proceedings in another court.[192] An employee who appears before the court confers jurisdiction on the court by his appearance, though the employee must be informed by the court of his right to object to the jurisdiction if it does not otherwise accord with these provisions.[193] An application may be made to the courts of another part of the UK for provisional measures.[194]

There is no definition of 'employee' or 'employer' in the CJJA. Problems dealing with forms of work disguised by the façade or sham of self-employment are likely to arise in the context of Section 15C.[195] It remains to be seen whether the persuasiveness of the CJEU's principles will be adhered to in relation to workers. English courts may depart from the jurisprudence of the CJEU where the European law on workers and their rights is at odds with English law.

In applying and interpreting these provisions, an English court is to have regard to principles laid down prior to Completion Day by the CJEU concerning Title II of the 1968 Brussels Convention or Chapter II of the Brussels Ia Regulation.[196] This means that decisions of the CJEU on the interpretation of the corresponding Articles of the Regulation will be treated as persuasive authority.[197] The courts may also consider and take account of the expert reports relating to the 1968 Brussels Convention.[198] There is inconsistency between the definition of retained EU law and the meaning and effect of a provision under Section 15(E)(2) CJJA. As a result, the interpretation of Sections 15A to 15D CJJA may lead to a greater and faster assimilation of common law concepts as compared to the retained Rome I and II Regulations.

As a result of the foregoing protective jurisdictional provisions, many or most English choice of court clauses in consumer and employment contracts will be rendered ineffective. Moreover, the Hague Convention applies only to exclusive choice

[190] Section 15C(2) CJJA.

[191] Section 15C(3) CJJA. The following sub-sections (4) and (5) preserve the 'exclusive' jurisdiction regime in Schedule 4 and provide for supplemental grounds of jurisdiction corresponding to those listed in Articles 20(1) and 22(2) of the Brussels Ia Regulation.

[192] Section 15C(6) CJJA.

[193] Section 15D(2)–(4) CJJA.

[194] Section 15D(7) CJJA.

[195] *Uber BV and others v Aslam and others* [2021] UKSC 5 (Lord Leggatt delivering the judgment of the Court).

[196] Section 15E(2)(a) CJJA.

[197] ibid.

[198] Section 15E(2)(b) CJJA.

of court agreements in civil and commercial matters.[199] Consumer and employment contracts are excluded from the scope of the Hague Convention.[200]

G. Choice of Court Agreements

1. Introduction

It has been observed that EU private international law in English courts has come full circle as a result of Brexit.[201] In particular, the venue and enforcement risk associated with choice of court agreements will be affected.[202] Article 25 of the Brussels Ia Regulation will no longer apply to determine the effect of a UK or EU Member State choice of court agreement in proceedings commenced after 1 January 2021, even if the agreement was concluded before that date.[203] Within its material scope,[204] the Hague Convention will apply to an 'exclusive choice of court agreement'[205] concluded from 1 October 2015[206] in favour of either a court in the UK[207] or an EU Member State court.[208] In other cases, the jurisdiction of a court in England and Wales based on a choice of court agreement may be established by service, either within or outside the jurisdiction. Service outside the jurisdiction in the case of a choice of court agreement will not require the court's permission.

The implications of Brexit for English choice of court agreements are settled to the extent that only a regional cross border civil judicial cooperation instrument such as the Lugano II Convention will displace the Hague Choice of Court Convention and the English common law rules to the periphery. The Hague Judgments Convention 2019 provides a complementary regime for the recognition and enforcement of judgments in civil and commercial matters. The Hague Judgments Convention makes special provision for the recognition and

[199] Article 1(1) of the Hague Choice of Court Convention; See RA Brand and PM Herrup, *The 2005 Hague Convention on Choice of Court Agreements* (Cambridge University Press 2008) ch 4 (hereafter Brand and Herrup, *Hague Convention*).

[200] Article 2(1) of the Hague Choice of Court Convention (hereafter Hague Convention).

[201] See Chapter 1 of this book.

[202] See Fentiman, *International Commercial Litigation* (n 163) ch 2. 'Venue risk' is a form of litigation risk arising from multistate transactions where the risk to each party is that any dispute will not be resolved in their preferred forum. Another species of litigation risk is 'enforcement risk'. This is the risk that a judgment debtor with worldwide assets will disperse or conceal those assets, and the risk that a judgment obtained in one court will be unenforceable elsewhere.

[203] cf Case 25/79 *Sanicentral GmbH v Collin* [1979] ECR 3423.

[204] Articles 1–2 of the Hague Convention.

[205] Article 3 of the Hague Convention.

[206] Article 16 of the Hague Convention.

[207] Article 5 of the Hague Convention.

[208] Article 6 of the Hague Convention.

enforcement of judgments based on non-exclusive choice of court agreements including unilateral or asymmetric choice of court agreements.[209] The 2019 Hague Convention also provides an exception to the recognition and enforcement of judgments procured in breach of a choice of court agreement.[210] This author has hitherto argued that the Hague Convention will apply between the UK and the EU Member States after Brexit rather than the Lugano II Convention or any bespoke deal between the UK and EU.[211]

In this area of private international law and in matters within the scope of the Hague Choice of Court Convention, there will be no reversion to the common law regime nor will a distinctly EU regime govern choice of court agreements. Instead, the substance and form of the Hague Convention may be emblematic of the future direction of private international law in English courts. A path that is neither well-trodden nor European but one that is forged at the Hague Conference of Private International Law and ushers in a different multilateral relationship between the UK and the EU in matters of private international law. It is a private international law relationship that is not premised on unilateralism or regionalism but one that is founded in internationalism.

This section will examine the changes to the law governing choice of court agreements in English private international law. An outline of the choice of court and conflicts of jurisdiction provisions in the Brussels Ia Regulation will assist us in comparing the pre-exit and post-exit regimes. This will be followed by an examination of the Hague Choice of Court Convention in the post-Brexit legal landscape. The English common law jurisdiction regime's approach to the regulation of choice of court agreements will be outlined. The relationship between the Hague Convention and the English common law jurisdiction regime will be analysed. It will reveal a synergy between the two regimes in the enforcement of choice of court agreements. The discussion will commence with a map of the nature and issues that arise from choice of court agreements.

[209] According to Article 5(1)(m) of the Hague Judgments Convention 2019, a judgment based on proceedings pursuant to a unilateral or asymmetric choice of court agreement is eligible for recognition and enforcement under the Convention.

[210] Article 7(1)(d) of the Hague Judgments Convention 2019 will ameliorate the venue and enforcement risk arising from pre-emptive torpedo proceedings by refusing to recognise or enforce any judgment given in breach of a choice of court agreement.

[211] See Ahmed, *Choice of Court Agreements* (n 7) ch 11; M Ahmed, 'BREXIT and English Jurisdiction Agreements: The Post-Referendum Legal Landscape' (2016) 27 European Business Law Review 989; M Ahmed and P Beaumont, 'Exclusive Choice of Court Agreements: Some Issues on The Hague Convention on Choice of Court Agreements and its Relationship with The Brussels Ia Regulation Especially Anti-Suit Injunctions, Concurrent Proceedings and The Implications of Brexit' (2017) 13 Journal of Private International Law 386–410 (hereafter Ahmed and Beaumont, 'Exclusive Choice of Court Agreements').

2. The Foundations and Anatomy of Choice of Court Agreements

The substantive and procedural aspects of a choice of court agreement warrant the classification of a 'hybrid' contract.[212] The dual nature of the choice of court agreement is manifested both as a private law contract and via the clause's procedural (jurisdictional) effects. The applicable law of a choice of court agreement reflects this dual classification.

Issues of interpretation, formal and substantive validity, and enforceability represent the anatomy of a choice of court agreement. There are two distinct aspects of interpretation: whether the clause is 'exclusive' or 'non-exclusive' and whether the claims in the proceedings are within the scope of the clause.[213] Formal validity is regulated by the instrument itself (ie Hague Convention or the Brussels Ia Regulation), which provides uniform and autonomous rules, whereas substantive validity is subject to the law of the chosen forum including its private international law rules. The enforcement of choice of court agreements is governed by the autonomous rules of the instruments.[214] Under the English common law regime and to the extent permitted by the autonomous system of the instruments,[215] anti-suit injunctions, actions for damages, and anti-enforcement injunctions may enforce the breach of a choice of court agreement.[216] English courts are no longer constrained by CJEU case law from granting anti-suit injunctions to restrain proceedings in the courts of EU Member States. Outside the scope of the Hague Convention,[217] English courts retain the power to decline jurisdiction based on

[212] Ahmed, 'Choice of Court Agreements' (n 7) 37; See also, Hartley, *Choice of Court Agreements* (n 8) 4–6, 129–30; Hartley, *Civil Jurisdiction* (n 173) 227.

[213] Article 25(1) of the Brussels Ia Regulation provides an autonomous presumption that the choice of court agreement shall be exclusive unless the parties have agreed otherwise. cf Article 3(b) of the Hague Convention. In relation to the scope of the clause, the CJEU has confirmed that questions of interpretation are a matter for Member State courts and the applicable national law: Case C-352/13 *Cartel Damage Claims (CDC) Hydrogen Peroxide SA v Evonik Degussa GmbH and Others* ECLI:EU:C:2015:335, [67]; Case C-214/89 *Powell Duffryn plc v Wolfgang Petereit* [1992] ECR I-01745 [36]-[37]; Case C-269/95 *Francesco Benincasa v Dentalkit Srl* [1997] ECR I-03767 [31]; *Roche Products v Provimi* [2003] EWHC 961 (Comm), [81] (Aikens J).

[214] Article 31(2) of the Brussels Ia Regulation; Articles 5 and 6 of the Hague Convention.

[215] In Case C-159/02 *Turner v. Grovit* [2005] ECR I-3565 and Case C-185/07 *Allianz SpA v West Tankers Inc* [2009] 1 Lloyd's Rep 413, the CJEU has held that the legal technique used by the English courts to prevent a party from commencing or continuing proceedings in breach of a jurisdiction or arbitration agreement, the anti-suit injunction, cannot be granted in circumstances where the foreign proceedings are before the courts of another EU Member State and are within the scope of the Brussels I Regulation. See M Ahmed, 'The Enforcement of Settlement and Jurisdiction Agreements and Parallel Proceedings in The European Union: *The Alexandros T* Litigation in The English Courts' (2015) 11 Journal of Private International Law 406, 412–15 (hereafter Ahmed, '*Alexandros T* Litigation').

[216] *Donohue v Armco Inc* [2001] UKHL 64, [2002] 1 Lloyd's Rep 425 (Anti-Suit Injunction); *Starlight Shipping Co v Allianz Marine & Aviation Versicherungs AG* [2014] EWCA Civ 1010 (Longmore LJ) (Damages); *Bank St Petersburg OJSC & Anor v Arkhangelsky & Ors* [2014] EWCA Civ 593, [2014] 1 CLC 670 (Longmore LJ) (Anti-enforcement Injunction). For the compatibility of remedies for breach of exclusive choice of court agreements with the Hague Convention, see, Ahmed and Beaumont, 'Exclusive Choice of Court Agreements' (n 211) 394–408.

[217] Article 5(2) of the Hague Convention.

a choice of court agreement, by staying proceedings if there are strong countervailing reasons.[218] The power to stay proceedings may also be used to give effect to a foreign exclusive choice of court agreement, including where the chosen court is in an EU Member State.[219] The law of the forum governs remedies for breach of choice of court agreements in the English common law regime.[220]

This broad-brush outline of interrelated issues will contextualise our discussion of choice of court agreements in the post-Brexit legal environment.

3. Choice of Court Agreements under the Brussels Ia Regulation

Before delving into the jurisdictional provisions of the Hague Convention, it is useful to summarise the pre-exit regime for choice of court agreements and the conflicts of jurisdiction. The cross-border civil and commercial judicial relationship between the UK and the EU Member States was governed by the Brussels Ia Regulation.[221] In basic terms, the Regulation provides that a choice of jurisdiction by the parties should be upheld[222] and that judgments given by the courts of one Member State should be recognised and enforced in all other Member States.[223]

The Brussels Ia Regulation effectively reversed the negative repercussions of the 'Italian torpedo'. The 'Italian torpedo' is a litigation tactic that relies on a combination of the Brussels I Regulation's (2001) rule on *lis pendens*[224] and the protracted delays in proceedings that occur in some EU Member States that allow opportunistic litigants to block proceedings against them in other Member States. The *lis pendens* rule applies where proceedings involving the same cause of action and between the same parties are brought in the courts of different Member States. Article 27 of the Brussels I Regulation (2001) requires the court second seised to stay its own proceedings before it until the jurisdiction of the court first seised is established. If the court first seised concludes that it has jurisdiction, the other court must decline jurisdiction.

Persons facing imminent patent infringement actions could protect themselves by commencing pre-emptive proceedings in Italy for a declaration of non-liability and effectively block proceedings against them in other EU Member States.[225]

218 *Donohue v Armco Inc* [2001] UKHL 64, [2002] 1 Lloyd's Rep 425.

219 *The Eleftheria* [1970] P 94; *The El Amria* [1981] 2 Lloyd's Rep 119; *The Sennar (No 2)* [1985] 1 WLR 490. See Ahmed, 'Choice of Court Agreements' (n 7) 2.

220 J Harris, 'Anti-Suit Injunctions—A Home Comfort' [1997] Lloyd's Maritime and Commercial Law Quarterly 413. cf A Briggs, 'The Unrestrained Reach of an Anti-Suit Injunction: A Pause for Thought' [1997] Lloyd's Maritime and Commercial Law Quarterly 90; C Sim, 'Choice of Law and Anti-Suit Injunctions: Relocating Comity' (2013) 62 International and Comparative Law Quarterly 703.

221 Article 81 of the Brussels Ia Regulation.

222 Article 25 of the Brussels Ia Regulation.

223 Articles 36(1) and 39 of the Brussels Ia Regulation.

224 Article 27 of the Brussels I Regulation.

225 M Franzosi, 'Worldwide Patent Litigation and the Italian Torpedo' [1997] European Intellectual Property Review 382.

Under the Brussels regime proceedings for a declaration of non-liability in one Member State and proceedings for the positive assertion of liability in another Member State have the same cause of action.[226] Thus, the *lis pendens* rule effectively blocks proceedings for a patent infringement action in any Member State other than the court first seised. Even if the party relying on the torpedo tactic is eventually bound to lose on the merits, the Italian proceedings could continue for many years, thus buying time to negotiate a settlement. It did not matter if the Italian courts lacked jurisdiction, since it would take a long time indeed for a definitive ruling to this effect to be obtained.[227]

The legitimacy of the torpedo came before the CJEU in the case of *Erich Gasser v MISAT*.[228] Gasser was an Austrian firm which entered into a contract with MISAT, an Italian company, under which Gasser sold children's clothing to MISAT. An exclusive choice of court agreement selected a court in Austria. When a dispute arose, MISAT brought proceedings before a court in Italy, claiming that the contract had been terminated and that MISAT had not breached it. After the Italian court was seised, Gasser brought proceedings before the Austrian court selected in the exclusive choice of court agreement. MISAT claimed that these proceedings were precluded as a result of its prior action in Italy.

An Austrian appeal court referred the matter to the CJEU. The main issue was the relationship between the *lis pendens*[229] provision and the provision on choice of court agreements.[230] The provision on choice of court agreements stated that the court designated by such agreements 'shall have exclusive jurisdiction' but what if another court is seised first? Is a court elected in a choice of court agreement required to stay proceedings whilst the court first seised rules on its jurisdiction including the validity and effectiveness of the choice of court agreement? The UK government made submissions that the designated court should be entitled to decide these questions for it and if it found that the choice of court agreement was valid, effective, and covered the case, it should go ahead without waiting for the other court to terminate the proceedings before it.

The CJEU held that the nominated court must stay the proceedings before it until the court first seised has established that it has no jurisdiction.[231] It made no difference if the court first seised is a Member State where legal proceedings take an inordinately long period of time.[232] The court designated in a choice of court

[226] Case C-144/86 *Gubisch Maschinenfabrik KG v Palumbo* [1987] ECR 4861; Case C-406/92 *The Tatry* [1999] QB 515.

[227] See Case C-159/97 *Transport Castelletti v Hugo Trumpy* [1999] ECR I-1597. The Italian court in this case took eight years to adjudicate on the issue of jurisdiction.

[228] Case C-116/02 *Erich Gasser Gmbh v MISAT Srl* [2004] 1 Lloyd's Rep 222.

[229] Article 21 of the Brussels Convention (Article 27 of the Brussels I Regulation and Article 29(1) of the Brussels Ia Regulation).

[230] Article 17 of the Brussels Convention (Article 23 of the Brussels I Regulation and Article 25 of the Brussels Ia Regulation).

[231] Case C-116/02 *Erich Gasser Gmbh v MISAT Srl* [2004] 1 Lloyd's Rep 222, [54].

[232] ibid [73].

agreement may also not consider whether the proceedings in the court first seised were brought in bad faith as a delaying tactic.[233] The ruling in *Gasser* seriously jeopardised the effectiveness of choice of court agreements in the EU.[234] It was even suggested that the decision would lead to a general preference for arbitration over litigation in the European Judicial Area.[235]

The provisions in the Brussels Ia Regulation that effectively reversed the negative effects of the *Gasser* decision were subject to considerable discussion.[236] The main provision on *lis pendens*[237] is subject to Article 31(2) of the Brussels Ia Regulation. Articles 31(2) to 31(4) of the Brussels Ia Regulation provide:[238]

2. Without prejudice to Article 26, where a court of a Member State on which an agreement as referred to in Article 25 confers exclusive jurisdiction is seised, any court of another Member State shall stay the proceedings until such time as the court seised on the basis of the agreement declares that it has no jurisdiction under the agreement.
3. Where the court designated in the agreement has established jurisdiction in accordance with the agreement, any court of another Member State shall decline jurisdiction in favour of that court.
4. Paragraphs 2 and 3 shall not apply to matters referred to in Sections 3, 4 or 5 where the policyholder, the insured, a beneficiary of the insurance contract, the injured party, the consumer or the employee is the claimant and the agreement is not valid under a provision contained within those Sections.

Article 31(2) is the provision which expressly overrides the *lis pendens* rule. It is itself subject to Article 26 which incorporates the principle of voluntary submission to jurisdiction. The result is that Article 31(2) provides that where an exclusive choice of court agreement selecting the courts of a Member State, a court in another Member State even if it was seised first must stay proceedings until such time as the selected court declares that it does not possess jurisdiction pursuant to the agreement. The selected court would declare that it lacked jurisdiction under a choice of court agreement if the clause was invalid or inapplicable. Article 31(3) provides

[233] ibid [48] and [53]; see Case C-351/89 *Overseas Union Insurance Ltd v New Hampshire Insurance Company* [1991] ECR I-3317, [25].

[234] See J Mance, 'Exclusive Jurisdiction Agreements and European Ideals' (2004) 120 Law Quarterly Review 357.

[235] ibid 358.

[236] See Beaumont and McEleavy, *Anton* (n 12) 258–60, note that the Brussels Ia Regulation in relation to choice of court agreements goes beyond the solution adopted by the Hague Convention on Choice of Court Agreements as it creates a rule on conflicts of jurisdiction (*lis pendens*) which accords priority to the chosen court. This is one example where the Brussels Ia Regulation will be able to make deference to party autonomy greater within the European Judicial Area than is possible globally under the Hague Convention.

[237] Article 29(1) of the Brussels Ia Regulation.

[238] Articles 31(2), 31(3) and 31(4) of the Brussels Ia Regulation.

that where the selected court finds that it has jurisdiction pursuant to the choice of court agreement, courts in other Member States must give up jurisdiction.

Article 31(2) enshrines a reverse *lis pendens* rule in that the court first seised must stay proceedings in deference to the selected court. The elected court determines the validity and applicability of the choice of court agreement. Article 25(1) provides that the substantive validity of a choice of court agreement is to be decided by the law of the designated court including its private international law rules.

Recital 22 clarifies that the designated court 'has priority to decide on the validity of the agreement and on the extent to which the agreement applies to the dispute pending before it', even if it is second seised and even if the other court has not already decided on the stay of proceedings.[239] Where, however, there is a conflict as to whether both courts have been chosen, then the court first seised will determine the validity of the choice of court clause.[240]

The risk of the solution adopted by the Brussels Ia Regulation was outlined by Advocate General Leger in his Opinion in *Gasser*.[241] He thought that such a solution might encourage delaying tactics by an unscrupulous party by alleging the existence of an agreement and bringing an action before the court allegedly chosen in order deliberately to delay judgment until that court had declared that it had no jurisdiction. The central issue is whether there is an agreement or disagreement to the jurisdiction of a court.[242] Briggs doubts whether we are justified in assuming, even generally and provisionally, that the party seeking to rely on a choice of court agreement is the one more likely to have right on his side.[243] Thus the presumption created in favour of party autonomy as an exception to the *lis pendens* mechanism presupposes the existence of a valid and effective choice of court agreement where they may be none.

In relation to the operation of the Article 31(2), the obligation on the non-designated court to stay proceedings arises only if the other court actually is nominated.[244] This essentially means that there is a dispute before the non-designated court as to whether there actually is a choice of court agreement. The obligation to stay does not come into operation on the mere empty claims of one of the parties

[239] Recital 22 of the Brussels Ia Regulation.
[240] ibid.
[241] Case C-116/02 *Erich Gasser GmbH v MISAT Srl* [2003] ECR I-14693, Opinion of AG Léger, [74]; A Briggs, 'What Should be Done about Jurisdiction Agreements' (2010) 12 Yearbook of Private International Law 311, 319–22 (hereafter Briggs, 'What Should be Done about Jurisdiction Agreements?'); cf TC Hartley, 'Choice-of-Court Agreements and the New Brussels I Regulation' (2013) 129 Law Quarterly Review 309, 312–13 (hereafter Hartley, 'Choice-of-Court Agreements and the New Brussels I Regulation').
[242] Briggs, 'What Should be Done about Jurisdiction Agreements?' (n 241) 319; A Briggs, 'The Brussels I bis Regulation Appears on the Horizon' [2011] Lloyd's Maritime and Commercial Law Quarterly 157, 162–164 (hereafter Briggs, 'Brussels I bis Regulation on the Horizon').
[243] Briggs, 'What Should be Done about Jurisdiction Agreements?' (n 241) 322; Briggs, Brussels I bis Regulation on the Horizon (n 242) 164.
[244] Hartley, 'Choice-of-Court Agreements and the New Brussels I Regulation' (n 241) 312.

as to the existence of a valid and effective choice of court agreement.[245] Something more substantial than empty claims is needed. However, the non-designated court cannot decide for itself whether the choice of court agreement is valid, effective, and covers the dispute.[246] Recital 22 expressly states that the nominated court has priority to adjudicate on these issues. This leaves the non-designated court with room to decide whether the claim that another court has been selected is entirely spurious. It can therefore require the party requesting a stay to present a *prima facie* case[247] that there was a choice of court agreement electing the court in question.[248] Once the standard of a *prima facie* case is met, the stay should be granted. However, it may be questioned whether a *prima facie* case that there was a choice of court agreement selecting the court would actually help where there was a genuine dispute as to the validity and effectiveness of the choice of court agreement requiring detailed examination. It may be that the court first seised where the *prima facie* case is made out has a genuine claim to jurisdiction in the event that the designated court eventually decides that there was no valid and effective choice of court agreement at all.

Article 25 of the Brussels Ia Regulation applies the law of the chosen court including its private international law rules to the issue of the substantive validity of a choice of court agreement.[249] The elected court shall have jurisdiction 'unless the agreement is null and void as to its substantive validity under the law of that Member State'.[250] The policy basis animating the selection of the law of the chosen court including its choice of law rules is to render the Brussels Ia Regulation compatible with the Hague Convention.[251] The rules for substantive validity for choice of court agreements in both instruments are phrased in an almost identical

[245] ibid 313.

[246] ibid.

[247] *Prima facie* (from Latin *prima facies*, first appearance) a case that has been supported by sufficient evidence for it to be taken as proved should there be no adequate evidence to the contrary. See J Law and EA Martin (ed), *Oxford Dictionary of Law* (7th edn, OUP 2009).

[248] Hartley, 'Choice-of-Court Agreements and the New Brussels I Regulation' (n 241) 313.

[249] Article 25(1) and Recital 20 of the Brussels Ia Regulation. In Case C-222/15 *Hoszig kft v Alstom Power Thermal Services* ECLI:EU:C:2016:224, [47], AG Szpunar examined the scope of the choice of law rule and suggested that the new formulation does not attempt to reverse the CJEU's case law on the autonomous determination of factual consent. For a similar argument, see U Magnus and P Mankowski, *Brussels Ibis Regulation* (2nd edn, Sellier European Law Publishers 2012) 628 (hereafter Magnus and Mankowski, *Brussels Ibis Regulation*). Briggs, *Private International Law* (n 163) 251–52, terms the reference to the law of the chosen court including its private international law rules to assess matters of substantive validity as 'retrograde'; A Dickinson, 'Surveying the Proposed Brussels I bis Regulation—Solid Foundations but Renovation Needed' (2010) 12 Yearbook of Private International Law 247, 301, contends that a solution to the issue is unnecessary and that the CJEU has already achieved a high level of legal certainty by affirming that the consent of the parties is to be determined solely by reference to the requirements of Article 23 of the Brussels I Regulation. Moreover, Dickinson argues that the new provision should not be used by Member State courts to permit a challenge to the validity of choice of court agreements on grounds which the CJEU has interpreted autonomously, ie CJEU jurisprudence should not be reversed.

[250] Article 25(1) and Recital 20 of the Brussels Ia Regulation.

[251] See Case C-222/15 *Hoszig kft v Alstom Power Thermal Services* (n 109) [49]–[50] (Opinion of AG Szpunar).

manner.[252] This has facilitated the approval of the Hague Convention by the EU and ensures the consistent treatment of issues of substantive validity of choice of court agreements in the Brussels Ia Regulation and the Hague Convention.

According to Recital 20 of the Brussels Ia Regulation the reference to the nominated court's law includes both its substantive law and its choice of law rules. Therefore, it is clear that the inclusion of *renvoi* within Article 25 is intended and the question whether a choice of court agreement is materially valid is therefore to be ascertained under the substantive law to which the choice of law rules of the Member State of the chosen court refer.[253]

Some commentators question whether *renvoi* should be applied in determining the substantive validity of a choice of court agreement.[254] They argue that contractual relations governed by party autonomy should exclude *renvoi* from the application of choice of law rules.[255] The exclusion of *renvoi* from the choice of law regimes of the Rome I and Rome II Regulations is evidence that certainty and predictability may be compromised by the application of *renvoi*.[256] However, in some cases it would be unreasonable to apply the substantive law of the chosen forum to the issue of capacity.[257] The forum chosen by the parties is often due to its neutrality and efficient dispute resolution and the chosen forum may have a tenuous connection with the actual dispute. In such cases it may be preferable to apply the choice of law rules of the chosen forum to determine the capacity of a party to enter into a choice of court agreement. The application of *renvoi* in these cases will lead to the application of a law closely connected to the dispute. In similar vein, where the parties have made an express choice of law that differs from the substantive law usually applied before the chosen forum, *renvoi* to the chosen law should be applied to respect the principle of party autonomy.[258] On the other hand, in cases of fraud, duress, and the plea of *non est factum*, it is not clear how *renvoi* can help in determining the substantive validity of a choice of court agreement. The substantive law of the chosen court may provide an appropriate legal regime to govern these issues, making a reference to the choice of law rules of the chosen court unnecessary. The factors pointing away from the law of the chosen forum in the case of matters of capacity may not exert the same pull in relation to issues of fraud, duress, and the

[252] Article 25(1) of the Brussels Ia Regulation; Article 5(1) of the Hague Convention.

[253] For a discussion of *renvoi*, see Collins and others, *Dicey, Morris & Collins* (n 86) ch 4.

[254] Briggs, *Private International Law* (n 163) 252; B Hess, 'The Brussels I Regulation: Recent Case Law of the Court of Justice and the Commission's Proposed Recast' (2012) 49 Common Market Law Review 1075, 1107; P Hay, 'Notes on the European Union's Brussels-I "Recast" Regulation' (2013) 13 The European Legal Forum 1, 3.

[255] PE Nygh, *Autonomy in International Contracts* (OUP 1999) 83–84.

[256] Article 20 of Regulation 593/2008 EC on the law applicable to contractual obligations [2008] OJ L177/6 (hereafter Rome I Regulation) and Article 24 of Regulation 864/2007 EC on the law applicable to non-contractual obligations [2007] OJ L199/40 (hereafter Rome II Regulation).

[257] T Ratković and D Zgrabljić Rotar, 'Choice-of-Court Agreements under the Brussels I Regulation (Recast)' (2013) 9 Journal of Private International Law 245, 258.

[258] Beaumont and McEleavy, *Anton* (n 12) ch 8, 254–55.

plea of *non est factum*. Indeed, the law of a neutral forum may negate any advantage available under a law closely connected to the dispute such as the applicable law of the main contract. The doctrines of severability[259] and *dépeçage*[260] allow the choice of court agreement to be governed by a law separate from the law governing the substantive contract. In fact, a separate law governing the choice of court agreement may ensure the continued validity of such agreements where the entire contract is impeached.

Difficult issues of proof of foreign law arise with the application of the doctrine of *renvoi*. Unlike civil law legal systems, foreign law is a question of fact in the English common law.[261] Therefore, the party relying on foreign law is required to plead and prove the content of foreign law.[262] When applying the doctrine of *renvoi*, evidence of the foreign rules on *renvoi* and foreign choice of law rules have to be pleaded and proved in the English common law courts.[263] In civil law legal systems, evidence of the foreign choice of law rules will suffice for the application of the doctrine of *renvoi*.[264] However, an inherent advantage of the English common law treating issues of proof of foreign law as questions of fact is that the parties can choose not to rely on the foreign law by not pleading it.[265] English law as the law of the forum is applied instead.[266] Secondly, the English courts usually apply English law by default where the content of the foreign law is not proved.[267] An analogy can be drawn between the parties not relying on the foreign law and a delayed choice of English law to govern the dispute.[268] A flexible approach to proof of foreign law in English courts may help the litigants ignore the doctrine of *renvoi* altogether by not pleading and proving the applicable law.

The Rome I Regulation does not apply to choice of court agreements.[269] National choice of law rules will govern the issue of the substantive validity of a choice of court agreement.[270] The lack of harmonisation of national choice of law rules may lead to uncertainty in the determination of the applicable law of the choice

[259] Article 25(5) of the Brussels Ia Regulation; Article 3(d) of the Hague Convention.

[260] See '*dépeçage*' ('Splitting the applicable law'); Article 3(1) of the Rome I Regulation and the Rome Convention; Collins and others, *Dicey, Morris & Collins* (n 86) ch 32, 1789–92.

[261] A Briggs, *The Conflict of Laws* (3rd edn, OUP 2013) ch 1, 7–13.

[262] ibid.

[263] Hartley, *Choice of Court Agreements* (n 8) ch 7, 165–67: reference to the 'foreign court' or 'double renvoi' or 'total renvoi' theory adopted by England and many other common law countries.

[264] ibid: reference to the 'single renvoi' theory adopted by France and Germany.

[265] Briggs, *Conflict of Laws* (n 54).

[266] ibid.

[267] ibid.

[268] See Article 3(2) of the Rome I Regulation and the Rome Convention; Collins and others, *Dicey, Morris & Collins* (n 86) ch 32, 1805–06.

[269] Article 1(2)(e) of the Rome I Regulation and Art 1(2)(d) of the Rome Convention; see M Giuliano and P Lagarde, 'Report on the Convention on the Law Applicable to Contractual Obligations' [1980] OJ C282/1, 11–12; Collins and others, *Dicey, Morris & Collins* (n 86) ch 32, 1788.

[270] B Hess, T Pfeiffer, and P Schlosser, 'Report on the Application of Regulation Brussels I in the Member States' (Study JLS/C4/2005/03, September 2007) [326]–[327], 92 (hereafter Heidelberg Report).

of court agreement. For instance, in English law the 'proper law' of the choice of court agreement, which is quite often the choice of law of the substantive contract, applies.[271] The proper law is the term which was used at common law to signify the law by which the validity of the contract was tested, and is used in this context to acknowledge that the identification of the law which governs a choice of court agreement is a matter for the common law rules of the conflict of laws.

Although the Rome I Regulation excludes choice of court agreements from its scope, it has been argued that the analogical application of the choice of law regime by the law of the forum would result in an optimal solution where the same law governs the validity of the choice of court agreement and the main contract.[272] In practice, this would secure a uniform standard for the applicable law rules of choice of court agreements. However, the underlying conceptual contradiction in this solution is that Article 20 of the Rome I Regulation explicitly excludes *renvoi* and Article 25 of the Brussels Ia Regulation has created a choice of law rule which expressly permits *renvoi*.

Article 25 of the Brussels Ia Regulation includes a provision on the severability of choice of court agreements:[273]

> An agreement conferring jurisdiction which forms part of a contract shall be treated as an agreement independent of the other terms of the contract.
>
> The validity of the agreement conferring jurisdiction cannot be contested solely on the ground that the contract is not valid.

Severability of choice of court agreements was established in the CJEU jurisprudence prior to the express provision in the Brussels Ia Regulation.[274] In *Benincasa v Dentalkit*, the CJEU found that a void provision of the contract does not render the choice of court agreement void without referring to the concept of severability.[275]

The technique of severability serves to insulate or protect the choice of court agreement from the invalidity of the main contract. A challenge to the existence and validity of the substantive contract will not on its own impugn the existence

[271] Collins and others, *Dicey, Morris & Collins* (n 86) ch 12, 603–04; D Joseph QC, *Jurisdiction and Arbitration Agreements and their Enforcement* (Sweet & Maxwell 2010) 182 (hereafter Joseph, *Jurisdiction and Arbitration*); see *Enka Insaat Ve Sanayi A.S. v OOO Insurance Company Chubb* [2020] UKSC 38; *Sulamerica CIA Nacional de Seguros SA and others v Enesa Engenharia SA and others* [2012] EWCA Civ 638, [2012] 1 All ER (Comm) 795.

[272] See F Garcimartin, 'Chapter 9—Article 25' in A Dickinson and E Lein (eds), *The Brussels I Regulation Recast* (OUP 2015) 297; Magnus and Mankowski, *Brussels Ibis Regulation* (n 249) 629.

[273] Article 25(5) of the Brussels Ia Regulation.

[274] Case C-214/89 *Powell Duffryn plc v Wolfgang Petereit* [1992] ECR I-01745; Case C-269/95 *Francesco Benincasa v Dentalkit Srl* [1997] ECR I-03767; Case C-159/97 *Trasporti Castelletti Spedizioni Internazionali SpA v Hugo Trumpy SpA* [1999] ECR I-01597.

[275] Case C-269/95 *Francesco Benincasa v Dentalkit Srl* [1997] ECR I-03767 [24]–[29]. See also, Case C-159/97 *Trasporti Castelletti Spedizioni Internazionali SpA v Hugo Trumpy SpA* [1999] ECR I-01597 [34], [49], [51].

and validity of the choice of court agreement. However, a specific attack on the existence and validity of the choice of court agreement may impeach it. The doctrine of severability and *dépeçage* allow the choice of court agreement to be governed by a law separate from the law governing the substantive contract. In fact a separate law governing the choice of court agreement may ensure the continued validity of such agreements where the entire contract is impugned. The principles of party autonomy and legal certainty provide the justification and legal basis for the technique of severability.

Article 25 of the Brussels Ia Regulation provides:[276]

> If the parties, *regardless of their domicile*, have agreed that a court or the courts of a Member State are to have jurisdiction to settle any disputes which have arisen or which may arise in connection with a particular legal relationship, that court or those courts shall have jurisdiction.

Two non-EU residents can choose a Member State court and if that choice is valid under the rules of the Regulation, the designated court will have jurisdiction over the dispute. This aspect of Article 25 reflects greater deference to the principle of party autonomy as the constraint of at least one of the parties being domiciled in the EU under Article 23 of the Brussels I Regulation is shed. The result is that the scope of application of the choice of court provision under Article 25 has widened.

4. Choice of Court Agreements under the Hague Convention on Choice of Court Agreements

a) Introduction

The Hague Choice of Court Convention is an emerging international commercial litigation regime, which enforces exclusive choice of court agreements at both the jurisdictional and recognition and enforcement stages.[277] On 1 October 2015, the Hague Convention entered into force in twenty-eight Contracting States, including Mexico and all the Member States of the EU, except Denmark.[278]

[276] Article 25(1) of the Brussels Ia Regulation (emphasis added).

[277] See generally, Hartley, *Choice of Court Agreements* (n 8); Brand and Herrup, *Hague Convention* (n 199); Ahmed and Beaumont, 'Exclusive Choice of Court Agreements' (n 211); M Weller, 'Choice of Court Agreements under Brussels Ia and under The Hague Convention: Coherences and Clashes' (2017) 13 Journal of Private International Law 91; P Beaumont, 'Hague Choice of Court Agreements Convention 2005: Background, Negotiations, Analysis and Current Status' (2009) 5 Journal of Private International Law 125 (hereafter Beaumont, 'Hague Choice of Court').

[278] On 4 December 2014, the Council adopted the decision to approve the Hague Convention on behalf of the European Union (2014/887/EU, [2014] OJ L353/5) after the European Parliament gave its consent to the approval of the Hague Convention by legislative resolution of 25 November 2014 ([2016] OJ C289/78). The Civil Jurisdiction and Judgments (Hague Convention on Choice of Court Agreements 2005) Regulations 2015, SI 2015/1644, brought the Hague Convention into force in the UK when the UK was a Member State of the EU.

Singapore ratified the Hague Convention on 2 June 2016 and the Convention applies between Singapore and the other Contracting States from 1 October 2016.[279] The Convention has entered into force in Montenegro and Denmark on 1 August 2018 and 1 September 2018 respectively.[280] China, North Macedonia, Ukraine, the United States, and Israel signed the Hague Convention but have not yet ratified it. Post Brexit, the Hague Convention has become a far more significant instrument because it regulates the enforcement of exclusive choice of court agreements in the civil judicial relationship between the UK and the EU.[281]

This section explains the concept and general scope of the Hague Convention, prior to presenting an outline of its defining provisions.

b) Concept

The Hague Convention is designed to create a mandatory international legal regime for the enforcement of exclusive choice of court agreements in commercial transactions and the recognition and enforcement of judgments resulting from proceedings based on such agreements. The Hague Convention operates in parallel with the very successful 1958 New York Convention on the Recognition and Enforcement of Foreign Arbitral Awards.[282] The choice of court agreement provisions in the Brussels Ia Regulation have been aligned with the Hague Convention in order to ensure better coordination and to secure the consistent enforcement of choice of court agreements both within the EU and globally.[283] The rules coordinating conflicts between the private international law regimes of the Hague

[279] See A Chong and M Yip, 'Singapore as a Centre for International Commercial Litigation: Party Autonomy to The Fore' (2019) 15 Journal of Private International Law 97. In *Ermgassen v Sixcap Financials* [2018] SGHCR 8, the Singapore High Court became the first court to recognise and enforce a judgment under the Hague Convention.

[280] See the Hague Conference on Private International law website for the status table in relation to the Convention, <https://www.hcch.net/en/instruments/conventions/status-table/?cid=98> accessed on 31 August 2021.

[281] This author has earlier argued that the Hague Choice of Court Convention will regulate the enforcement of exclusive choice of court agreements between the UK and the EU. See M Ahmed, 'The Validity of Choice of Court Agreements in International Commercial Contracts under the Hague Choice of Court Convention and the Brussels Ia Regulation' in M Furmston (ed.), *The Future of the Law of Contract* (Informa Law from Routledge 2020) ch 11; Ahmed, *Choice of Court Agreements* (n 7) ch 11.

[282] United Nations Convention on the Recognition and Enforcement of Foreign Arbitral Awards, 10 June 1958, 330 UNTS 4739 ('New York Convention'). T Hartley, 'Is the 2005 Hague Choice-of-Court Convention Really a Threat to Justice and Fair Play? A Reply to Gary Born' (*EAPIL Blog*, 30 June 2021) <https://eapil.org/2021/06/30/is-the-2005-hague-choice-of-court-convention-really-a-threat-to-justice-and-fair-play-a-reply-to-gary-born/> accessed 31 August 2021. cf R Garnett, 'The Hague Choice of Court Convention: Magnum Opus or Much Ado about Nothing?' (2009) 5 Journal of Private International Law 161, 171–73, doubts whether the Hague Convention is a true litigation counterpart of the New York Convention. This may be attributed to the presence of a wider range of excluded subject matter under Article 2 compared to international arbitration, the potentially wider defences to enforcement of agreements (particularly the 'manifest injustice' ground) and the scope for Contracting States to remove certain areas from the Convention under Article 21. Moreover, international arbitration offers advantages to parties relating to the process itself including neutrality, judicial support, and arbitral institutions of the seat of arbitration, procedural flexibility, privacy, and confidentiality.

[283] Heidelberg Report [338]–[344], [390], 95–7, 112.

Convention and the Brussels Ia Regulation have been referred to as 'tertiary rules' forming part of an increasingly multi-layered, multilateral, and multi-speed regional and international legal order.[284] According to the Hague Convention, the Convention will take precedence over the Brussels Ia Regulation if there is an actual incompatibility between the two instruments but excluding the situations where the parties reside exclusively within EU Member States and where recognition or enforcement of a judgment by an EU court is being sought within the EU.[285]

c) Scope

The Hague Convention is a narrow instrument when compared to the Brussels Ia Regulation or the Lugano II Convention. The Hague Convention applies to exclusive choice of court agreements in international cases in civil or commercial matters.[286] The Hague Convention does not apply to non-exclusive choice of court clauses including unilateral or asymmetric choice of court agreements.[287] Consumer and employment contracts are excluded from the scope of the Hague Convention.[288] Together with further exclusions under Article 2(2), this leads to the result that the Hague Convention primarily applies in 'business-to-business' or commercial cases. The Hague Convention excludes *inter alia* personal injury cases,[289] the carriage of goods and passengers,[290] anti-trust (competition) matters,[291] and marine pollution, limitation of liability for maritime claims, general average, and emergency towage and salvage.[292] Therefore, the Convention does not apply to a bill of lading or a voyage charterparty. The Hague Convention does, however, apply to other maritime contracts such as ship finance contracts, ship mortgages and liens, ship building contracts, ship sale and purchase contracts, time charterparties, and contracts of marine insurance and reinsurance that relate to maritime matters, including cargo insurance.[293] As a result, not all choice of court agreements concluded in favour of the English courts in civil or commercial matters will fall within the scope of the Hague Convention. The common law

[284] A Mills, 'Variable Geometry, Peer Governance, and the Public International Perspective on Private International Law' in H Muir Watt and DP Fernandez Arroyo (eds), *Private International Law and Global Governance* (OUP 2014) 245, 257.

[285] Article 26(6) of the Hague Convention; Permanent Bureau of the Conference, *Convention of 30 June 2005 on Choice of Court Agreements: Text and Explanatory Report by Trevor Hartley and Masato Dogauchi* (HCCH Publications 2013) [267] <https://assets.hcch.net/docs/0de60e2f-e002-408e-98a7-5638e1ebac65.pdf> accessed 31 August 2021; Hartley, *Choice of Court Agreements* (n 8) ch 6, 121–26.

[286] Article 1(1) of the Hague Convention; see Brand and Herrup, *Hague Convention* (n 199) ch 4.

[287] Articles 1(1) and 3(a) of the Hague Convention and the Explanatory Report by Professors T Hartley and M Dogauchi (n 285) [105]–[106].

[288] Article 2(1) of the Hague Convention.

[289] Article 2(2)(j) of the Hague Convention.

[290] Article 2(2)(f) of the Hague Convention.

[291] Article 2(2)(h) of the Hague Convention.

[292] Article 2(2)(g) of the Hague Convention.

[293] Article 17 of the Hague Convention.

jurisdiction regime will apply to choice of court agreements not covered by the Hague Convention.

The Hague Convention only applies in international cases. The definition of what is an international case differs between jurisdictional issues (Chapter II) and recognition and enforcement issues (Chapter III). For the Hague Convention's jurisdictional rules to apply, a case is international unless the parties are resident in the same Contracting State and the relationship of the parties and all other elements relevant to the dispute, regardless of the location of the chosen court, are connected only with that State.[294] For the purposes of obtaining the recognition and enforcement of a judgment in a Contracting State, it is sufficient that the judgment presented is foreign.[295]

Post Brexit, the UK has replicated the EU's declaration limiting the application of the Hague Convention in relation to certain insurance contracts.[296] It has been argued that the UK should withdraw this declaration and enable the UK insurance services market to effectively utilise choice of court agreements in business-to-business cases.[297] The declaration prevents the Hague Convention from applying to a significant class of insurance contracts.[298] As a result, exclusive choice of court agreements in insurance contracts covered by the declaration are not given effect to under the Hague Convention in the UK and UK judgments on matters within the scope of the declaration do not benefit from recognition and enforcement under the Hague Convention in other Contracting States.[299] This creates complications for UK cross-border insurance law. While the UK was a Member State of the EU it consistently opposed these protective provisions on insurance which go beyond the accepted need to protect consumers.[300] The UK was consistently outvoted as this was a qualified majority file in the Council of the EU. It is ironic that after Brexit the UK is following the EU approach to insurance in its declaration in the Hague Choice of Court Convention when it is not bound to do so.

For matters that *are* covered however, the Hague Convention does offer legal certainty. It obliges Contracting States to decline jurisdiction in the face of a relevant English *exclusive* choice of court clause, *and* to recognise and enforce judgments from chosen courts in other Contracting States.

[294] Article 1(2) of the Hague Convention.

[295] Article 1(3) of the Hague Convention.

[296] See Article 21 of the Hague Convention and <https://www.hcch.net/en/instruments/conventions/status-table/notifications/?csid=1044&disp=resdn> accessed 31 August 2021.

[297] Beaumont, 'Private International Law after Brexit' (n 18) 7.

[298] The Memorandum on Use of Delegated Powers accompanying the Private International Law (Implementation of Agreements) Bill suggested (at [22]) that the UK will continue to exclude insurance contracts.

[299] See Article 21(2) of the Convention. For a discussion of the lawfulness and appropriateness of the EU declaration on insurance contracts see P Beaumont, 'The Revived Judgments Project in The Hague' (2014) Nederlands Internationaal Privaatrecht 532–39.

[300] Beaumont, 'Private International Law after Brexit' (n 18).

d) Defining provisions

The basic principles of the Hague Convention can be outlined in a few sentences.[301] The chosen court in an exclusive choice of court agreement shall have jurisdiction to decide a dispute which falls within its purview, unless the agreement is null and void under the law of that state.[302] Any court other than the chosen court shall suspend or dismiss proceedings to which an exclusive choice of court agreement applies.[303] Articles 5 and 6 of the Hague Convention are emblematic of the *substantive law* and *internationalist* paradigms of party autonomy at work in tandem.[304] A judgment given by a chosen court shall be recognised and enforced in other Contracting States and recognition and enforcement may be refused only on the grounds specified in the Hague Convention.[305] Article 22 provides an optional fourth basic rule allowing each Contracting State the opportunity to declare that, on the basis of reciprocity, its courts will recognise and enforce judgments given by courts of other Contracting States designated in a non-exclusive choice of court agreement.[306] Article 22 is based on the assumption that some Contracting States may opt for enhanced judicial cooperation beyond the minimum mandatory framework of the Hague Convention.

The Hague Convention gives effect to the principle of severability:[307]

> An exclusive choice of court agreement that forms part of a contract shall be treated as an agreement independent of the other terms of the contract. The validity of the exclusive choice of court agreement cannot be contested solely on the ground that the contract is not valid.

The substantive validity of the exclusive choice of court agreement in the Hague Convention is subject to the law of the state of the chosen court including its private international law rules.[308] There is an indication in the Explanatory Report to the Hague Convention that most 'consent' questions are governed by the choice of law rules established to determine substantive validity and capacity but that some issues require the basic factual requirements of consent to

301 Hartley, *Choice of Court Agreements* (n 8) ch 1, 21–22; Brand and Herrup, *Hague Convention* (n 199) ch 2, 11–14; Explanatory Report by Professors T Hartley and M Dogauchi [1].

302 Article 5 of the Hague Convention.

303 Article 6 of the Hague Convention.

304 For a discussion of the *substantive law* and *internationalist* paradigms of party autonomy featuring as dialectically opposite categories converging into a new and more reconciled transnationalist paradigm of party autonomy, see ch 2 of Ahmed, *Choice of Court Agreements* (n 7).

305 Article 8 of the Hague Convention.

306 Article 22 of the Hague Convention.

307 Article 3(d) of the Hague Convention; Brand and Herrup, *Hague Convention* (n 199) ch 4, 46–47.

308 Article 5(1) of the Hague Convention; Explanatory Report by Professors T Hartley and M Dogauchi (n 285) [126]; Hartley, *Choice of Court Agreements* (n 8) ch 7, 165–71; Brand and Herrup, *Hague Convention* (n 199) ch 5, 80–82.

exist before there is an agreement.[309] However, it has previously been rejected that issues of 'consent' are governed by either 'the law of the forum—including its choice of law rules'[310] or by an independent interpretation of 'agreement' or by an independent evaluation of the factual requirements of consent in order to establish an agreement.[311] Instead, the Hague Convention provides a complete system of rules to determine whether there is an exclusive choice of court agreement for the purposes of the Convention. Formal validity issues are governed by the harmonised rules in Article 3(c), substantive validity issues are governed by the law of the State of the chosen court including its private international law rules, and capacity issues are governed by the law of the court seised including its private international law rules.[312]

A court designated by a choice of court agreement has no power under the Hague Convention to stay its proceedings on *forum non conveniens* grounds or to stay its proceedings on the basis of the *lis alibi pendens* doctrine.[313] This should be interpreted as the conferral of a right on the parties to invoke the jurisdiction of the chosen court. Fundamentally, the jurisdiction of the chosen court under the Hague Convention is mandatory as opposed to the common law regime's discretionary jurisdiction over choice of court agreements. Notwithstanding, under the common law rules, there appears to be no reported case where the English court has failed to assume jurisdiction where the parties concluded an English exclusive choice of court agreement.[314] In relation to non-international cases, Article 19 of the Hague Convention allows a Contracting State to declare that its courts will not exercise jurisdiction when, except for the location of the chosen court, there is no connection between that State and the parties or the dispute. Thus, if a declaration pursuant to Article 19 has been made, the possibility of declining jurisdiction effectively trumps the rule in Article 5(2).[315]

It is now time to turn our attention towards issues that may arise in the post-Brexit application of the Hague Convention by the English courts. Practical measures are suggested by the author to mitigate the impact of such issues.

[309] Explanatory Report by Professors T Hartley and M Dogauchi (n 285) [94]–[96].

[310] Brand and Herrup, *Hague Convention* (n 199) 79.

[311] Beaumont, 'Hague Choice of Court Agreements' (n 277) 138–40.

[312] ibid. cf Hartley, *Choice of Court Agreements* (n 8) 133.

[313] Article 5(2) of the Hague Convention; see Brand and Herrup, *Hague Convention* (n 199) ch 5, 82–84; RA Brand and SR Jablonski, *Forum Non Conveniens: History, Global Practice, and Future Under the Hague Convention on Choice of Court Agreements* (OUP 2007) ch 9, 208.

[314] cf There is a reported decision where English proceedings were stayed on the claimant's application, regardless of an English choice of court clause: *Bouygues Offshore SA v Caspian Shipping Company* [1998] EWCA Civ 1077, [1998] 2 Lloyd's Rep 461. See A Briggs, *Agreements on Jurisdiction and Choice of Law* (OUP 2008) ch 6 (hereafter Briggs, *Agreements*); Hill and Shúilleabháin, *Clarkson & Hill* (n 115) 138.

[315] Brand and Herrup, *Hague Convention* (n 199) ch 5, 84; Beaumont, 'Hague Choice of Court' (n 277) 149. No party to the Convention has made the Article 19 declaration so far.

e) A legal lacuna in the application of the Hague Convention to English exclusive choice of court agreements concluded between 1 October 2015 and 1 January 2021?

The UK and the EU Member States are Contracting States of the 2005 Hague Convention on Choice of Court Agreements.[316] This position is not, however, without potential transitional wrinkles. The Hague Convention states the Convention applies to exclusive choice of court agreements concluded after its entry into force for the state of the chosen court and that the Convention does not apply to proceedings instituted before its entry into force in the state of the court seised.[317] The Hague Convention has, however, already entered into force in the UK because of the EU's ratification of the Convention.[318]

The UK is now a party to the Hague Convention as an independent Contracting State. Primary legislation has been adopted to implement the UK's obligations under the Hague Convention.[319] The new Section 3D CJJA provides that the Hague Convention is to have the force of law.[320] The Hague Convention is to be read together with the reservations and declarations made by the UK when acceding to it, although these are not separately reproduced in the legislation.[321] The implementing legislation explicitly affirms the UK's position that its accession as an independent Contracting State guarantees that the Convention will continue to apply seamlessly in the UK from 1 October 2015, when the UK originally acceded to the Convention as an EU Member State.[322] Notably, the Hague Conference on Private International Law (the depositary of the Convention and ratifications by participating states) states that the 2005 Convention entered into force for the UK in October 2015.

The position of the UK government, as set out in the Private International Law (Implementation of Agreements) Act 2020, is that the provisions in the Convention will continue to apply to the UK post Completion Day without interruption. While this will mean that UK courts can find jurisdiction under the Convention for agreements that pre-date 1 January 2021, this is contrary to the position as set out in the EU Notice to Stakeholders dated 27 August 2020.[323] That document states

[316] Concluded at the 20th Session of the Hague Conference on Private International Law, The Hague, 30 June 2005.

[317] Article 16 of the Hague Convention.

[318] The Civil Jurisdiction and Judgments (Hague Convention on Choice of Court Agreements 2005) Regulations 2015, SI 2015/1644, brought the Hague Convention into force in the UK when the UK was an EU Member State.

[319] Section 1 of the Private International Law (Implementation of Agreements) Act 2020 and Schedule 5, [3], [7], and [9], amending CJJA and substantially replacing earlier legislation (SI 2018/1124) made under the Withdrawal Act.

[320] The English language text of the Hague Convention is set out in Schedule 3F to the 1982 Act.

[321] Section 3E(2) CJJA.

[322] Schedule 5, [7] of the Private International Law (Implementation of Agreements) Act 2020 referring to Article 16 of the Hague Convention.

[323] European Commission, 'Notice to Stakeholders: Withdrawal of the United Kingdom and EU Rules in the Field of Civil Justice and Private International Law', Brussels, 27 August 2020, [3.3] <civil_justice_en.pdf> accessed 31 August 2021.

the European Commission's view that the Convention will only apply to UK exclusive choice of court agreements if they are concluded after the Convention enters into force for the UK in its own right as an independent Contracting State.

This may have implications for the enforcement for a UK judgment in an EU Member State or an EU Member State may refuse to stay proceedings in favour of an English exclusive choice of court agreement concluded after 1 October 2015 but before 1 January 2021, if EU Member State courts take the approach set out in the EU Notice 2020. In those circumstances, where the English court's jurisdiction was based on an exclusive choice of court clause pre-dating 1 January 2021, EU Member State courts will not enforce the judgment pursuant to the Convention, though the judgment may still be enforceable under local rules in the relevant Member State.

The Hague Convention applies to exclusive choice of court agreements concluded after the convention's 'entry into force' for the state of the chosen court. The European Commission has not given any basis for its view that the 'entry into force' date for the UK should be taken to refer to the date the Convention enters into force for the UK in its own right, rather than the earlier date (1 October 2015) when the Convention entered into force for the UK by virtue of its EU membership.

It is not clear that the European Commission's view is correct, and it is not binding on the courts that will decide this question in future. The proper interpretation of the Convention in this regard will fall to be determined by EU Member State courts asked to apply the Convention to enforce a UK judgment based on an exclusive jurisdiction pre-dating 1 January 2021 and ultimately by the CJEU if any such Member State court sends a preliminary reference to the CJEU under Article 267 of the Treaty on the Functioning of the European Union (TFEU). An EU Member State court may decline to stay proceedings under Article 6 of the Hague Convention because the English exclusive choice of court agreement predates 1 January 2021. A preliminary reference to the CJEU under Article 267 TFEU may also arise from such proceedings in an EU Member State court.

However, in light of the European Commission's view, unless and until this question is finally determined, there is a litigation risk that a UK judgment would not be enforced under the Convention in these circumstances. How serious a risk that is for a given claimant will depend on the likelihood of a UK judgment being enforced, if the Convention does not apply, under local rules in the EU Member State(s) where the defendant has its assets.

The potential litigation risk of non-enforcement and the refusal to stay proceedings by a Member State court can be avoided by the claimant. If a dispute has arisen under the relevant choice of court agreement during the transition period, a claimant should protect its position by commencing proceedings in the English courts prior to 1 January 2021. In those circumstances, the rules on jurisdiction and enforcement of judgments under the Brussels Ia Regulation will apply.

If a dispute has not arisen, then the options available depend on whether the agreement containing the exclusive choice of court clause has already been entered into. If so, the parties are advised to rewrite (ie re-date) the choice of court agreement after 1 January 2021 in such a way that it is clearly within the scope of the Hague Convention.

If the agreement has not been entered into, then the obvious question is whether it can be delayed until after 1 January 2021. If that is not feasible, and if there are likely to be significant risks enforcing a UK judgment in the relevant EU Member State(s) if the Convention does not apply, then the party concerned may want to consider alternatives to the exclusive jurisdiction of the English courts. Alternatives include arbitration, which is not affected by Brexit, a unilateral or non-exclusive choice of court clause in favour of the English courts, to hedge the parties' choice of jurisdiction till the dispute arises, or potentially a choice of jurisdiction in favour of an EU Member State court or a Lugano II Convention Contracting State. These alternatives are discussed in Chapter 3, Section D.

It is widely expected that the differing positions of the UK and the European Commission on the 'lacuna' in the application of the Hague Convention will come before the CJEU.[324] The Member State court may either refuse to enforce a UK judgment under Article 8 or refuse to stay proceedings based on an English exclusive choice of court agreement under Article 6 concluded between 1 October 2015 and 1 January 2021. If the English exclusive choice of court agreement has already been entered into in a contract, parties are advised to rewrite (ie re-date) the choice of court agreement after 1 January 2021 in such a way that it is clearly within the scope of the Hague Convention.

f) Choice of Court Agreements and Service of Proceedings outside Jurisdiction after Brexit

A claimant who relies upon the Hague Choice of Court Convention to establish the jurisdiction of a court in England or Wales may serve the claim form abroad without needing the court's prior permission.[325] With effect from 6 April 2021, this provision will be extended to all cases in which a contract contains a term giving the court jurisdiction to determine the claim, whether or not the choice of court agreement is one to which the Convention applies.[326]

Claimants in English proceedings no longer have to apply for the court's permission to serve those proceedings out of jurisdiction where the claims fall within an English choice of court clause. This is a pragmatic development as it removes the procedural hurdle of having to make an application to serve out in disputes

324 As a preliminary reference from a Member State court under Article 267 TFEU.

325 CPR 6.33(2B).

326 Civil Procedure (Amendment) Rules (SI 2021/117), reg 6. In both cases, the claimant must file a notice stating the grounds of the entitlement to serve the claim form out of the jurisdiction (CPR 6.34).

where the parties have agreed that the English courts should have jurisdiction. Significantly, the new regime will now apply to service on defendants located in any jurisdiction in the world (not limited largely to countries in the EU, European Economic Area (EEA), or signatories to the 2005 Hague Convention as was the case prior to Brexit) and appears to cover exclusive, non-exclusive, asymmetric, or unilateral choice of court agreements. In view of the increasingly competitive market for cross-border dispute resolution, this is a change to the law that should augment the attractiveness of the English courts in the post-Brexit world.

i) Pre-exit regime

Prior to 1 January 2021, an English court's permission to serve a claim out of jurisdiction based on a choice of court clause was not required if it had jurisdiction under the Brussels Ia Regulation, the Lugano II Convention, the Hague Convention, or in a small number of other circumstances. If those provisions did not apply, the claimant had to apply for permission to serve the claim outside of the jurisdiction under CPR 6.36. This included establishing a good arguable case that the claim falls within one of the common law gateways for service out, there is a serious issue to be tried on the merits, England is clearly or distinctly the appropriate forum to try the claim, and that the English court should exercise its discretion to permit the claim to be served out. This was often a costly process and was done without notice to the defendant which meant that the claimant had to comply with the duty of full and frank disclosure, including highlighting the weaknesses in its own case. Generally, this is not something that a party is eager to do upon commencement of proceedings.

ii) The position prior to 6 April 2021

From 1 January 2021 and until 6 April 2021, given that the UK is no longer party to the Brussels Ia Regulation or the Lugano II Convention, a party to an English choice of court clause needs to apply for permission to serve a claim out of the jurisdiction unless that claim falls within the Hague Convention (or in limited other circumstances). However, the 2005 Hague Convention's remit is relatively narrow geographically and covers exclusive choice of court clauses only. In particular, it does not cover non-exclusive, asymmetric, or unilateral choice of court clauses (where all or one of the parties have a choice in which jurisdiction to bring proceedings respectively) or exclusive choice of court clauses entered into before 1 October 2015 (date of entry into force of the 2005 Hague Convention in the UK as a Member State of the EU).

iii) New regime

Further to the Lord Chancellor's Advisory Committee on Private International Law and the Law Society's proposals, at its October 2020 meeting the Civil Procedure Rules Committee proposed to make changes to the service out rules where there is an English choice of court agreement. Those changes were finalised and implemented via the Civil Procedure (Amendment) Rules 2021 (SI 117/2021) which comes into effect on 6 April 2021.

As a result of those changes, the new wording of CPR 6.33(2B) provides that the claimant may serve the claim form on the defendant outside of the UK without permission where, for each claim made against the defendant to be served and included in the claim form,

> (a) the court has power to determine that claim under the 2005 Hague Convention and the defendant is a party to an exclusive choice of court agreement conferring jurisdiction on that court within the meaning of Article 3 of the 2005 Hague Convention; or (b) a contract contains a term to the effect that the court shall have jurisdiction to determine that claim.

In light of these changes, a claimant in English proceedings can proceed to serve its claim form on the defendant out of the jurisdiction upon issue without any applications to the English court provided there is a clause in an agreement between the parties specifying that the English courts shall have jurisdiction to determine that claim. Although it is highly likely that an English court would have given permission to serve out in such circumstances prior to this rule change in any case, the removal of the requirement to do so is of clear benefit to claimants in terms of saving costs and the speed with which proceedings can be served on the defendant. At the same time, the defendant still has the ability to challenge jurisdiction upon being served (eg to challenge the validity of the choice of court agreement). From a policy perspective, it is difficult to see the prejudice of these changes to the defendant in the circumstances where the parties had already agreed jurisdiction.

More notably, assuming that there is a valid choice of court agreement covering the claim, the changes also mean that a claimant no longer has to apply for permission to serve out on defendants in jurisdictions outside the EU Member States covered by the previous EU linked regimes, for instance defendants in Russia, the Caribbean, and European offshore jurisdictions, the Middle East etc. Further, the new rules mean that the claimant can avoid the requirements of full and frank disclosure in applications for service out of jurisdiction which are generally done on an *ex parte* basis.

If and when the UK becomes a Contracting State of the Lugano II Convention, claimants will not need permission for claims based on English choice of court clauses provided the defendant is domiciled within a relevant state (the EU Member States, Norway, Switzerland, and Iceland). However, the new rules in force from 6 April 2021 will continue to be relevant as regards defendants located outside of those European states.

These efficient amendments will save costs for parties choosing the English courts as the forum to resolve their disputes. The fact that the new regime also applies to non-exclusive choice of court clauses means that parties across the globe are more likely to choose the English courts for one-stop-shop dispute resolution.[327]

g) The enforcement of English exclusive choice of court agreements under the Hague Convention

All references to Contracting States in this section include by implication the EU Member States because all EU Member States are Contracting States of the Hague Convention.

The Hague Convention does not comprehensively address the *Gasser*[328] problem of who should interpret the choice of court agreement as it does not confer sole competence on the court putatively chosen to do so.[329] Where the parties have agreed to the exclusive jurisdiction of the English courts, and the courts of another Contracting State are seised, the other court must normally decline to exercise jurisdiction.[330] The court other than the chosen court must decline jurisdiction if it is established that there is a valid and exclusive choice of court agreement in favour of the English courts and the claim falls within the scope of the choice of court agreement and the Hague Convention. At the least, the other court would need to establish a *prima facie* case that such an agreement confers jurisdiction on the English courts. It need not decline jurisdiction, however, principally in the following situations:

(1) if the agreement is invalid under the law of the state of the chosen court;
(2) a party lacked the capacity to conclude the agreement under the law of the state of the court seised;
(3) if giving effect to the agreement would lead to a manifest injustice or would be manifestly contrary to the public policy of the state of the court seised;[331]

[327] For the presumption that arbitration is chosen as a one-stop method of adjudication for the determination of all disputes, see, *Premium Nafta Products Limited and others v Fili Shipping Company Limited and others* [2007] UKHL 40, [13] (Lord Hoffmann) and [27] (Lord Hope). cf Where two dispute resolution clauses conflict as to forum, the English courts will look at the center of gravity of the dispute in question, in order to decide which forum is the most appropriate for that dispute: *Trust Risk Group SpA v AmTrust Europe Ltd* [2015] EWCA Civ 437. In *Deutsche Bank AG v Comune di Savona* [2018] EWCA Civ 1740, [31], the Court of Appeal stated that the 'one stop adjudication is only a presumption' and that it was 'desirable that potentially conflicting jurisdiction clauses should be given a mutually exclusive construction'.

[328] See Case C-116/02 *Erich Gasser Gmbh v MISAT Srl* [2003] ECR I-14693. In *Gasser*, The CJEU decided that the court first seised (Italy) should determine whether the choice of court agreement giving exclusive jurisdiction to the Austrian courts was valid and applicable. The Austrian courts were obliged to wait for the decision of the Italian court even if the Italian court took an inordinately long period of time to adjudicate on the jurisdictional issue.

[329] Articles 5 and 6 of the Hague Convention. cf Article 31(2) of the Brussels Ia Regulation.

[330] Article 6 of the Hague Convention.

[331] The ruling in *Carvalho v Hull, Blyth (Angola) Ltd* [1979] 1 WLR 1228, where the English court allowed the claimant to sue in England in breach of an Angolan choice of court clause would probably be decided in the same manner under Article 6(c) of the Hague Convention. Explanatory Report by Professors T Hartley and M Dogauchi (n 285) [151]–[153]; Hartley, *Choice of Court Agreements* (n 8) ch 8, 184;

(4) if for exceptional reasons beyond the control of the parties, the agreement cannot reasonably be performed.[332]

Therefore, the litigation risk of pre-emptive 'torpedo' proceedings in breach of an English exclusive choice of court agreement in the courts of a Contracting State is reduced but not removed in cases subject to the Hague Convention on Choice of Court Agreements.[333] The future cross-border civil judicial relationship between the UK and the EU may give rise to a reincarnation of pre-emptive torpedo litigation where a Member State court may be seised in breach of an English exclusive choice of court clause. However, the availability of anti-suit injunctions in the English court's armoury may be relied upon by a disgruntled party to swiftly and effectively neutralise any threat posed by such rogue proceedings. The interpretation of the scope for pre-emptive torpedo litigation in relation to the threshold issue and the exceptions to the obligation to decline jurisdiction may come under judicial scrutiny and as a result acquire further clarity in the emergent jurisprudence of the Hague Convention.[334]

The Hague Convention does not counter the potential for pre-emptive proceedings in every situation. First, the Hague Convention can only apply if an English exclusive choice of court agreement is challenged in a Contracting State. Second, it does not apply to asymmetric choice of court agreements, which are frequently encountered in international commercial and financial transactions.[335] Although there is no requirement that the parties should have equal rights, it was agreed by the Diplomatic Session that in order to be covered by the Hague Convention, the agreement must be exclusive irrespective of the party bringing the proceedings.[336]

J Landbrecht, 'The Concepts of "Injustice" and "Public Policy" in Article 6(c) of the Hague Choice of Court Convention' (2019) 15 Journal of Private International Law 339.

332 The exceptions in (c) and (d) are intended to apply 'only in the most exceptional circumstances': see Explanatory Report by Professors T Hartley and M Dogauchi (n 285) [148]; Hartley, *Choice of Court Agreements* (n 8) ch 8, 183.

333 Fentiman, *International Commercial Litigation* (n 163) 97.

334 For the scope for pre-emptive torpedo litigation on the threshold issue and the non-chosen court's need to establish whether its duty to stay proceedings is engaged in the different context of Article 31(2) of the Brussels Ia Regulation, see Ahmed, *Choice of Court Agreements* (n 7) 228; Fentiman, *International Commercial Litigation* (n 163) 100.

335 Explanatory Report by Professors T Hartley and M Dogauchi (n 285) [105]–[106]; Hartley, *Choice of Court Agreements* (n 8) ch 7, 143–44; The Court of Appeal in *Etihad Airways PJSC v Prof. Dr. Lucas Flöther* [2020] EWCA Civ 1707, [85] (Henderson LJ) referred in *obiter* comments to [106] of the Explanatory Report as 'a strong indication' that asymmetric clauses fall outside the Hague Convention. cf In *Etihad Airways PJSC v Prof. Dr. Lucas Flöther* [2019] EWHC 3107 (Comm), [2020] QB 793, [215]–[217] (Jacobs J) and *Commerzbank Aktiengesellschaft v Pauline Shipping and Liquimar Tankers* [2017] EWHC 161 (Comm), [71]–[74] (Cranston J) it was noted that there are 'good arguments' that the definition of exclusive choice of court clauses in Article 3(a) of the Hague Convention covers asymmetric choice of court clauses. However, it should be observed that these *obiter* remarks are not supported by either the text of the Official Explanatory Report or the minutes of the Diplomatic Session.

336 Minutes No 3 of the Second Commission Meeting of Wednesday 15 June 2005 (morning) in *Proceedings of the Twentieth Session of the Hague Conference on Private International Law* (Permanent Bureau of the Conference, Intersentia, 2010) 577, 577–78.

Outside the scope of the Hague Convention, English courts have traditionally enforced asymmetric choice of court agreements by anti-suit injunctions.[337] The Court of Appeal in *Etihad Airways PJSC v Prof. Dr. Lucas Flöther* has confirmed that the protective cover of Article 31(2) of the Brussels Ia Regulation extends to asymmetric choice of court clauses.[338]

The grounds for displacing an agreement provided in the Hague Convention offer significant opportunities to undermine a choice of court agreement, and to create uncertainty as to their status. Despite the enhancement of the enforcement of choice of court agreements in some cases, the potential for tactical forum shopping remains along with the burden on a defendant in foreign proceedings to launch a defence and incur costs and expenses in those proceedings.

The lack of a *lis alibi pendens* provision[339] to coordinate proceedings and the apparent tolerance of 'parallel proceedings'[340] suggests that the Hague Convention does not adhere to the strict multilateral jurisdiction and judgments model of the Brussels Ia Regulation premised on the mutual trust principle. Therefore, the issue of whether national private law remedies such as anti-suit injunctions and damages for breach of choice of court agreements might be relied upon may receive a different answer under the Hague Convention than under the Brussels Ia Regulation.

The referral of issues relating to material validity, a substantive element of a choice of court agreement, to the law of the chosen forum including its private international law rules recognises the complex 'hybrid' nature of a choice of court agreement incorporating a mix of substantive and procedural components. Article 3(d) of the Hague Convention offers an additional layer of protection for choice of court agreements by emphasising that an attack on the validity of the substantive contract does not by itself impeach the validity of the independent choice of court agreement. This ensures that the forum 'chosen' by the parties exercises adjudicatory authority even where the very existence of the substantive contract is in dispute. The principles of party autonomy and legal certainty justify the exercise

[337] See *Continental Bank NA v Aeakos Compania Naviera SA* [1994] 1 WLR 588, 592F-594G (CA) (Steyn LJ); *Mauritius Commercial Bank Limited v Hestia Holdings Limited and Sujana Universal Industries Limited* [2013] EWHC 1328 (Comm), [2013] 2 Lloyds Rep 121, [37] (Popplewell J); *Bank of New York Mellon v GV Films* [2009] EWHC 2338, [14]; *Credit Suisse First Boston (Europe) Ltd v MLC (Bermuda) Ltd* [1999] 1 All ER 237, 249G-250A.

[338] *Etihad Airways PJSC v Prof. Dr. Lucas Flöther* [2020] EWCA Civ 1707, [93] (Henderson LJ); *Etihad Airways PJSC v Prof. Dr. Lucas Flöther* [2019] EWHC 3107 (Comm), [2020] QB 793 (Jacobs J); In *Commerzbank Aktiengesellschaft v Pauline Shipping and Liquimar Tankers* [2017] EWHC 161 (Comm), [52], [64], Cranston J decided that Article 31(2) covered asymmetric choice of court clauses even though the clause was exclusive in relation to the defendant's claim only. In *Perella Weinberg Partners UK LLP, Perella Weinberg Partners (Europe) LP v Codere SA* [2016] EWHC 1182 (Comm), [18], Walker J had also made an *obiter* remark that Article 31(2)'s protective cover extends to asymmetric choice of court clauses. See I Bergson, 'The Death of the Torpedo Action?' (2015) 11 Journal of Private International Law 1, 22. For a critique of the view that Article 31(2) applies to exclusive choice of court agreements, see M Ahmed, 'The Legal Regulation and Enforcement of Asymmetric Jurisdiction Agreements in the European Union' (2017) 28 European Business Law Review 403.

[339] Article 5(2) of the Hague Convention; cf Article 29 of the Brussels Ia Regulation.

[340] Explanatory Report by Professors T Hartley and M Dogauchi (n 285) [132]–[134].

of jurisdiction by the chosen court where the validity of the substantive contract is impugned.

Article 7 of the Hague Convention states that the Convention does not affect the granting of interim measures of protection:[341]

> Interim measures of protection are not governed by this Convention. This Convention neither requires nor precludes the grant, refusal or termination of interim measures of protection by a court of a Contracting State and does not affect whether or not a party may request or a court should grant, refuse or terminate such measures.

Although anti-suit injunctions might be characterised as interim measures of protection, they are not specified as such in the Official Explanatory Report.[342] However, the Explanatory Reports of the Draft Conventions on Choice of Court Agreements have cited an anti-suit injunction precluding a party from bringing proceedings in a court other than that chosen as an example of an interim measure of protection.[343]

A plenary discussion between official delegates recorded in Minutes No 9 of a Second Commission meeting at the Diplomatic Session which finalised the Hague Choice of Court Convention provides support to the argument that anti-suit injunctions may be awarded to support the enforcement of choice of court agreements by Contracting States.[344] Significantly, Mr Paul R Beaumont of the UK delegation sought to clarify the position in relation to anti-suit injunctions by differentiating the formal 'process' from the desired 'outcome'.[345] Where anti-suit injunctions enforce choice of court agreements and thus help to achieve the intended outcome of the Convention, there was a consensus among the delegates

[341] Article 7 of the Hague Convention; see Brand and Herrup, *Hague Convention* (n 199) ch 5, 95–96.

[342] Hartley, *Choice of Court Agreements* (n 8) ch 10, 215–16; Explanatory Report by Professors T Hartley and M Dogauchi (n 285) [160]–[163]; cf B Hess, 'The Draft Hague Convention on Choice of Court Agreements, External Competencies of the European Union and Recent Case Law of the European Court of Justice' in A Nuyts and N Watté (eds), *International Civil Litigation in Europe and Relations with Third States* (Bruylant 2005) 263, 281–82, argues that, in principle, anti-suit injunctions should be allowed as the EU notion of mutual trust does not apply between Contracting States of the Hague Convention. He even suggests that an express exclusive jurisdiction of the designated court to order such measures together with a corresponding obligation on all courts of the Contracting States to recognise and enforce such orders should be incorporated into the Hague Convention.

[343] TC Hartley and M Dogauchi, 'Explanatory Report on the Preliminary Draft Convention on Exclusive Choice of Court Agreements' (Preliminary Document No 26 of December 2004) in Proceedings of the Twentieth Session of the Hague Conference on Private International Law (Permanent Bureau of the Conference, Intersentia, 2010) 167, 195–97, [131]; TC Hartley and M Dogauchi, 'Explanatory Report on the Preliminary Draft Convention on Choice of Court Agreements' (Preliminary Document No 25 of March 2004) <www.hcch.net/upload/wop/jdgm_pd25e.pdf>, 24, [101].

[344] Minutes No 9 of the Second Commission Meeting of Monday 20 June 2005 (morning) in Proceedings of the Twentieth Session of the Hague Conference on Private International Law (Permanent Bureau of the Conference, Intersentia, 2010) 622, 623–24.

[345] ibid, 624.

in the meeting that the Convention did not limit or constrain national courts of Contracting States from granting the remedy.[346]

The primary meaning of interim measures of protection is measures intended to protect the position of the parties while the proceedings are pending.[347] After mentioning freezing orders, interim injunctions, and orders for the production of evidence the Official Explanatory Report states:[348]

> All these measures are intended to support the choice of court agreement by making it more effective. They thus help to achieve the objective of the Convention. Nevertheless, they remain outside its scope.

Tellingly the Explanatory Report goes on to say that:

> If an interim measure—for example, an injunction—granted by that court is subsequently made permanent, it will be enforceable under the Convention in other Contracting States.

Arguably, an anti-suit injunction granted for breach of an English exclusive choice of court clause is a measure intended to make the choice of court agreement more effective.[349] This opens the possibility for a party faced with proceedings brought in clear breach of an English exclusive choice of court agreement to apply to the English courts for an anti-suit injunction in Hague Convention cases.[350] The law of the forum will govern the issue of remedies for breach of English exclusive choice of court agreements as the Hague Convention is *sub silento* on the matter.[351] If the English court is the chosen court and has at some point made the anti-suit injunction permanent then it would seem from the Explanatory Report that the permanent injunction is an enforceable judgment within the scope of the

[346] ibid. The delegates who clearly held a view that anti-suit injunctions to enforce choice of court agreements were compatible with the Hague Convention included Mr Paul R Beaumont (United Kingdom), Mr Trevor C Hartley (co-Reporter), Mr J Kovar (United States of America), Mr David Bennett (Australia), and Mr Gottfried Musger (Austria). The Chair (Mr Andreas Bucher (Switzerland)) noted that the co-Reporters would make what had been said on this clear, and that there would also be a process for commenting on the Explanatory Report. Sadly, his wish on this point that the co-Reporters would make the matter clear in the final Explanatory Report was not fulfilled.

[347] Hartley, *Choice of Court Agreements* (n 8) ch 10, 216.

[348] Explanatory Report by Professors T Hartley and M Dogauchi (n 285) [160].

[349] cf Principle 7.1 of the *Leuven/London Principles on Declining and Referring Jurisdiction in Civil and Commercial Litigation* accepts that there is no place for anti-suit injunctions where both states are parties to an international convention specifying common rules for the exercise of original jurisdiction. Indeed, no such remedy should be ordered where the court is satisfied that the other court will apply the Principles (Principle 7.2). Ordinarily deference should be given to the court seised of the substantive proceedings, at least where that court has rules permitting it to decline jurisdiction in certain cases. Significantly, Principle 7.3 qualifies Principles 7.1 and 7.2 by permitting an exception in the case of a 'manifest' breach of an exclusive choice of court clause under the law of both states.

[350] Joseph, *Jurisdiction and Arbitration* (n 271) 410–11.

[351] ibid.

Convention. On the other hand, the operation of national law in relation to interim measures of protection is not completely unfettered by the Hague Convention.[352] Considerations of general treaty law may place constraints on the operation of national law. Thus, there is a legitimate question as to whether a court not chosen could issue an anti-suit injunction against proceedings in a court chosen in an exclusive choice of court agreement.[353] It is submitted, that in these circumstances, the use of anti-suit injunctions will actually impede the sound operation of the Hague Convention and jeopardise the enforcement of jurisdictional party autonomy. Thus, there is a strong argument that the Hague Convention will not permit the use of anti-suit injunctions to render choice of court agreements ineffective.[354]

It has been observed that anti-suit injunctions granted for breach of English exclusive choice of court clauses are measures intended to make such agreements more effective. However, the principal method of enforcing choice of court agreements in both the Hague Convention and the Brussels Ia Regulation is jurisdictional or procedural and not contractual in nature. The nominated court in a choice of court agreement shall exercise jurisdiction whilst all other courts are required to stay and eventually decline jurisdiction.[355] In the case of the Brussels Ia Regulation a 'reverse *lis pendens* rule'[356] according primacy to the choice of court agreement

[352] Brand and Herrup, *Hague Convention* (n 199) ch 5, 96; Hartley and Dogauchi, 'Explanatory Report on the Preliminary Draft Convention on Exclusive Choice of Court Agreements' (December 2004) (n 343) 167, 193, [120]–[121]; Hartley and Dogauchi, 'Explanatory Report on the Preliminary Draft Convention on Choice of Court Agreements' (March 2004) (n 343) 22, [88]–[89]; see also, A Schulz, 'Reflection Paper to Assist in the Preparation of a Convention on Jurisdiction and Recognition and Enforcement of Foreign Judgments in Civil and Commercial Matters' (Preliminary Document No 19 of August 2002) in *Proceedings of the Twentieth Session of the Hague Conference on Private International Law* (Permanent Bureau of the Conference, Intersentia, 2010) 11, 25, [77], who identified whether the Convention should contain a rule prohibiting the courts of a Contracting State from issuing anti-suit injunctions with regard to proceedings before the court in another Contracting State which was designated by an exclusive choice of court clause.

[353] Under public international law treaty interpretation is based on the requirements of Articles 31 and 32 of the Vienna Convention on the Law of Treaties at least for states bound by the Convention. Resort to the preparatory work is allowed under Article 32 if the meaning of a Convention is 'ambiguous or obscure' from the application of Article 31 or if it confirms the meaning arrived at from the application of Article 31. Arguably the circumstances in which anti-suit injunctions can be used in relation to the Hague Convention are not clear from reading the wording of the Convention and taking account of its context and its object and purpose but even if they are clear the preparatory work in terms of the discussion of this issue at the Diplomatic Session confirms the correct interpretation. Therefore resort to the preparatory work on the use of anti-suit injunctions in relation to the Hague Convention—in particular the published discussion on this issue at the Diplomatic Session—is appropriate for a court seeking to interpret the Hague Convention in a uniform manner as required by Article 23 of that Convention.

[354] Brand and Herrup, *Hague Convention* (n 199) ch 5, 96; see Minutes No 9 of the Second Commission Meeting of Monday 20 June 2005 (morning) in *Proceedings of the Twentieth Session of the Hague Conference on Private International Law* (Permanent Bureau of the Conference, Intersentia, 2010) 622, 623–24. The delegates who clearly held a view that anti-suit injunctions preventing parties from bringing proceedings in the chosen court were incompatible with the Hague Convention were the same as those listed in n 639 above.

[355] Article 6 of the Hague Convention; Articles 31(2) and 31(3) of the Brussels Ia Regulation.

[356] Hartley, *Choice of Court Agreements* (n 8) 228, [11.17]; Hartley, 'Choice-of-Court Agreements and the New Brussels I Regulation' (n 241) 312.

rather than the court first seised is the envisaged method of enforcing jurisdictional party autonomy within the EU.[357] The prospects of remedies enforcing choice of court agreements making much headway in the EU is necessarily curtailed by a multilateral jurisdictional system that prizes the overarching principle of mutual trust and systemic objectives more than the enforcement of private rights and obligations embodied in an exclusive choice of court agreement.

In contrast, the Hague Convention is premised on a system of qualified or partial mutual trust which suggests that the arguments for enforcing choice of court agreements through anti-suit injunctions may be pursued here with a greater likelihood of success.[358] However, it should be noted, that anti-suit injunctions as opposed to a more general class of injunctions were not specifically discussed as a method for enforcing exclusive choice of court agreements in the final Explanatory Report.[359] The judgment of a Contracting State which rules on the validity of a choice of court agreement selecting that state itself shall be recognised and enforced in other Contracting States.[360] However, the judgment of a Contracting State which rules on the validity of a choice of court agreement selecting another Contracting State will not be entitled to recognition and enforcement in other Contracting States.[361] The application of an anti-suit injunction and the damages remedy may be justified in the case of the assumption of jurisdiction by a Contracting State without regard to the presence of a valid choice of court agreement in favour of another Contracting State. Thus, the Hague Convention might allow an English court to second guess the findings of another Contracting State as to the validity and effectiveness of an English choice of court agreement and award damages for breach of the choice of court clause. The Hague Convention complemented by the common law's remedies for breach of exclusive choice of court agreements synergises the enforcement of jurisdictional party autonomy in English courts.

[357] For criticism of the kompetenz-kompetenz of the 'allegedly' chosen forum in a choice of court agreement, see Case C-116/02 *Erich Gasser GmbH v MISAT Srl* 2003] ECR I-14693, Opinion of AG Léger, [74]; Briggs, 'What Should be Done about Jurisdiction Agreements?' (n 241) 319–22; Briggs, 'Brussels I bis Regulation on the Horizon' (n 242) 162–64.

[358] J Harris, 'Agreements on Jurisdiction and Choice of Law: Where Next?' [2009] Lloyd's Maritime and Commercial Law Quarterly 537, 560. There is a risk that if a case is referred to the CJEU concerning an anti-suit injunction from a non-EU Hague Contracting State that is trying to enforce an exclusive choice of court agreement in favour of the courts of the state granting the injunction that the CJEU will regard such an injunction as contrary to the Convention. Hopefully the CJEU will not do so because it carefully considers the *travaux préparatoires* of the Convention and accepts that there is no obligation on non-EU Contracting States to the Convention not to grant such injunctions and that such an obligation cannot be inferred from a notion of 'mutual trust' in this context. There is some hope for this outcome given that in Case C-536/13 *Gazprom OAO* EU:C:2015:316, esp [35]–[44], the CJEU recognised that there is no obligation on arbitral bodies not to grant anti-suit injunctions in relation to proceedings pending in the courts of an EU Member State.

[359] See Explanatory Report by Professors T Hartley and M Dogauchi (n 285).

[360] Article 8(1) of the Hague Convention.

[361] Brand and Herrup, *Hague Convention* (n 199) ch 6, 100; Hartley, *Choice of Court Agreements* (n 8) ch 9, 195; Explanatory Report by Professors T Hartley and M Dogauchi (n 285) [164]–[181].

It should be noted that the Hague Convention is a codified regime regulating the validity and effectiveness of choice of court agreements globally.[362] The application of remedies to enforce choice of court agreements by some Contracting States may create a rift in the yet to develop jurisprudence of the Hague Convention and without an international court interpreting the meaning of the global Convention it is likely that the uniform application of the Convention might be compromised.

H. UK–EU Jurisdictional Conflicts

1. Anti-suit Injunctions

Post Brexit, so far as the EU Member States are concerned the UK is a third state. Before Articles 33 and 34 were added to the Brussels Ia Regulation, there were no express provisions addressing the position of non-EU courts. Article 33 of the Brussels Ia Regulation provides that courts in EU Member States may stay proceedings in favour of courts outside the EU if three conditions are met: first, the non-EU court was first seised; secondly, the non-EU court can give a judgment capable of enforcement in the EU Member State in question; and, thirdly, a stay is necessary for the proper administration of justice.[363] The EU Member State court has discretion to stay proceedings in favour of the court outside the EU. Articles 33 and 34 of the Regulation have codified the instances where prior parallel proceedings outside the EU may result in a stay of proceedings. There is evidence of some Member State courts' practice which gives effect to the jurisdiction of non-EU courts under the guise of giving 'reflexive effect' to the Regulation's provisions.[364] However, as the Brussels Ia Regulation now specifically addresses the position of non-EU courts, an attempt to circumvent the operation of the Brussels Ia Regulation by staying proceedings on other grounds may be harder to justify in principle.

A second seised EU Member State court may decline to stay proceedings under Articles 33 or 34 in favour of prior English proceedings. Notwithstanding, English

[362] See Article 23 of the Hague Convention, which highlights its international character and the need to promote uniformity in its application; Explanatory Report by Professors T Hartley and M Dogauchi (n 285) [256]. The equivalent provision in the preliminary draft Convention 1999 is Article 38(1). The commentary on this issue is in P Nygh and F Pocar, 'Report on the preliminary draft Convention on Jurisdiction and Foreign Judgments in Civil and Commercial Matters' Prel Doc 11, August 2000, 118–19 <FAX MESSAGE (1 page) (hcch.net)> accessed 31 August 2021.

[363] According to Articles 33 and 34 of the Brussels Ia Regulation, a second seised EU court may in the interests of the proper administration of justice (in a discretionary way somewhat analogous to *forum non conveniens*) decline jurisdiction in favour of the first seised non-EU court. See P Beaumont, 'Forum Non Conveniens and the EU rules on Conflicts of Jurisdiction: A Possible Global Solution' [2018] Revue critique de droit international privé 447 (hereafter Beaumont, 'Forum Non Conveniens').

[364] cf Case C-281/02 *Owusu v Jackson* [2005] ECR I-1383; see A Layton, 'The Brussels I Regulation in the International Legal Order: Some Reflections on Reflectiveness' in E Lein (ed), *The Brussels I Review Proposal Uncovered* (BIICL 2012) 75.

courts are no longer constrained by EU law from granting anti-suit injunctions to restrain proceedings in EU Member States.[365] The grounds on which an anti-suit injunction may be granted include the breach of a legal or equitable right,[366] non-contractual wrongs,[367] or interference with the jurisdiction of the English court.[368] As an equitable remedy, the English court has discretion whether to grant an anti-suit injunction to restrain a party from commencing or continuing with litigation abroad.[369] Failure to obey an anti-suit injunction will constitute a contempt of court, which could lead to a fine, imprisonment, and, ultimately, sequestration of assets.[370] A party with any presence or assets in the England and Wales would have to comply with the injunction or reconcile itself to the loss of those assets. The negative function of comity serves as a short-hand expression for the rules of jurisdiction in public international law, that limit the extent to which one state may

[365] See generally, T Raphael QC, *The Anti-Suit Injunction* (2nd edn, OUP 2019); A Dickinson, 'Taming Anti-suit Injunctions' in Dickinson and Peel (eds), *A Conflict of Laws Companion* (n 54) ch 4; Section 37(1) of the Senior Courts Act 1981; Section 50 of the Senior Courts Act 1981 restates the power to grant damages in lieu of an injunction originally granted to the Court of Chancery by Section 2 of the Chancery Amendment Act 1858, commonly known as Lord Cairns' Act. The mutual trust constraints laid down by the CJEU in Case C-159/02 *Turner v Grovit* [2004] ECR I-3365 and Case C-185/07 *Allianz SpA v West Tankers Inc* [2009] ECR I-663, no longer prevent an English court from granting anti-suit injunctive relief or alternative remedies.

[366] This includes the breach of a right not to be sued in the non-elected forum arising under a choice of court agreement or arbitration agreement. See *Donohue v Armco Inc* [2001] UKHL 64, [2002] 1 Lloyd's Rep 425; *Ust-Kamenogorsk Hydropower Plant JSC v AES Ust-Kamenogorsk Hydropower Plant LLP* [2013] UKSC 35, [2013] 1 WLR 1889, [2013] 1 CLC 1069, [21]–[28] (Lord Mance). In *Masri v Consolidated Contractors* [2008] EWCA Civ 625, [2009] QB 503, Lawrence Collins LJ, who accepted *obiter* with some reluctance that the authorities supported the existence of a legal or equitable right in 'single forum' cases, held after full argument that there was no relevant equitable right in 'alternative forum' cases.

[367] *Turner v Grovit* [2001] UKHL 65, [2002] 1 WLR 107.

[368] *SAS Institute Inc v World Programming* [2020] EWCA Civ 599; *Masri v Consolidated Contractors International (UK) Ltd (No 3)* [2008] EWCA Civ 625, [2009] QB 503 (Lawrence Collins LJ); *Ahmed v Mehmet* [2014] EWCA Civ 277 (instituting proceedings in respect of a matter which has already been adjudicated in England with a view to undermining the English judgment).

[369] *Airbus Industrie GIE v Patel* [1998] UKHL 12, [1999] 1 AC 119 (Lord Goff); *The Angelic Grace* [1995] 1 Lloyd's Rep 87, 96 (CA) (Millett LJ). cf *Highland Crusader LP v Deutsche Bank AG* [2009] EWCA Civ 725, [50] (Toulson LJ); *Re Maxwell Communications Corporation plc* (No 2) [1992] BCC 757 (Hoffmann J).

[370] In *Dell Emerging Markets (EMEA) Ltd v Systems Equipment Services SARL* [2020] EWHC 561 (Comm), Mr Justice Henshaw handed down sentences of between nine and 18 months to the directors of one of Dell's Lebanese distributors for procuring breaches of anti-suit injunctions. A party who fails to comply with an anti-suit injunction will be in contempt of an English court order, which is a criminal offence punishable by up to two-years' imprisonment. Committal orders may be made against directors of a company to which an injunction is addressed (CPR 81.4(3)), provided a copy of the order containing the injunction has been served in accordance with CPR 81.5–81.8 and was brought to the attention of the relevant director. See also, *Hin-Pro International Logistics Limited v Compania Sud Americana De Vapores S.A.* [2015] EWCA Civ 401, [6] (Christopher Clarke LJ) An application for committal against a director of the company who was actively involved in the breach of an anti-suit injunction also succeeded in *Trafigura Pte Ltd v Emirates General Petroleum Corp (EMARAT)* [2010] EWHC 3007 (Comm) (Teare J), where the director was committed to prison for a period of twelve months. Furthermore, any foreign judgment obtained in breach of anti-suit injunction will not be enforceable in England.

permissibly intervene in the affairs of another. It is in this sense that English courts have used comity as a factor limiting the grant of anti-suit injunctions.[371]

English courts are aware that anti-suit injunctions can be perceived as inherently opposed to comity and have always endeavoured to reconcile anti-suit injunctions with comity. Lord Hobhouse in *Turner v Grovit* emphasised that English law attaches high importance to comity and the English court has in mind how the 'restraining order'[372] will be perceived by foreign courts.

English case law reveals the existence of two competing conceptions of comity. The development of the anti-suit injunction in English law is premised on a narrow interpretation of the principle of comity.[373] According to this approach, the demands of comity are satisfied provided that the English court has a sufficient interest in granting the relief.[374] Inspired by judicial authority from other common law jurisdictions English courts have sometimes adopted a broader interpretation of comity. This approach considers that the 'sufficient interest' or connection principle enunciated by Lord Goff in *Airbus Industrie GIE v Patel* imposes a necessary but not sufficient condition for compliance with comity.[375] The broad theory of comity limits anti-suit injunctions to situations where the foreign court has exercised an exorbitant jurisdiction, save to protect its own jurisdiction, or otherwise enforce public policy. The strong conception potentially precludes the restraint of foreign proceedings except in cases involving an abuse of process of the English courts, and where the enforcement of contractual rights is sought. Lord Goff's position in *Airbus Industrie v Patel* prevails as a matter of authority, and only that view is consistent with the current approach of the English courts. But it remains possible that the interface between anti-suit injunctions and comity will in the future come before the UK Supreme Court.[376]

It has been doubted whether comity is a consideration where relief is sought to enforce an English arbitration agreement or exclusive choice of court agreement.[377] In such cases it has been said that 'the true role of comity is to ensure that

[371] C McLachlan, *Lis Pendens in International Litigation* (Martinus Nijhoff 2009) ch 2, 172–79 (hereafter McLachlan, *Lis Pendens*).

[372] 'Restraining order': alternative terminology for an anti-suit injunction adopted by Lord Hobhouse in *Turner v Grovit*. However, subsequent English decisions have not adopted the term 'restraining order' and have continued to utilise the conventional nomenclature.

[373] L Collins, 'Comity in Modern Private International Law' in J Fawcett (ed), *Reform and Development of Private International Law: Essays in Honour of Sir Peter North* (OUP 2002) 89; A Briggs, 'The Principle of Comity in Private International Law' (2012) 354 Recueil des Cours 65, 181–82.

[374] *Airbus Industrie GIE v Patel* [1998] UKHL 12, [1999] 1 AC 119 (Lord Goff).

[375] *Amchem Products Inc v British Columbia (Workers Compensation Board)* (1993) 102 DLR (4th) 96 [29]–[30], [61] (Supreme Court of Canada) (Sopinka J); *Highland Crusader LP v Deutsche Bank AG* [2009] EWCA Civ 725 (Toulson LJ); *Star Reefers Pool Inc v JFC Group Co Ltd* [2012] EWCA Civ 14 (Rix LJ); *Re Maxwell Communications Corporation plc* (No 2) [1992] BCC 757 (Hoffmann J); McLachlan, *Lis Pendens* (n 664) 161–63.

[376] Fentiman, *International Commercial Litigation* (n 163) 537.

[377] Collins, 'Comity in Modern Private International Law' (n 373) 102; Fentiman, *International Commercial Litigation* (n 163) 528; R Fentiman, 'Comity and Antisuit Injunctions' (1998) 57 Cambridge Law Journal 467, 467.

the parties' agreement is respected', not to inhibit the grant of relief. In a significant passage, Millett LJ drew a distinction between cases where breach of contract is alleged, and those where the abusive nature of the respondent's conduct is in issue. In the latter case, comity may be an issue, but not it seems in the former:[378]

> In my judgment, the time has come to lay aside the ritual incantation that this is a jurisdiction which should only be exercised sparingly and with great caution. There have been many statements of great authority warning of the danger of giving an appearance of undue interference with the proceedings of a foreign court. Such sensitivity to the feelings of a foreign court has much to commend it where the injunction is sought on the ground of forum non conveniens or on the general ground that the foreign proceedings are vexatious or oppressive but where no breach of contract is involved. In the former case, great care may be needed to avoid casting doubt on the fairness or adequacy of the procedures of the foreign court. In the latter case, the question whether proceedings are vexatious or oppressive is primarily a matter for the court before which they are pending. But in my judgment there is no good reason for diffidence in grating an injunction to restrain foreign proceedings on the clear and simple ground that the defendant has promised not to bring them.

The role of comity in cases involving the enforcement of contractual dispute resolution clauses has been touched upon by the UK Supreme Court.[379] The UK Supreme Court confirmed the exercise of the power to grant the injunction enforcing the arbitration agreement even where no arbitration was contemplated or afoot.[380] However, Lord Mance observed that there will be cases involving the breach of such agreements where 'the appropriate course will be to leave it to the foreign court to recognise and enforce the parties' agreement on forum'.[381] The Supreme Court also clarified that the reference in Section 44(2)(e) of the Arbitration Act 1996 to the granting of an interim injunction was not intended either to exclude the court's general power to act under Section 37 of the Senior Courts Act 1981 in circumstances outside the scope of Section 44 of the 1996 Act or to duplicate part of the general power contained in Section 37 of the 1981 Act.[382]

The near irrelevance of comity in cases involving a breach of an exclusive choice of court agreement or arbitration agreement can be hard to justify in principle. The English court has derived its right to intervene from the parties' contractual choice of England as the forum for the substantive dispute. However, from a truly

[378] *The Angelic Grace* [1995] 1 Lloyd's Rep 87, 96 (CA) (Millett LJ).
[379] *Ust-Kamenogorsk Hydropower Plant JSC v AES Ust-Kamenogorsk Hydropower Plant LLP* [2013] UKSC 35, [2013] 1 WLR 1889, [2013] 1 CLC 1069 (Lord Mance).
[380] ibid [60].
[381] ibid [61].
[382] ibid [48].

international systemic perspective this may not be enough to justify the award of an anti-suit injunction or damages for breach of an exclusive choice of court agreement.

It has been argued that in order for an anti-suit injunction or the damages remedy in such a case to be reconcilable with comity, there would at least have to be some system-transcendent reason why it was appropriate for English private international law rules to be given overriding effect, and for the English courts to intervene.[383] Possible contenders for a system-transcendent rationale include the principle of freedom of contract or *pacta sunt servanda*: if the parties have elected to contract under a particular system of law, including that system's conflict of laws rules, and for the exclusive jurisdiction of that system's courts, then their personal choices should be respected, and their personal obligations enforced, and it is legitimate for the chosen court to enforce those obligations.

However, the existence of a 'system-transcendent rationale' underpinning the enforcement of exclusive choice of court agreements via anti-suit injunctions and the damages remedy may be challenged.[384] First, the use of the term 'system-transcendent rationale' alludes to the fact that the justification offered is descriptive and of general applicability. However, the very concept of a system-transcendent postulate is undermined by the relative inability of any legal system to overcome its own normative biases and prejudices. Therefore, it may not be appropriate at all to use the term 'system-transcendent rationale' where a legal system's approach towards a seemingly 'neutral' or 'value-free' concept is laden with normative and interpretive meaning. For instance, the conception that exclusive choice of court agreements are ordinary contractual obligations that can be enforced in the same way as other contractual obligations is not adhered to in many civil law legal systems.[385] Notwithstanding any argument premised on a fallacious system-transcendent rationale, the right to rely on the foreign court's law and policy choices still cannot be overridden.

Having realised the futility of postulating and relying on a 'system-transcendent rationale', it essentially comes down to a fundamental choice between values: does the importance that comity places on the sovereignty of other legal systems and their right to impose their own law and policy choices require non-intervention, irrespective of any system-transcendent rationale? Or will the importance of

[383] Raphael, *The Anti-Suit Injunction* (n 365) 19–20, 201–03.

[384] Raphael acknowledges that a system-transcendent rationale will ultimately reflect the English courts' view of transcendence: Raphael, *The Anti-Suit Injunction* (n 365) 19. In *Hin-Pro International Logistics Limited v Compania Sud Americana De Vapores SA* [2015] EWCA Civ 401 (Christopher Clarke LJ), the application of common law principles of contractual interpretation to a choice of court clause contained in a bill of lading rendered it 'exclusive' and the continuation of the anti-suit injunction was affirmed. There is a danger that the principle of comity may become undermined in such cases. See FWH Chan, 'Anti-suit Injunctions and the Doctrine of Comity' (2016) 79 Modern Law Review 341.

[385] cf The 'procedural contract' conception of choice of court agreements examined in Ahmed, *Choice of Court Agreements* (n 7) ch 4.

achieving practical justice, and enforcing a party's personal obligations, according to the originating system's own perception of what is right (tempered, of course, by the widest possible conception of a system-transcendent rationale that is necessarily 'internationalist' in spirit), be sufficient to warrant an order against the party concerned, even at the price of tensions with comity? The English common law conflict of laws chooses the latter result.

The courts' previous tendency to overlook the jurisdiction to grant relief, and the more current failure to recognise the importance of comity, reflect the idea that jurisdiction is supplied by the existence of a ground for relief and that comity can be no problem if that is the case.[386] The principles of equity persuade us that the court can do as it likes to prevent unconscionable conduct.[387] To adapt a phrase, we may assume that extremism in the pursuit of material justice in the individual instance is no vice. However, there is a difference—between an equitable approach, led by the imperative of achieving material injustice *inter partes* in the individual case, and an international approach, driven by concerns about jurisdictional connection, comity, and conflicts justice.[388] A practical example of viewing the same decision from different perspectives and value systems is offered by *West Tankers*:[389] is it a question of whether the English court trusts the Italian court or whether English private international law rules should be applied to determine whether the English arbitration clause is applicable, valid, and effective?

If the UK accedes to the Lugano II Convention at some point in the future, there can be little doubt that English courts will not be able to grant anti-suit injunctions against proceedings in Lugano II Convention Contracting States.[390] The prohibition against anti-suit injunctions is based on an inherent principle of the Brussels

[386] For the difference between 'jurisdiction to prescribe' (subject matter jurisdiction) and 'jurisdiction to adjudicate' and the negative international repercussions of relying exclusively on the existence of the latter in cross-border civil and commercial litigation before the English courts, see *Masri v Consolidated Contractors (No 2)* [2008] EWCA Civ 303, [2009] 2 WLR 621, [35] (Lawrence Collins LJ), a Court of Appeal decision concerning a receivership order in respect of foreign assets of a foreign company: 'Consequently the mere fact that an order is in personam and is directed towards someone who is subject to the personal jurisdiction of the English court does not exclude the possibility that the making of the order would be contrary to international law or comity, and outside the subject matter jurisdiction of the English court'; TC Hartley, 'Jurisdiction in Conflict of Laws—Disclosure, Third-party Debt and Freezing Orders' (2010) 126 Law Quarterly Review 194, 194–202; A Johnson, 'Morrison v National Australia Bank: Foreign Securities and the Jurisdiction to Prescribe' in D Fairgrieve and E Lein (eds), *Extraterritoriality and Collective Redress* (OUP 2012) 379, 384–85.

[387] The reference to 'just and convenient to do so' in Section 37(1) of the Senior Courts Act 1981 is indicative of the context in which the provision operates: 'The High Court may by order (whether interlocutory or final) grant an injunction or appoint a receiver in all cases in which it appears to the court to be *just and convenient to do so*' (emphasis added).

[388] For a discussion of the difference between 'conflicts justice' and 'material justice', see, SC Symeonides, *The American Choice-of-Law Revolution: Past, Present and Future* (Martinus Nijhoff 2006) 404–11.

[389] A Briggs, 'The Impact of Recent Judgments of the European Court on English Procedural Law and Practice' (2005) II (124) Zeitschrift fur Schweizerisches Recht 231–62.

[390] Briggs, *Civil Jurisdiction* (n 21) 641; Hartley, *Civil Jurisdiction* (n 173) 375.

regime[391] that no court is better placed to determine the jurisdiction of a Member State court than the courts of that Member State.[392] The minor differences between the Lugano II Convention and the Brussels Ia Regulation do not have an impact on this fundamental principle.[393] In any case, *West Tankers* was decided under the Brussels I Regulation (2001) and the Lugano II Convention is equivalent to the Brussels I Regulation in this matter. Notwithstanding, it would be difficult to fathom that the EU would permit the UK to join the Lugano II Convention if there was any possibility of anti-suit injunctions being granted in relation to proceedings to which it applies.

The International Law Association's *Leuven/London Principles on Declining and Referring Jurisdiction in Civil and Commercial Litigation*[394] adopt a restrictive approach to anti-suit injunctions. Subject to the exception in Principle 7.3, Principle 7.1 accepts that there is no place for such a remedy where both states are parties to an international convention specifying common rules for the exercise of original jurisdiction. Nor indeed should such a remedy be ordered where the court is satisfied that the other court will apply the Principles.[395] In this way, the Committee sought to build the idea that ordinarily deference should be given to the court seised of the substantive proceedings, at least where that court has rules permitting it to decline jurisdiction in certain cases.[396] Significantly, Principle 7.3 qualifies both of the previous principles by permitting an exception in the case of a manifest breach of an exclusive choice of court clause under the law of both states.

The International Law Institute's *Resolution on The Principles for Determining when the Use of the Doctrine of Forum Non Conveniens and Anti-suit Injunctions is Appropriate*[397] adopts a more liberal approach towards anti-suit injunctions:[398]

[391] Case C-185/07 *West Tankers Inc v Allianz SpA* EU:C:2009:69, [2009] 1 AC 1138, [35]: 'It is incompatible with [the Brussels I Regulation] ... for a court of a Member State to make an order to restrain a person from commencing or continuing proceedings before the courts of another Member State on the ground that such proceedings would be contrary to an arbitration agreement.'

[392] See Case C-185/07 *West Tankers Inc v Allianz SpA* EU:C:2009:69, [2009] 1 AC 1138, [29]; Case C-159/02 *Turner v Grovit* [2004] ECR I-3565, [26]; Case C-116/02 *Erich Gasser GmbH v MISAT Srl* [2003] ECR I-14693, [48]; Case C-351/89 *Overseas Union Insurance and Others* [1991] ECR I-3317, [23]–[24].

[393] There is no equivalent in the Lugano II Convention to Article 73(2) and Recital 12 of the recast Brussels Ia Regulation.

[394] Resolution 1/2000, (2000) 69 ILA Rep Conf 13; Report (2000), 69 ILA Rep Conf 137.

[395] Principle 7.2.

[396] *Amchem Products Inc v Workers Compensation Board* (1993) 102 DLR (4th) 96 (Supreme Court of Canada) (Sopinka J).

[397] International Law Institute, Bruges Session 2003, Second Commission, 2 September 2003 (Rapporteur: Sir Lawrence Collins, Co-rapporteur: M Georges Droz) in 'Texts, Materials and Recent Developments' (2003) 5 Yearbook of Private International Law 337, 338.

[398] ibid, Principle 5; ML Niboyet, 'Le Principe de Confiance Mutuelle et Les Injonctions Anti-Suit' in P de Vareilles-Sommieres (ed), *Forum Shopping in the European Judicial Area* (Hart Publishing 2007) 77, 85, highlights that the 2003 Bruges Resolution states that anti-suit injunctions are not, in principle, contrary to international law. It is the exercise of the power to grant the anti-injunction that determines whether their use is appropriate.

> Courts which grant anti-suit injunctions should be sensitive to the demands of comity, and in particular should refrain from granting such injunctions in cases other than (a) a breach of a choice of court agreement or arbitration agreement; (b) unreasonable or oppressive conduct by a plaintiff in a foreign jurisdiction; or (c) the protection of their own jurisdiction in such matters as the administration of estates and insolvency.

The systemic conception of private international law as an international system for the allocation of adjudicatory authority reduces the need to control international parallel proceedings unilaterally through the pre-emptory exercise of exorbitant jurisdiction. However, international judicial cooperation in civil and commercial matters is an emergent phenomenon. Therefore, the 'jungle of separate, broadly based, jurisdictions all over the world'[399] may necessitate the use of anti-suit injunctions, damages, and anti-enforcement injunctions to achieve material justice between the parties in individual instances.

It has been observed that the broad concept of comity accommodates anti-suit injunctions to curb the exercise of exorbitant and extraterritorial jurisdiction by a foreign court:[400] 'The foreign court, not having, itself, observed the rules of comity, cannot expect its decision to be respected on the basis of comity.' The broad concept will also permit the English courts to restrain the breach of an exclusive choice of court agreement or arbitration agreement. Moreover, a court is also entitled to preserve the integrity of its own process. It remains possible that the compatibility of anti-suit injunctions with the two unresolved conceptions of comity will come before the UK Supreme Court after Brexit.

2. *Forum Non Conveniens*

Outside the scope of the Hague Choice of Court Convention, the English court may decide that it will not exercise adjudicatory authority over the dispute by declining jurisdiction. Unlike the mandatory direct rules of jurisdiction of the Brussels–Lugano regime, the English common law rules draw a distinction between the *existence* and *exercise* of jurisdiction. Where the claimant invokes the jurisdiction of the English court on the basis of the defendant's presence in England or the claimant is seeking permission under CPR 6.36 for process to be served abroad, the court has discretion whether or not to assume jurisdiction. Originally, the approaches in the two types of case were very different. During the first three-quarters of the twentieth century, the court would not stay proceedings

[399] *Airbus Industrie GIE v Patel Airbus Industrie GIE v Patel* [1998] UKHL 12, [1999] 1 AC 119, 132–33 (Lord Goff).

[400] *Amchem Products Inc v Workers Compensation Board* (1993) 102 DLR (4th) 96.

brought against a defendant who was present in England unless the commencement of proceedings was vexatious or oppressive.[401] The traditional attitude of the English courts encouraged forum shopping which was elegantly encapsulated by Lord Denning: 'if the forum is England, it is a good place to shop in, both for the quality of the goods and the speed of the service'.[402] By contrast, in cases brought under CPR 6.36, it has been established since the nineteenth century that permission to serve out of jurisdiction requires the claimant to show that England is the appropriate forum.[403]

As a result of a series of decisions,[404] the House of Lords moved from the position that a stay would be granted only if the English proceedings were vexatious or oppressive to the modern position that a stay should be granted if there is an available forum which is more appropriate than the English court. Lord Goff's speech in *The Spiliada* is the cornerstone of the modern law on *forum non conveniens*.[405]

Section 49 CJJA provides that nothing in the Act shall prevent the UK courts from staying, striking out, or dismissing any proceedings on the ground of *forum non conveniens* or otherwise, where to do so is not inconsistent with the Hague Choice of Court Convention.[406] Outside the scope of the Hague Convention, the English courts will revert to the broader application of the doctrine of *forum non conveniens* even in cases where previously it could not be employed as a result of the limitations of EU civil procedural law.[407] Post Brexit, an English court may decide not to exercise jurisdiction by staying proceedings where the preponderance of connecting factors point towards the availability of another forum that is more appropriate for the trial of the dispute. The two pronged *Spiliada* approach to *forum non conveniens* has provided a fine-tuned response to jurisdictional battles in international commercial litigation by balancing the demands of a natural forum abroad with the interests of justice requiring the matter to be nevertheless heard in England.[408] If the UK accedes to the Lugano II Convention at some point in the future, the doctrine of *forum non conveniens* would almost certainly be prohibited if an English court has jurisdiction under the Convention.[409]

401 *St Pierre v South American Stores (Gath and Chaves) Ltd* [1936] 1 KB 382.

402 *The Atlantic Star* [1973] QB 364, 382.

403 *Societe Generale de Paris v Dreyfus Bros* (1885) 29 Ch D 239.

404 *The Atlantic Star* [1973] QB 364; *MacShannon v Rockware Glass Ltd* [1978] AC 795; *Amin Rasheed Shipping Corporation v Kuwait Insurance Co* [1984] AC 50; *The Abidin Daver* [1984] AC 398.

405 [1987] AC 460.

406 Article 5(2) of the Hague Convention.

407 *Kennedy v The National Trust for Scotland* [2019] EWCA Civ 648, [2020] QB 663; In *Cook v Virgin Media* [2015] EWCA Civ 1287, [25], the Master of the Rolls refers to Professor Adrian Briggs QC in *Civil Jurisdiction and Judgments* (6th edn) at 2.28: 'a matter is demonstrably wholly internal to the United Kingdom ... is not one in which the Regulation is designed to have any role'. cf Case C–281/02 *Owusu v Jackson* [2005] ECR I-1383.

408 *Spiliada Maritime Corpn v Cansulex Ltd (The Spiliada)* [1987] AC 460 (Lord Goff).

409 Hartley, *Civil Jurisdiction* (n 173) 374.

The *lis pendens* rule coordinates the multilateral jurisdictional regime of the Brussels Ia Regulation by minimising the risk of irreconcilable judgments.[410] The English common law jurisdictional regime does not possess a first come, first served coordination mechanism. Indeed, the unilateral nature of the common law jurisdictional regime and the relative tolerance of parallel proceedings obviate the need for such multilateral coordination. However, where proceedings between the same parties arising out of the same dispute are also pending in a foreign court the English court will often be a less appropriate forum than it would have been in the absence of the foreign proceedings.[411] *Lis pendens* is only one factor which has to be weighed against the other connecting factors in the search for the natural forum.[412] Where foreign proceedings have progressed significantly and judgment is expected the argument that the foreign court is the more appropriate forum is very substantial.[413] The first limb of *The Spiliada forum non conveniens* test enables an English court to stay its proceedings if it considers that the existence of the international parallel proceedings, amongst other factors, renders the foreign forum better placed to resolve the dispute.[414]

The Spiliada forum non conveniens test relies on litigating parties providing a list of connecting factors to the trial judge to consider where the court would not be referred to other decisions on other facts and that submissions would be measured in 'hours and not days'.[415] It was expected that an appeal should be rare and

[410] cf The UK Supreme Court's majority decision in *The Alexandros T* [2013] UKSC 70; [2014] 1 All ER 590 (Lord Clarke with whom Lord Sumption and Lord Hughes agree) confirms a narrow approach to the 'same cause of action' issue and ensures that the *lis pendens* provision bites in relatively straightforward situations where the causes of action are 'mirror images' of one another. The proceedings may fall within Article 28 of the Brussels I Regulation (Article 30 of the Recast Regulation), being a related action, but the UK Supreme Court confirmed the line of authority that the existence of the choice of court agreement has the effect that a court will not exercise its discretion to stay its proceedings: *Nomura International Plc v Banca Monte Dei Paschi Di Siena SpA* [2013] EWHC 3187 (Comm) (Eder J); *Nordea Bank Norge ASA, Vasonia Shipping Company Limited v Unicredit Corporate Banking SpA, Banca di Roma SpA* (2011) EWHC 30 (Comm) (Gloster J); *JP Morgan Europe Ltd v Primacom AG* [2005] 2 Lloyd's Rep 665 (Cooke J); Fentiman, *International Commercial Litigation* (n 163) 398; T Kruger, *Civil Jurisdiction Rules of the EU and their Impact on Third States* (OUP 2008) 309–11. cf J Hill and A Chong, *International Commercial Disputes* (4th rev edn, Hart Publishing 2010) 291; Joseph, *Jurisdiction and Arbitration* (n 271) 494–95. Proceedings in both the English and the Greek courts were allowed to continue in parallel. It should be observed that the UK Supreme Court's overly narrow and instrumental conception of the 'same cause of action' may give rise to irreconcilable judgments, which the *lis pendens* provision in the Brussels I Regulation is designed to eliminate from the very outset.

[411] In *The Abidin Daver* [1984] AC 398, the House of Lords held that the English proceedings should be stayed in the face of prior Turkish proceedings between the Turkish ship-owners and Cuban ship-owners for damage arising from a collision between their ships in Turkish waters.

[412] AT von Mehren and E Gottschalk, *Adjudicatory Authority in Private International Law* (Martinus Nijhoff 2007) 363 (hereafter von Mehren and Gottschalk, *Adjudicatory Authority*). See *Stonebridge Underwriting Ltd v Ontario Municipal Insurance Exchange* [2010] 2 CLC 349; *Faraday Reinsurance Co Ltd v Howden North America Inc* [2012] 2 CLC 956; *Niche Products Ltd v Macdermid Offshore Solutions LLC* [2014] FSR 21.

[413] *Cleveland Museum of Art v Capricorn Art International SA* [1990] 2 Lloyd's Rep 166.

[414] A Arzandeh, 'Should the *Spiliada* Test Be Revised?' (2014) 10 Journal of Private International Law 89, 92.

[415] *Spiliada Maritime Corpn v Cansulex Ltd (The Spiliada)* [1987] AC 460, 465. (Lord Templeman).

the appellate court should be reluctant to interfere.[416] The practical experience of courts in England has been to the contrary. The time, cost, and court resources expended in jurisdictional disputes have been highlighted by the senior judiciary over the years.[417]

In the context of human rights and environmental damage litigation by foreign claimants against UK based multinational companies the availability of *forum non conveniens* may help the courts to ward off jurisdictional challenges at the outset. However, in exceptional cases, the claimant's lack of financial and litigation strength in the natural forum may be considered under the interests of justice limb of *The Spiliada* test which may lead to an English court deciding not to stay proceedings.[418] English law does not expressly endorse a 'forum of necessity' doctrine but in the latter instance English courts might demonstrate a willingness to function as such.[419]

It is argued that if the Australian 'clearly inappropriate forum'[420] test is adopted in this context, it is unlikely that a foreign claimant seeking compensation from a parent company in an English court would see the case dismissed on *forum non conveniens* grounds.[421] Under the Australian *Voth* test, the judge's focus should

416 ibid.

417 *Voth v Manildra Flour Mills Pty Ltd* (1990) 171 CLR 538, 565, 571 (HC); *Societe Commerciale de Reassurance v Eras International Ltd.* [1992] 1 Lloyd's Rep. 570, 614. (Mustill LJ, Nourse LJ, and Nicholls LJ); *Hindocha & Ors v Gheewala & Ors (Jersey)* [2003] UKPC 77; *Deripaska v Cherney (No 2)* [2009] EWCA Civ 849, [2010] 2 All ER (Comm) 456, [6]–[7] (Waller LJ); *VTB Capital plc v Nutritek International Corp* [2013] UKSC 5, [2013] 2 AC 337, [82]–[83] (Lord Neuberger); *Altimo Holdings and Investment Limited v Kyrgyz Mobil Tel Limited* [2011] UKPC 7, [2012] 1 WLR 1804, [7] (Lord Collins); *Vedanta v Lungowe* [2019] UKSC 20, [6]–[14] (Lord Briggs); *Okpabi v Shell* [2021] UKSC 3, [107] (Lord Hamblen).

418 See *Connelly v RTZ Corpn plc (No 2)* [1998] AC 854, 873 (Lord Goff); *Lubbe v Cape plc* [2000] 1 WLR 1545, 1555 (Lord Bingham). cf Lord Hoffman in his dissenting judgment reasoned that the refusal of a stay due to the lack of financial and litigation strength of the claimant in the natural forum cannot be based upon any defensible principle. 'It means that the action of a rich plaintiff will be stayed while the action of a poor plaintiff in respect of precisely the same transaction will not': *Connelly v RTZ Corpn plc (No 2)* [1998] AC 854, [39]. At [41], Lord Hoffman also referred to the floodgates argument with respect to the liability of a parent company in England: 'any multinational with its parent company in England will be liable to be sued here in respect of its activities anywhere in the world'. See also, *Vedanta v Lungowe* [2019] UKSC 20, [93].

419 For an example of a *forum necessitatis* provision, see, Article 3 of the Swiss Federal Act on Private International Law (1987). The European Commission considered including a *forum necessitatis* provision in the Brussels Ia Regulation (2012) but no consensus was reached and the proposal was not part of the final version.

420 *Voth v Manildra Flour Mills Pty Ltd* (1990) 171 CLR 538 (HC); *Regie National des Usines Renault SA v Zhang* [2002] HCA 10 (HC); *CSR Ltd v Cigna Insurance Australia Ltd* (1997) 189 CLR 345 (HC).

421 M Ahmed, 'Private International Law and Substantive Liability Issues in Tort Litigation against Multinational Companies in the English Courts: Recent UK Supreme Court Decisions and Post-Brexit Implications' (2022) 18 Journal of Private International Law ; P Prince, 'Bhopal, Bougainville and Ok Tedi: Why Australia's Forum Non Conveniens Approach is Better' (1998) 47 International and Comparative Law Quarterly 573, 597 (hereafter Prince, 'Australia's Forum Non Conveniens'). The converse of this approach has been adopted in the cross-border defamation law of England and Wales. The jurisdictional rule in Section 9 of the Defamation Act 2013 provides that England and Wales should be 'clearly the most appropriate place' in which to bring an action in respect of a libelous statement. The curtailment of the phenomena of 'libel tourism' in English courts is the statutory intent of this jurisdictional provision.

be upon the inappropriateness of the local court and not the appropriateness or comparative appropriateness of the suggested foreign forum. The evaluative process under *Voth* should simply be about assessing whether enough of the relevant factors indicate that the forum is clearly inappropriate. A diminished, but acceptable, global role for *forum non conveniens* is also based on a 'clearly inappropriate' forum test.[422] The International Law Association's *Leuven/London Principles on Declining and Referring Jurisdiction in Civil and Commercial Litigation*[423] and the International Law Institute's *Principles for Determining when the Use of the Doctrine of Forum Non Conveniens and Anti-suit Injunctions is Appropriate*[424] support a 'manifestly more appropriate' and 'clearly more appropriate' *forum non conveniens* test respectively. The 'clearly inappropriate forum' test applies the relatively strict standard that a stay should only be granted if proceedings would cause a serious injustice by being oppressive and vexatious to the defendant. The Australian *forum non conveniens* approach in effect acts as a barrier against Australian multinationals seeking to escape the jurisdiction of Australian courts in relation to their overseas conduct.[425]

Indeed, jurisdictional certainty and efficiency will be fostered as a result of a test whose methodologically pluralist parameters are less discretionary than the wide ranging evaluative enquiry undertaken in the quest for the natural forum.[426] If *forum non conveniens* is confined to cases where the other forum is clearly more appropriate, relatively little predictability is lost as claimants have the opportunity to bring their actions in the more appropriate forum.[427] The augmented predictability that results from acceptance of the 'clearly more appropriate' test could well channel litigation to that forum without the need to invoke *forum non conveniens*.[428] From a comparative law standpoint, the adoption of the Australian common law variant of *forum non conveniens* will effectively synthesise *The Spiliada*'s evaluative enquiry

[422] See Article 22 in the Summary of the Outcome of the Discussion in Commission II of the First Part of the Diplomatic Conference 6–20 June 2001 Interim Text Prepared by the Permanent Bureau and the Co-reporters <jdgm2001draft_e.PDF> accessed 31 August 2021. Beaumont, 'Forum Non Conveniens' (n 363) 447, advances a global solution to the conflicts of jurisdiction by balancing the EU *lis pendens* rule with a clearly circumscribed and exceptionally applicable *forum non conveniens*.

[423] Principle 4.3 of Resolution 1/2000, (2000) 69 ILA Rep Conf 13; Report (2000), 69 ILA Rep Conf 137.

[424] Principles 1, 2, and 4 of the International Law Institute, Bruges Session 2003, Second Commission, 2 September 2003 (Rapporteur: Sir Lawrence Collins, Co-rapporteur: M Georges Droz) in 'Texts, Materials and Recent Developments' (2003) 5 Yearbook of Private International Law 337, 338.

[425] Prince, 'Australia's Forum Non Conveniens' (n 421) 597; Briggs, *Civil Jurisdiction* (n 21) 445; A Reed, 'To Be or Not To Be: The Forum Non Conveniens Performance Acted out on Anglo-American Courtroom Stages' (2000) 29 Georgia Journal of International and Comparative Law 31, 125.

[426] See *Vedanta v Lungowe* [2019] UKSC 20, [6]–[14] and *Okpabi v Shell* [2021] UKSC 3, [107]. The need to overhaul the costly and time consuming Goffian *forum conveniens* model in the post-Brexit legal environment has been suggested in Dickinson, 'Walking Solo' (n 59). Dickinson suggests that the wide-ranging evaluative enquiry can be reined in by shifting the burden of proof in its entirety to the defendant and requiring a clearly more appropriate forum than England for a stay of proceedings.

[427] von Mehren and Gottschalk, *Adjudicatory Authority* (n 412) 350.

[428] ibid.

with the certainty and efficiency inherent in the mandatory rules of direct jurisdiction of the Brussels–Lugano regime.

It should be observed that the High Court of Australia has chosen to amend or replace the *Voth* test in contexts where it was felt to be unworkable, notably in cases involving parallel proceedings and exclusive choice of court agreements.[429] This solution may be criticised for increasing the litigation risk for UK-domiciled companies in this context but it has become imperative that alternatives to the *forum non conveniens* status quo are explored because otherwise access to justice for disadvantaged foreign litigants may be delayed and denied.

The reasons why it has been suggested that Lord Templeman's aspiration in *Spiliada* as to how applications would be dealt with have not been realised are echoed in some of the reasons identified in *Voth* for not adopting the *Spiliada* test:[430] in some cases, the question 'what is the natural and appropriate forum' will be 'by no means easy to answer, particularly at an interlocutory stage of proceedings'; 'the complexity of modern transnational transactions and relationships between parties is such as to indicate that in a significant number of cases there is more than one forum with an arguable claim to be the natural forum'; it is desirable to discourage the litigation of such a potentially difficult question; and that 'there are powerful policy considerations which militate against Australian courts sitting in judgment upon the ability or willingness of the courts of another country to accord justice to the plaintiff in the particular case'.[431]

In hard cases,[432] there may be no easy answers as to the natural forum. In theory, a hard case presupposes that the law is identified, understood, evaluated, and applied by a judge of Herculean stature which would always yield the same ultimate result. In reality, it is impossible to find a perfect judge and there may be more

[429] R Garnett, 'Stay of Proceedings in Australia: A "Clearly Inappropriate" Test?' (1999) 23 Melbourne University Law Review 30.

[430] *Voth v Manildra Flour Mills Pty Ltd* (1990) 171 CLR 538, 558–59 (HC); See A Bell, 'The Natural Forum Revisited' in Dickinson and Peel (eds), *A Conflict of Laws Companion* (n 54) ch 1, 21 (hereafter Bell, 'The Natural Forum Revisited').

[431] In *Amin Rasheed Shipping Corp v Kuwait Insurance Co* [1984] AC 50, 67, Lord Diplock commented on the procedural laws of different countries by referring to the: '[i]nvidious task of making a comparison of the relative efficiency of the civil law and common law procedures for the determination of disputed facts. In my opinion, it would have been wholly wrong for an English court, with quite inadequate experience of how it works in practice in a particular country, to condemn as inferior to that of our own country a system of procedure for the trial of issues of fact that has long been adopted by a large number of both developed and developing countries in the modern world.'

[432] Dworkin defines a 'hard case', as follows: when a certain case cannot be resolved by the use of an unequivocal legal rule, set out by the appropriate body prior to the event, 'then the judge has, accordingly to that theory, a 'discretion' to decide the case either way'. See R Dworkin, *Taking Rights Seriously* (Duckworth 1978) 81. cf Hart uses the problem of 'the core and the penumbra' to illustrate the idea that laws must be related to the meaning of the words, not any natural or moral belief. A 'core' case would be one that the statute is intended to cover. In the classic example, a statute that bans vehicles from a park is obviously intended to cover cars. A 'penumbra' case would be one not considered by the creators of the law, such as a skateboard in the example cited earlier. See HLA Hart, *The Concept of Law* (2nd edn, OUP 1994) 121–50; HLA Hart, 'Positivism and the Separation of Law and Morals' (1958) 71 Harvard Law Review 593.

than one way of identifying, understanding, and weighing inconsistent principles. Eventually, a judge may not arrive at a result approximating to the identity of a singular natural forum. It has been aptly observed that if a supreme court was itself subject to further appeal, there could be little doubt that many of its decisions would be overruled.[433]

It has been argued that the *Spiliada* test has not fared particularly well as times have changed.[434] The success of the *Spiliada* doctrine depends largely on its mutual adoption in states that share a common legal tradition. It has not lived up to the expectations of those who thought that its application would be short, simple, and straightforward.[435]

3. Choice of Court Agreements

Let us suppose that an EU Member State court is first seised and an English court is second seised of proceedings pursuant to a choice of court agreement outside the scope of the Hague Convention.[436] Under the Brussels Ia Regulation, the English courts cannot grant an anti-suit injunction to restrain a party from commencing or continuing with proceedings in the courts of another EU Member State brought in breach of the exclusive choice of court agreement.[437] However, the mutual trust constraints of European civil procedural law no longer apply and the English courts are free to grant anti-suit injunctions ordering parties to stop legal proceedings brought in breach of contract. English courts retain the power to decline jurisdiction based on a choice of court agreement by staying proceedings if there are strong countervailing reasons.[438] Contrary to the position under the Brussels regime,[439] the power to stay proceedings may also be used to give effect to a foreign exclusive choice of court agreement, including where the chosen court is in an EU Member State.[440]

433 See Lord Mance, 'Should the Law Be Certain?' (The Oxford Shrieval Lecture given in the University Church of St Mary The Virgin, Oxford, 11 October 2011). On the veracity of Supreme Court decisions, where the documentary evidence contains a sharp clash of evidence about the facts, the exercise carried out by the judge is an evaluative one, sometimes with a 'predictive' element, and with more than one possible 'right' answer: *AmTrust Europe Ltd v Trust Risk Group SpA* [2015] EWCA Civ 437, [2016] 1 All ER Comm 325 [33] (Beatson LJ).

434 Bell, 'The Natural Forum Revisited' (n 430) 30.

435 ibid.

436 Article 5(2) of the Hague Convention.

437 Case C-159/02 *Turner v Grovit* [2004] ECR I-03565; Case C-116/02 *Erich Gasser Gmbh v MISAT Srl* [2003] ECR I-14693; see Ahmed, '*Alexandros T* Litigation' (n 215) 412–15.

438 *Donohue v Armco Inc* [2001] UKHL 64, [2002] 1 Lloyd's Rep 425. Briggs, *Agreements* (n 314) ch 6.

439 In *Catalyst Investment Group v Lewinsohn* [2009] EWHC 1964 (Ch), [2010] Ch 218, Barling J interpreted *Owusu v Jackson* and decided that the English courts have no power to decline jurisdiction, properly founded on one of the Brussels I grounds of jurisdiction, in favour of a court outside the EU even if it was seised first of an action; cf *Ferrexpo AG v Gilson Investments Limited and ors* [2012] EWHC 721 (Comm) (Andrew Smith J).

440 *The Eleftheria* [1970] P 94; *Evans Marshall & Co Ltd v Bertola SA* [1973] 1 WLR 349; *The El Amria* [1981] 2 Lloyd's Rep 119; *The Sennar (No 2)* [1985] 1 WLR 490. See Ahmed, *Choice of Court Agreements*

The Hague Choice of Court Convention's disconnection clause provides that the EU Member States shall apply the Hague Convention externally[441] but shall apply the EU rules amongst each other. As a consequence, Articles 5 and 6 of the Hague Convention have codified the reflexive effect of the Brussels Ia Regulation in relation to exclusive choice of court agreements in matters within the scope of the Convention. Under Articles 33 and 34 of the Brussels Ia Regulation, the courts of an EU Member State have no power to stay proceedings in favour of English courts despite an English exclusive choice of court clause.

If, contrary to the assumption made above, the Hague Convention was applicable, the courts of an EU Member State that are seised of proceedings in breach of an English exclusive choice of court agreement should defer to the English courts.[442] Moreover, the Hague Convention's system of qualified mutual trust will also permit the use of anti-suit injunctions, the damages remedy for breach of exclusive choice of court agreements and anti- enforcement injunctions where such relief furthers the objective of the Convention.[443] The Hague Convention complemented by the common law's remedies for breach of exclusive choice of court agreements synergises the enforcement of exclusive choice of court clauses in English courts.

I. Interim Conclusion

One might take comfort in the fact that there is nothing in the rules described here that is truly novel. The effect of Brexit will be to extend to the domain formerly occupied by the Brussels–Lugano regime to the private international law rules for situations lacking an EU connection, with which many cross-border lawyers will be familiar. Some will welcome, for instance, the increased role for the doctrine of *forum non conveniens* or the UK courts' unfettered ability to grant anti-suit injunctions. Others will see the transition from a codified and harmonised regime to a complex and piecemeal set of rules as a regression. Notwithstanding, these complexities create an opportunity to review and reform English private international law.[444] The case for reform is even more pertinent now that the UK's application to rejoin the Lugano II Convention has been unsuccessful.

(n 7) 2; E Peel, 'Exclusive Jurisdiction Agreements: Purity and Pragmatism in the Conflict of Laws' [1998] Lloyd's Maritime and Commercial Law Quarterly 182.

441 Article 26(6) of the Hague Convention.
442 Article 6 of the Hague Convention.
443 Ahmed and Beaumont, 'Exclusive Choice of Court Agreements' (n 211).
444 A thoroughly rational roadmap for the future development of private international law in England is sketched in Dickinson, 'Walking Solo' (n 59).

The Hague Choice of Court Convention offers a comprehensive regime for exclusive choice of court agreements within its scope. It provides legal certainty and substantial protection to the jurisdiction of English courts designated in a choice of court clause that will be respected in the rest of the EU Member States. It has been observed that the Hague Convention complemented by the common law's remedies for breach of exclusive choice of court agreements synergises the enforcement of exclusive choice of court clauses in English courts.

3

Recognition and Enforcement of Judgments

A. Introduction

Enforcement risk is a form of litigation risk arising from multistate transactions where a judgment debtor with worldwide assets may disperse or conceal those assets and that a judgment obtained in one court may be unenforceable elsewhere.[1] The rules for the recognition and enforcement of judgments reduce enforcement risk by giving effect to a foreign judgment in the legal order of the state addressed. Foreign judgments may be entitled to recognition and enforcement under one of a number of different legal regimes. The common law rules are applicable to judgments given by the courts of many countries. The Administration of Justice Act 1920 applies to the enforcement of some Commonwealth judgments. The Foreign Judgments (Reciprocal Enforcement) Act 1933, which is a codification of the common law, governs the recognition and enforcement of judgments of some Commonwealth countries and judgments given by some non-Commonwealth countries (including countries in Western Europe and Israel). The 1933 Act was superseded, in civil and commercial matters, by the Brussels Ia Regulation and the Lugano II Convention but the revocation of these instruments in the wake of Brexit may lead to a revival of the bilateral treaties. As regards matters within the scope of Article 1 of the Brussels Ia Regulation, Chapter III applies to judgments given by the courts of EU Member States. There is also provision for the recognition and enforcement in England of judgments granted by the courts of Scotland and Northern Ireland.[2]

Whereas, at common law, foreign judgments are enforced by bringing ordinary proceedings on the judgment, under the various statutory regimes there are special procedures prescribed leading to registration of the judgment. Once registered, a foreign judgment may be enforced in the same way as a judgment of the English court. However, there is no special procedure for the recognition of foreign judgments.

The law on recognition and enforcement of judgments is based on 'an acknowledgement that the society of nations will work better if some foreign judgments

[1] cf 'Venue risk' is a form of litigation risk arising from multistate transactions where the risk to each party is that any dispute will not be resolved in their preferred forum. See R Fentiman, *International Commercial Litigation* (2nd edn, OUP 2015) ch 2 (hereafter Fentiman, *International Commercial Litigation*).

[2] Schedules 6 and 7 of the Civil Jurisdiction and Judgments Act 1982 (CJJA).

Brexit and the Future of Private International Law in English Courts. Mukarrum Ahmed, Oxford University Press.
 DOI: 10.1093/oso/9780192848116.003.0003

are taken to create rights which supersede the underlying cause of action, and which may be directly enforced in countries where the defendant or his assets are to be found'.[3] There are two broad theories that justify the law in this area. The theory of obligation is based on the concept that if the original court assumed jurisdiction on a proper basis the court's judgment should *prima facie* be regarded as creating an obligation between the parties to the foreign proceedings which the English court ought to recognise and where appropriate enforce. In effect, a foreign judgment which orders a judgment debtor to pay damages is to be regarded as creating a debt which the judgment creditor can enforce in England. The alternative theory is based on the idea of reciprocity between states in the recognition and enforcement of judgments. The theory of obligation was adopted by English courts in the nineteenth century and still forms the basis of recognition and enforcement at common law and the statutory schemes premised on the common law.[4] The Brussels Ia Regulation provides for the reciprocal recognition and enforcement of judgments granted by the courts of the EU Member States.[5]

The recognition and enforcement of judgments is limited by a range of defences. Recognition and enforcement is a two-stage process. Once the basic conditions of recognition and enforcement are satisfied, is there a defence due to which the foreign judgment should nevertheless not be recognised or enforced?

Notwithstanding the significance of jurisdictional disputes in English courts, the fundamental purpose of the Brussels regime is to facilitate the free movement of judgments between the EU Member States. The harmonisation of jurisdictional rules was considered necessary in order to achieve the primary objective of the Brussels Ia Regulation. Under the common law rules, it is a necessary requirement for recognition and enforcement that the court of origin of the judgment is a court of competent jurisdiction according to English private international law rules. The Brussels Ia Regulation obviates the need for such an enquiry by simplifying the recognition and enforcement of judgments with uniform direct rules of jurisdiction in civil and commercial matters.

The recognition and enforcement of judgments under the Brussels Ia Regulation is built on the principle of mutual trust between the courts of the Member States.[6] A judgment that is recognised under the Brussels Ia Regulation should in principle have the same effects in the state in which the recognition is sought as it does in the

[3] *Adams v Cape Industries plc* [1990] Ch 433, 552 (Slade LJ).

[4] *Schibsby v Westenholz* (1870) LR 6 QB 155.

[5] Denmark entered into an agreement with the EU so that, under international law, the provisions of Council Regulation (EU) 1215/2012 of the European Parliament and of the Council of 12 December 2012 on jurisdiction and the recognition and enforcement of judgments in civil and commercial matters (recast) [2012] OJ L351/1 (hereafter Brussels Ia Regulation) apply to relations between Denmark and the other EU Member States: OJ 2013 L79/4.

[6] Recital 26 of the Brussels Ia Regulation; Case C-302/13 *flyLAL-Lithuanian Airlines AS v Starptautiskā lidosta Rīga VAS and Air Baltic Corporation AS* EU:C:2014:2319.

state of origin.[7] If a judgment contains a measure or an order which is not known in the law of the Member State addressed, that measure or order shall, to the extent possible, be adapted to a measure or an order known in the law of that Member State which has equivalent effects attached to it and which pursues similar aims and interests.[8]

B. Recognition and Enforcement of Judgments during the Transition Period

During the Brexit transition period, Articles 66 to 69 of the Agreement on the withdrawal of the United Kingdom of Great Britain and Northern Ireland from the European Union and the European Atomic Energy Community, 19 October 2019,[9] contains provisions on jurisdiction, recognition and enforcement of judgments, and the applicable law. The EU Withdrawal Agreement stipulates that the recognition and enforcement of judgments given in legal proceedings instituted before the end of the transition period and authentic instruments formally drawn up or registered and court settlements approved or concluded before the end of the transition period will be governed by the Brussels Ia Regulation.[10] Therefore, English courts will continue to render judgments where jurisdiction is governed by the Brussels Ia Regulation for the foreseeable future. It follows that the judgments provisions of the Brussels–Lugano regime will apply in England for much longer than the jurisdictional rules of those instruments.

C. Recognition and Enforcement of Judgments in the Post-Brexit Landscape: The Common Law Regime

In the absence of the Brussels–Lugano regime for recognition and enforcement of judgments in proceedings commenced after 1 January 2021, it remains necessary to apply national law to recognise and enforce a judgment from an EU Member State court or Lugano II Convention Contacting States in England. This means that the English common law rules relating to the recognition and enforcement of judgments apply where the foreign jurisdictions do not have applicable treaties in place with the UK or in the absence of any applicable UK statute. In most cases, judgment creditors and those seeking recognition of a judgment as *res judicata* will need to rely on the English common law rules for the recognition and enforcement

[7] Case 145/86 *Horst Ludwig Martin Hoffmann v Adelheid Krieg* [1988] ECR -00645; Case C-456/11 *Gothaer Allgemeine Versicherung AG and Others v Samskip GmbH* EU:C:2012:719.
[8] Article 54 of the Brussels Ia Regulation.
[9] EU Withdrawal Agreement.
[10] Article 67(2)(a) of the EU Withdrawal Agreement.

of judgments. However, a judgment given by a court of a Member State designated in an exclusive choice of court agreement shall be recognised and enforced in the UK in accordance with Chapter III of the Hague Choice of Court Convention.[11]

The High Court of England and Wales (Queen's Bench Division) is the relevant court in which to bring an application for the recognition and enforcement of a foreign judgment in England and Wales. Summary judgment procedures will usually be available. The procedures for the enforcement of foreign judgments are governed by Part 74 of the Civil Procedure Rules.

For the purposes of recognition, a judgment must be final and conclusive[12] and on the merits.[13] The recognition of a judgment will generally give rise to an estoppel by binding the parties on any matter of fact or law which was a necessary part of the reasons for the foreign judgment.[14] The extended doctrine of *res judicata* based on abuse of process provides that the parties to litigation before a court of competent jurisdiction must bring forward their whole case and cannot later reopen the litigation by relying on matters which ought to have been brought forward but were omitted owing to negligence, inadvertence, or accident.[15]

For enforcement by an ordinary civil claim based on the judgment debt, a judgment must be final and conclusive and for a definite sum of money. Other judgments, such as provisional judgments or non-money judgments, will not be enforced at common law. The judgment must not have been issued in respect of

[11] Article 8(1) of the Hague Convention.

[12] Final and conclusive means that the judgment is *res judicata* and 'would have precluded the unsuccessful party from bringing fresh proceedings in the [foreign] jurisdiction': *Joint Stock Company 'Aeroflot-Russian Airlines' v Berezovsky and anr* [2014] EWCA Civ 20, [29] (Arden LJ); *Nouvion v Freeman* (1889) 15 App Cas 1 (HL)).

[13] For a particular claim or issue, establishing facts as proved and stating and applying the law to those facts to reach a conclusion (*The Sennar (No 2)* [1985] 1 WLR 490, 499 (Lord Brandon)). So defined, it may be questioned whether this adds anything to the requirement that the judgment be conclusive (ibid, 494 (Lord Diplock)). If anything, it emphasises the need to examine carefully whether the foreign court has, in fact, adjudicated upon a particular matter. *The Sennar (No 2)* [1985] 1 WLR 490, 494 (HL) (Lord Diplock): 'What [on the merits] means in the context of judgments delivered by courts of justice is that the court has held that it has jurisdiction to adjudicate upon an issue raised in the cause of action to which the particular set of facts give rise.' The significance of the use of the word 'adjudicate' as opposed to dismissing the matter procedurally should be noted. For the general principle that an issue estoppel can arise from an interlocutory or interim finding by a foreign court on a procedural or non-substantive matter, see *Desert Sun Loan Corp v Hill* [1996] CLC 1132.

[14] Estoppel includes cause of action estoppel, issue estoppel, and the extended doctrine of *res judicata* based on abuse of process. Section 34 CJJA. See *Republic of India v India Steamship Co Ltd; The Indian Endurance and The Indian Grace* [1998] AC 878 (HL) (Lord Steyn); A Briggs, 'Foreign Judgments and res judicata' (1997) 68 British Yearbook of International Law 355; Fentiman, *International Commercial Litigation* (n 1) 471. For an in-depth discussion of the preclusive effect of the plea of former recovery under Section 34 of the CJJA 1982, see P Barnett, *Res Judicata, Estoppel, and Foreign Judgments: The Preclusive Effects of Foreign Judgments in Private International Law* (OUP 2001) 98–116 (hereafter Barnett, *Foreign Judgments*).

[15] For the domestic doctrine of abuse of process in English law, see *Henderson v Henderson* (1843) 3 Hare 100 (Wigram V-C); *Johnson v Gore Wood & Co* [2002] AC 1 (Lord Bingham). For the international dimension of the doctrine of abuse of process, see *House of Spring Gardens v Waite* [1991] 1 QB 241, 251; *Desert Sun Corp v Hill* [1996] 2 All ER 847, 859, 864; see Fentiman, *International Commercial Litigation* (n 1) 478–79; Barnett, *Foreign Judgments* (n 14) ch 6.

taxes, penalties, or multiple damages awards. A judgment under the Brussels Ia Regulation is defined 'any judgment given by a court or tribunal of a Member State, whatever the judgment may be called, including a decree, order, decision or writ of execution, as well as a decision on the determination of costs or expenses by an officer of the court'.[16] In contrast with the common law, this wide definition of a judgment under the Brussels Ia Regulation includes procedural judgments,[17] interim injunctions, consent orders, and decrees of specific performance. A judgment may be a judgment for the purposes of the Regulation even though it does not determine the substantive merits of the parties' dispute such as a procedural judgment declining jurisdiction on the basis of a foreign choice of court agreement.[18]

In both the recognition and enforcement of judgments, the judgment must have originated from a court of competent jurisdiction according to English private international law rules.[19] These indirect jurisdictional rules are narrowly and closely defined. The defendant must either have been present in the territory of the foreign court when the proceedings in the court of origin were commenced,[20] or must have submitted to the foreign court's jurisdiction, either by prior agreement[21] or by defending the case on the merits without challenging the jurisdiction (or after an unsuccessful challenge), or by counterclaiming in the proceedings.[22] The residence of the defendant within the territory over which the foreign court exercises jurisdiction at the time of commencement of proceedings may also be considered a court of competent jurisdiction.[23] For corporate defendants, the test of presence requires something more than the transitory presence of a representative. Usually a fixed place of business through which the activity in question has arisen will satisfy the requirement of jurisdictional connection.[24]

[16] Article 2(a) of the Brussels Ia Regulation.

[17] Case C-456/11 *Gothaer Allgemeine Versicherung AG and Others v Samskip GmbH* EU:C:2012:719.

[18] ibid.

[19] *Schibsby v Westenholz* (1870) LR 6 QB 155. In general, the competence of the court of origin to adjudicate on the cause of action is irrelevant to the recognition and enforcement of its judgment in England (*Pemberton v Hughes* [1899] 1 Ch 781).

[20] *Adams v Cape Industries plc* [1990] Ch 433 (CA).

[21] *Vizcaya Partners Ltd v Picard and another* [2016] UKPC 5, [2016] 3 All ER 181 (Lord Collins), settled the uncertainty in the common law in relation to whether an agreement to submit must be express, or can also be implied or inferred. The Privy Council adjudicated that consent to jurisdiction can be implied. cf For the position prior to the Privy Council decision, see L Collins and others (eds), *Dicey, Morris & Collins The Conflict of Laws* (15th edn, Sweet and Maxwell, 2012) [14-079]: 'It may be laid down as a general rule that an agreement to submit to the jurisdiction of a foreign court must be express: it cannot be implied.'

[22] *Rubin v Eurofinance SA* [2012] UKSC 46, [2013] 1 AC 236; Section 33 CJJA. cf Section 34 CJJA: 'No proceedings may be brought by a person in England and Wales or Northern Ireland on a cause of action in respect of which a judgment has been given in his favour in proceedings between the same parties, or their privies, in a court in another part of the United Kingdom or in a court of an overseas country, unless that judgment is not enforceable or entitled to recognition in England and Wales or, as the case may be, in Northern Ireland.'

[23] *State Bank of India v Murjani Marketing Group Ltd*, unreported 27 March 1991 (CA).

[24] J Hill and M Ní Shúilleabháin, *Clarkson & Hill's Conflict of Laws* (5th edn, OUP 2016) 175.

If these requirements are met, the judgment will be entitled to recognition or enforcement unless one or more of the defences is established including fraud, infringement of natural justice, public policy, the judgment is invalid under the foreign law, or a dispute resolution agreement has been breached.[25] Section 32 of the Civil Jurisdiction and Judgments Act 1982 (CJJA) can be said to provide a more comprehensive solution to the enforcement of choice of court agreements as compared to the Brussels Ia Regulation. The English common law jurisdiction and judgments regime protects choice of court agreements at both the jurisdictional and the recognition and enforcement stage. At the jurisdiction stage, an anti-suit injunction or the damages remedy coupled with declaratory relief may enforce the choice of court agreement. At the recognition and enforcement stage, Section 32 does not permit the recognition and enforcement of judgments in breach of an English choice of court agreement. This can be supplemented by an anti-enforcement injunction and declaratory relief.

Inconsistency with a prior judgment entitled to recognition and, if appropriate, enforcement in England will also counteract a foreign judgment's enforceability. Subject to these defences, the substance of the foreign judgment will not be reviewed for error.[26] The Hague Choice of Court Convention provides for the recognition and enforcement of judgments based on exclusive choice of court agreements but the defences to recognition and enforcement are more restrictive than the Brussels–Lugano regime.[27]

The absence of the Brussels–Lugano regime may give rise to the question whether the common law is capable of evolving to fill the lacuna by patching together a rule for the reception of foreign authentic instruments into the English legal system.[28] It has been argued that an authentic instrument may arrive for enforcement in England via registration in the Books of Council and Session in Scotland. This registration in accordance with Scots law is then liable to be enforced in England as a Scottish judgment under the CJJA.[29] Apart from this rather unlikely case of double exequatur, the common law cannot recognise authentic instruments because they are not within the common law's definition of judgments. However, they can be used as notarial evidence of the obligation to which they attest so that the claimant can sue on the obligation but this defeats the purpose of a rule for the reception of authentic instruments. As the Brussels–Lugano regime is no longer the law of the land, nothing in the common law can replicate their reception of authentic instruments.

The UK maintains a number of pre-Brussels Convention bilateral treaties for the reciprocal recognition and enforcement of judgments in civil matters with certain

[25] Section 32 CJJA.
[26] *Godard v Gray* (1871) LR 6 QB 139.
[27] Article 9 of the Hague Convention.
[28] J Fitchen, *The Private International Law of Authentic Instruments* (Hart Publishing 2020) 99.
[29] Section 18 CJJA.

EU and EFTA states, which were incorporated into English law under the Foreign Judgments (Reciprocal Enforcement) Act 1933 and the Administration of Justice Act 1920.[30] While it may be arguable that these conventions have not ceased to exist and judgments from these states should be enforceable under the Foreign Judgments (Reciprocal Enforcement) Act 1933, this is likely to be the subject of litigation as these conventions were largely superseded by EU rules and have not been applied since 1987, when the Brussels Convention took effect in the UK.[31]

In the UK, enforcement of judgments from those European jurisdictions may once more need to be effected pursuant to the Foreign Judgments (Reciprocal Enforcement) Act 1933. All other cases will fall under common law according to which a foreign judgment is not directly enforceable in the English courts but can be the subject of a fresh action for enforcement of a debt in the High Court.

These conventions were superseded by the provisions of the Brussels Convention,[32] preserving their effect only for matters falling outside the Convention's scope.[33] The Brussels I Regulation and the Brussels Ia Regulation contain similarly phrased superseding provisions.[34]

After Brexit, the status in international law of these bilateral treaties and the Brussels Convention[35] is unsettled. The revival of the revoked Brussels Convention is in the highest degree unlikely[36] as it would require the courts of the Member States and the Court of Justice of the European Union (CJEU) to agree to the analysis. Moreover, the flaws in the fundamental architecture and territorial scope of the Brussels Convention constitute major impediments.[37]

[30] See the bilateral treaties listed in Article 55 of the 1968 Brussels Convention on jurisdiction and the enforcement of judgments in civil and commercial matters OJ L 299, 31.12.1972, 32 (hereafter Brussels Convention). For example, the bilateral treaties between the UK and France (1934), Germany (1961), Austria (1962), Italy (1964), and the Netherlands (1969).

[31] A Briggs, *Civil Jurisdiction and Judgments* (7th edn, Informa Law from Routledge 2021) 23.

[32] Article 54 of the Brussels Convention.

[33] Article 56, [1] of the Brussels Convention.

[34] Articles 69 and 70(1) of Council Regulation (EC) 44/2001 on jurisdiction and the recognition and enforcement of judgments in civil and commercial matters (Brussels I) [2001] OJ L12/1 (hereafter Brussels I Regulation); Articles 69 and 70(1) of the Brussels Ia Regulation.

[35] A Dickinson, 'No Coming Back?' (*EAPIL Blog*, 19 February 2021) <https://eapil.org/2021/02/19/dickinson-on-the-fate-of-the-1968-brussels-convention-no-coming-back/> accessed 31 August 2021.

[36] A Briggs, 'Secession from the European Union and Private International Law: The Cloud with a Silver Lining' (Commercial Bar Association Brexit Lecture, 24 January 2017) <adrian_briggs_brexit_lecture.pdf> accessed 31 August 2021.

[37] For instance, the Brussels Convention lacks a uniform test for establishing the date of seisin for *lis pendens* purposes (Case 129/83 *Zelger v Salinitri* [1984] ECR 2397; cf Article 32 of the Brussels Ia Regulation; Article 30 of the Lugano II Convention) and the CJEU's commercially inept decision in Case C-116/02 *Erich Gasser GmbH v Misat Srl* [2003] ECR I-14693 will survive. cf Article 31(2)–(4) and Recital 22 of the Brussels Ia Regulation. The special jurisdictional rules for sale of goods and provision of services contracts involving delivery and performance in the EU will also be very different (Article 5(1) of the Brussels Convention; cf Article 7(1)(b) of the Brussels Ia Regulation; Article 5(1)(b) of the Lugano II Convention). It should also be noted that fifteen Member States are Contracting States to the Brussels Convention so the geographic reach of civil judicial cooperation will be significantly reduced.

In contrast with the revoked Brussels Convention, the legislation adopted to give effect to the bilateral treaties remains on the statute book.[38] Although EU law might have displaced the bilateral treaties in so far as the Brussels Ia Regulation also provided a mechanism for the recognition and enforcement of judgments, the Vienna Convention on the Law of Treaties suggests that they remain in effect and are no longer superseded.[39] In any case, suspension was only partial and the bilateral treaties continue to apply to matters falling outside the scope of the Brussels regime such as judgments giving effect to an arbitral award[40] and to judgments ordering repayment of an unfair preference.[41] Significantly, the question whether the bilateral treaties are still in force will be determined ultimately by the UK Supreme Court or the final court of appeal of the Member State concerned and not the CJEU.

If a judgment creditor were to seek to rely upon one of these bilateral treaties in proceedings to secure the recognition and enforcement of a judgment emanating from one of the six Member States before an English court in respect of a matter formerly within the scope of the Brussels regime, the court would need to enquire whether the relevant provisions of the Brussels Convention, alternatively the two Regulations, impliedly repealed[42] the operation of earlier legislation giving effect to the bilateral conventions with respect to matters falling within the Brussels regime at the time when those provisions were given effect in UK law by means of the CJJA[43] and the European Communities Act 1972.[44] As part of that enquiry, the English court would inevitably need to examine the conventions' status in international law and possibly the related question as to the status of the Brussels Convention. The resuscitated operation of the Brussels Convention in the UK would require practical reciprocity on the part of the other Contracting States and may well require changes to legislation or rules of court in those States, which may in the circumstances not be readily forthcoming.

[38] See the statutory instruments made under Section 1 of the Foreign Judgments (Reciprocal Enforcement) Act 1933: Austria (SI 1962/1339), Belgium (SR&O 1936/609), France (SR&O 1936/1169), Germany (SI 1961/1199), Italy (SI 1973/1894), The Netherlands (SI 1979/1063, as amended).

[39] Article 59 of the Vienna Convention on the Law of Treaties.

[40] Section 1(2A) of the Foreign Judgments (Reciprocal Proceedings) Act 1933.

[41] *New Cap Reinsurance Corp Ltd v Grant* [2012] UKSC 46, [2013] 1 AC 236.

[42] The doctrine of implied repeal means that where an Act of Parliament conflicts with an earlier one, the later Act takes precedence and the conflicting parts of the earlier Act become legally inoperable. The latest Act of Parliament will therefore prevail. This notion is linked with the principle of Parliamentary sovereignty and that no Parliament can bind its successor. However, the principle of supremacy of EU law created an exception to the doctrine of implied repeal. In *Thoburn v Sunderland City Council* [2002] EWHC 195 (Admin), Laws LJ held that some constitutionally significant statutes hold a higher status in UK law and are not subject to the doctrine of implied repeal. The case specifically dealt with Section 2(2) of the European Communities Act, but in his judgment Laws LJ also held the view that the Parliament Acts and the Human Rights Act are 'constitutional statutes' and in his opinion may not be subject to the doctrine of implied repeal. In *BH v The Lord Advocate (Scotland)* [2012] UKSC 24, [30], Lord Hope held that 'the Scotland Act can only be expressly repealed; it cannot be impliedly repealed; that is because of its "fundamental constitutional nature"'.

[43] Brussels Convention.

[44] Brussels I Regulation and the Brussels Ia Regulation.

On 29 January 2021, the UK government informed the European Council of its view that the Brussels Convention has ceased to apply to the UK and Gibraltar with the expiry of the transition period on 1 January 2021:[45]

> The Government of the United Kingdom hereby notifies the Secretary-General of the Council of the European Union that it considers that the Brussels Convention 1968 and the 1971 Protocol, including subsequent amendments and accessions, ceased to apply to the United Kingdom and Gibraltar from 1 January 2021, as a consequence of the United Kingdom ceasing to be a Member State of the European Union and of the end of the Transition Period.

In a notable development, the UK and Norway concluded an agreement on the continued application of the pre-existing (1961) bilateral convention on reciprocal recognition and enforcement between them pending the outcome of the UK's application to rejoin the 2007 Lugano II Convention.[46] The agreement on the continued application of the bilateral convention has been given effect by legislation in the UK.[47] The basic premise of the new UK–Norway Convention, and of the legislation giving effect to it, would appear to be that the UK's pre-existing bilateral reciprocal recognition and enforcement conventions do not automatically revive to fill the lacuna left by the Brussels–Lugano regime in relations between the UK and European states.

The German Federal Court of Justice has provided some clarity on the question whether any of the old multilateral or bilateral treaties still apply.[48] The Federal Court of Justice apparently does not treat either the 1968 Brussels Convention on Jurisdiction and the Enforcement of Judgments in Civil and Commercial Matters or the Convention between the United Kingdom and Northern Ireland and the Federal Republic of Germany for the Reciprocal Recognition and Enforcement of Judgments in Civil and Commercial Matters as relevant post Brexit.[49]

45 Letter of the UK Mission to the European Union dated 29 January 2021. <https://conflictoflaws.net/2021/uk-notifies-that-it-considers-the-brussels-and-rome-convention-to-no-longer-apply-to-it/> accessed 31 August 2021.

46 Agreement on the Continued Application and Amendment of the Convention between the Government of the United Kingdom of Great Britain and Northern Ireland and the Government of the Kingdom of Norway Providing for the Reciprocal Recognition and Enforcement of Judgments in Civil Matters signed at London on 12 June 1961 Oslo, 13 October 2020 (CP 314). <https://assets.publishing.service.gov.uk/government/uploads/system/uploads/attachment_data/file/932354/CS_Norway_2.2020_UK_Norway_Agreement_Enforcement_Judgement_Civil_Matters.pdf> accessed 31 August 2021.

47 Reciprocal Enforcement of Foreign Judgments (Norway) (Amendment) (England and Wales and Northern Ireland) Order 2020 (SI 2020/1338); Reciprocal Enforcement of Foreign Judgments (Norway) Amendment (Scotland) Order 2020 (SSI 2020/371).

48 Bundesgerichtshof (BGH), 1 March 2021, X ZR 54/19.

49 ibid.

In any event, it should also be pointed out that the bilateral conventions and the UK legislation giving effect to them were modelled on the rules of the common law, so the differences in substance between the two regimes are relatively small.[50] Procedurally, the bilateral conventions offer the advantage of a streamlined enforcement mechanism by registration, subject to the judgment debtor's right to apply to set aside the judgment on the grounds set out.[51] The status of the bilateral conventions may, therefore, be more significant when it comes to recognition and enforcement of English judgments in the six Member States concerned.

Commonwealth judgments from Cyprus and Malta may be enforced by registration under the Administration of Justice Act 1920, the requirements for which are also modelled on the rules of the common law.

The nineteenth-century common law rules for the recognition and enforcement of judgments need to be reviewed. The rules allow the enforcement of foreign default judgments based only on the defendant's transient presence in the foreign jurisdiction at the time of service. However, a 'real and substantial connection' which could serve as an indirect jurisdictional rule such as the place of performance of a contract or the place where a tort occurred is deemed irrelevant for the purposes of recognition and enforcement.[52] The jurisdictional filters in the Hague Judgments Convention 2019 resemble the connecting factors which justify exorbitant jurisdiction in some legal systems. As a result, the grounds for recognition and enforcement under the Convention are wider than the traditional requirement of a court of competent jurisdiction according to English private international law rules. Legislation will likely be needed if a better set of rules is to be formulated.

D. EU Enforceability: The Hague Convention on Choice of Court Agreements

The comprehensive jurisdictional and recognition and enforcement regime of the Brussels Ia Regulation is not replicated in the Hague Choice of Court Convention which only provides for double convention based on 'exclusive' choice of court agreements. Article 8 provides the general requirements for recognition and

[50] Significantly, mere presence within the territory over which the foreign court exercises jurisdiction does not establish the court's competence under Section 4(2) of the Foreign Judgments (Reciprocal Enforcement) Act 1933, by contrast with the position at common law.

[51] CPR, Part 74, Section I.

[52] A Arzandeh, 'Reformulating the Common Law Rules on the Recognition and Enforcement of Foreign Judgments' (2019) 39 Legal Studies 56, 67, argues that the scope of international jurisdictional competence in common law recognition and enforcement cases should be broadened to include the jurisdictional gateways codified in CPR PD 6B para 3.1. cf A Briggs, *Private International Law in English Courts* (OUP 2014) 497. See also, J Walker, 'The Great Canadian Comity Experiment Continues' (2004) 120 Law Quarterly Review 365 and SGA Pitel, 'A Modern Approach to Enforcing Foreign Judgments' [2004] Lloyd's Maritime and Commercial Law Quarterly 289.

enforcement of judgments under the Hague Convention.[53] The judgment has to be rendered by a court of a Contracting State and the court has to be designated in an exclusive choice of court agreement.[54] The concept of an exclusive choice of court agreement is defined in terms of the formal requirement laid down in Article 3(c) of the Hague Convention and these requirements are imported into Article 8. The position under the Hague Convention is different from the Brussels–Lugano regime because the court addressed decides for itself whether the choice of court agreement is valid but it is bound by any relevant findings of fact by the court of origin.

Once the general requirements have been satisfied, the judgment must be recognised unless there is some reason to the contrary. A review of the merits of the judgment is not permitted.[55] However, this does not prevent recognition from being refused on the basis of public policy. If the proceedings were commenced in the chosen court but that court transferred the matter to another court in the same state,[56] the obligation to recognise the judgments applies unless a party objected to the transfer in a timely manner in the state of origin.[57]

In the post-Brexit legal environment, the English courts may choose to broadly interpret asymmetric choice of court agreements as exclusive choice of court agreements under the Hague Convention to align with the common law and the Brussels Ia Regulation approach and ensure that a greater number of choice of court agreements are brought within the fold of the Hague Convention.[58] However, both the text of the Hague Convention and the Official Explanatory Report only consider mutually exclusive choice of court agreements to be exclusive choice of court agreements for the purposes of the Convention.[59] Significantly, it may be argued that in relation to English proceedings based on an English asymmetric choice of court agreement under Article 5 of the Hague Convention, the other court may not stay

[53] Permanent Bureau of the Conference, *Convention of 30 June 2005 on Choice of Court Agreements: Text and Explanatory Report by Trevor Hartley and Masato Dogauchi* (HCCH Publications 2013) [164]–[181] <https://assets.hcch.net/docs/0de60e2f-e002-408e-98a7-5638e1ebac65.pdf> accessed 31 August 2021. See T Hartley, *Civil Jurisdiction and Judgments in Europe* (OUP 2017) ch 20.

[54] Article 8 covers situations where the court of origin is chosen in an exclusive choice of court agreement but jurisdiction in the court of origin is based on some other ground: Explanatory Report by Professors T Hartley and M Dogauchi (n 53) [164].

[55] Article 8(2) of the Hague Convention.

[56] Article 5(3) of the Hague Convention.

[57] Article 8(5) of the Hague Convention.

[58] In *Etihad Airways PJSC v Prof. Dr. Lucas Flöther* [2019] EWHC 3107 (Comm), [2020] QB 793, [215]–[217] (Jacobs J) and *Commerzbank Aktiengesellschaft v Pauline Shipping and Liquimar Tankers* [2017] EWHC 161 (Comm), [71]–[74] (Cranston J) it was noted that there are 'good arguments' that the definition of exclusive choice of court clauses in Article 3(a) of the Hague Convention covers asymmetric choice of court clauses. However, it should be observed that these *obiter* remarks are not supported by either the text of the Official Explanatory Report or the minutes of the Diplomatic Session. cf The Court of Appeal in *Etihad Airways PJSC v Prof. Dr. Lucas Flöther* [2020] EWCA Civ 1707, [85] (Henderson LJ) referred in *obiter* comments to [106] of the Explanatory Report as 'a strong indication' that asymmetric clauses fall outside the Hague Convention.

[59] Articles 1(1) and 3(a) of the Hague Convention; Explanatory Report by Professors T Hartley and M Dogauchi (n 53) [105]–[106].

proceedings under Article 6 of the Convention and that the English judgment may not be entitled to recognition and enforcement under Article 8 of the Convention. In relation to the latter, the Hague Convention provides that Contracting States may make reciprocal declarations for the recognition and enforcement of judgments based on non-exclusive choice of court agreements.[60] It is recommended that the UK and the EU (as a Regional Economic Integration Organisation)[61] should make a reciprocal declaration under Article 22 of the Convention to enable enhanced judicial cooperation in civil and commercial matters between the UK and the EU within the minimum mandatory framework of the Hague Convention. There has been no positive indication of any reciprocal declarations to date.

If the court first seised adjudicates that the choice of court clause is inapplicable, ineffective, or invalid and arrives at a decision prior to the commencement of proceedings in the chosen court or if no proceedings are instituted in the chosen court at all,[62] there is nothing in the Brussels Ia Regulation expressly providing that the non-chosen court's judgment is not entitled to recognition under Chapter III and the CJEU's ruling in *Gothaer* suggests that such a judgment would be binding.[63] Article 31(2) of the Brussels Ia Regulation only protects exclusive choice of court agreements at the *lis pendens* stage. A judgment contrary to an exclusive choice of court agreement may be recognised and enforced under the Brussels Ia Regulation if Article 31(2) of Brussels Ia is not invoked.[64] However, only a judgment of a chosen court is entitled to recognition and enforcement under the Hague Convention.[65] Recognition or enforcement may be refused only on the grounds specified in the Hague Convention.[66]

If the general requirements for recognition and enforcement are satisfied, the judgment must be recognised and enforced, unless one of the specified grounds for refusal is established.[67] Recognition or enforcement may be refused if:[68]

[60] Article 22 of the Hague Convention.

[61] Article 29 of the Hague Convention.

[62] Q Forner-Delaygua, 'Changes to Jurisdiction Based on Exclusive Jurisdiction Agreements under the Brussels I Regulation Recast' (2015) 11 Journal of Private International Law 379, 392.

[63] Case C-456/11 *Gothaer Allgemeine Versicherung AG v Samskip GmbH* EU:C:2012:719, [2013] QB 548. See C Heinze and B Steinrotter, 'The Revised Lis Pendens Rules in the Brussels Ibis Regulation' in in V Lazic and S Stuij (eds), *Brussels Ibis Regulation: Changes and Challenges of the Renewed Procedural Scheme* (TMC Asser Press/Springer 2017) 1, 22; P Rogerson, 'Chapter 11—Arts 29–30' in A Dickinson and E Lein, *The Brussels I Regulation Recast* (OUP 2015) 330; cf In Case C-438/12 *Weber v Weber* EU:C:2014:212, [55], the CJEU decided that in relation to exclusive jurisdiction under Article 22 of the Brussels I Regulation (Article 24 of the Brussels Ia Regulation): 'if the court first seised gives a judgment which fails to take account of Article 22(1) of Regulation No 44/2001, that judgment cannot be recognised in the member state in which the court second seised is situated'; Recital 12 of the Brussels Ia Regulation clarifies that rulings on the validity or scope of arbitration agreements are no longer to be recognised under the Regulation's provisions, but rulings on the validity of choice of court agreements are not similarly protected.

[64] Case C-456/11 *Gothaer Allgemeine Versicherung AG and Others v Samskip GmbH* EU:C:2012:719.

[65] Article 8(1) of the Hague Convention.

[66] ibid.

[67] Explanatory Report by Professors T Hartley and M Dogauchi (n 53) [182]–[193].

[68] Article 9 of the Hague Convention.

a) the agreement was null and void[69] under the law of the State of the chosen court,[70] unless the chosen court has determined that the agreement is valid;
b) a party lacked the capacity to conclude the agreement under the law of the requested State;
c) the document which instituted the proceedings or an equivalent document, including the essential elements of the claim,
   i) was not notified to the defendant in sufficient time and in such a way as to enable him to arrange for his defence, unless the defendant entered an appearance and presented his case without contesting notification in the court of origin, provided that the law of the State of origin permitted notification to be contested; or
   ii) was notified to the defendant in the requested State in a manner that is incompatible with fundamental principles of the requested State concerning service of documents;
d) the judgment was obtained by fraud in connection with a matter of procedure;
e) recognition or enforcement would be manifestly incompatible with the public policy of the requested State, including situations where the specific proceedings leading to the judgment were incompatible with fundamental principles of procedural fairness of that State;
f) the judgment is inconsistent with a judgment given in the requested State in a dispute between the same parties; or
g) the judgment is inconsistent with an earlier judgment given in another State between the same parties on the same cause of action, provided that the earlier judgment fulfils the conditions necessary for its recognition in the requested State.

In contrast, the Lugano II Convention does not even protect exclusive choice of court agreements at the *lis pendens* stage[71] let alone denying recognition and enforcement to a judgment procured in breach of a choice of court agreement. The future accession of the UK and the EU to the Hague Judgments Convention 2019 will assist in abating pre-emptive torpedo proceedings by enabling the refusal of recognition or enforcement of any judgment given in breach of a choice of court agreement.[72] Moreover, a judgment based on proceedings pursuant to a unilateral

[69] This does not include formal validity of a choice of court agreement. It is intended to encompass fraud, mistake, misrepresentation, duress, and lack of capacity. Explanatory Report by Professors T Hartley and M Dogauchi (n 53) [126].

[70] The law of the chosen forum includes the choice of law rules of that state (*renvoi*). Explanatory Report by Professors T Hartley and M Dogauchi (n 53) [125].

[71] Case C-116/02 *Erich Gasser Gmbh v MISAT Srl* [2003] ECR I-14693; cf Articles 31(2)– (4) and Recital 22 of the Brussels Ia Regulation.

[72] Article 7(1)(d) of the Hague Judgments Convention 2019.

or asymmetric choice of court agreement will be eligible for recognition and enforcement under the Hague Judgments Convention.[73]

E. EU Enforceability: Alternatives to English Exclusive Choice of Court Agreements

If enforceability of a judgment throughout the EU Member States is a significant priority, there are alternative solutions in circumstances where exclusive jurisdiction would have been given to the English courts.

First, select the jurisdiction to the courts of an EU Member State or a Lugano II Convention Contracting State (Norway, Iceland, and Switzerland). This would depend upon being comfortable with proceedings in that court, including as to its procedures, costs, speed, and quality of outcomes. This is already sometimes done in, for example, security agreements where the security in question is located in another EU Member State.

Second, select the non-exclusive jurisdiction of the English courts. This cautious approach hedges the parties' choice of jurisdiction and allows the position to be reconsidered at the time when legal proceedings are commenced. If at that time enforcement remains an important consideration, the non-exclusive choice of court clause will allow the use of a Member State court of competent jurisdiction. A variant of non-exclusive choice of court clauses is the asymmetric or unilateral choice of court agreement, which is commonly used in cross-border finance contracts.[74] This binds one party to sue exclusively in the primary non-exclusive forum but allows the other party to commence proceedings in that court or in any other court of competent jurisdiction.

The French Cour de Cassation called into question the validity of these clauses under Article 23 of the Brussels I Regulation in *Mme X v Rothschild*[75] and Article 23 of the Lugano II Convention in *ICH v Credit Suisse*.[76] The position was ameliorated by the Cour de Cassation's decision in *Apple Sales International v eBizcuss*.[77] However, the first chamber of the Cour de Cassation issued two more decisions, in *Crédit Suisse II*[78] and *Saint-Joseph*,[79] where it reaffirmed its opposition to

[73] Article 5(1)(m) of the Hague Judgments Convention 2019.

[74] See M Ahmed, 'The Legal Regulation and Enforcement of Asymmetric Jurisdiction Agreements in the European Union' (2017) 28 European Business Law Review 403 (hereafter Ahmed, *Asymmetric Jurisdiction Agreements*); L Merrett, 'The Future Enforcement of Asymmetric Jurisdiction Agreements' (2018) 67 International and Comparative Law Quarterly 37.

[75] *Ms X v Banque Privee Edmond de Rothschild Europe (Societe)* Cass civ, 1ere, 26.9.2012, No 11-26.022, [2013] ILPr 12.

[76] *ICH (Societe) v Credit Suisse (Societe)* Cass civ, 1ere, 25.3.2015, No 13– 27.264, [2015] ILPr 39.

[77] *Apple Sales International v eBizcuss* Cass 1ere Civ, 7.10.2015, No 14– 16.898.

[78] Cass. civ. 1e., 7 feb. 2018, n° 16-24.497, D. 2018, 1934, S. Bollée; JDI 2018, comm. 16, note M.-E. Ancel et L. Marion.

[79] Cass. civ. 1e., 3 oct. 2018, n° 17-21.309, JDI 2018, comm. 16, note M.-E. Ancel et L. Marion, JCP G 2018, note F. Mailhé.

asymmetric choice of court clauses.[80] The Cour de Cassation chose to quash the decisions that had refused to set the clause aside (Saint-Joseph) and confirmed that which had accepted to do it (Crédit Suisse II). The decisions are both justified at length, but the most interesting is the latter one. Referring to the 'high degree of predictability' that such clauses should ensure and to the CJEU's *Coreck Maritime* decision about the necessity of 'objective elements' to allow for the determination of the designated courts,[81] the higher court decides that the fact that the clause 'did not correspond to the objective of predictability' because it 'did not hold any reference to a rule of competence applicable in a Member-State (of the European Union) nor any objective element precise enough to allow for the identification of the courts which could be seised'.[82]

Under the present state of the law in France, unless such clauses therefore refine the option offered to one of the parties to limit it to a specific connecting factor (even as vague as 'the place of the harm' from the eBizcuss case) or to specific rules of jurisdiction (Article 7(1) of the Brussels Ia Regulation on contractual matters, as may be supposed, for example), they may be set aside.

Significantly, the Court of Appeal of England and Wales in *Etihad Airways PJSC v Prof. Dr. Lucas Flöther* has confirmed that the protective cover of Article 31(2) of the Brussels Ia Regulation extends to asymmetric choice of court clauses.[83] Nonetheless, doubts as a matter of EU law are not of significance now that the UK is outside the EU and English courts have traditionally enforced these clauses.[84] It could, however, affect EU Member States' courts' approach to the choice of court

[80] Mailhé highlights that France is in dire need of reconciliation between two diverging case law trends regarding the validity of asymmetric choice of court clauses in F Mailhé, 'France: A Game of Asymmetries, Optional and Asymmetrical Choice of Court Agreements Under French Case Law' in M Keyes (ed), *Optional Choice of Court Agreements in Private International Law* (Ius Comparatum, Global Studies in Comparative Law, Springer 2019) <https://doi.org/10.1007/978-3-030-23914-5_8> accessed 31 August 2021.

[81] Case C-387/98 *Coreck Maritime GmbH v Handelsveem BV* [2000] ECR I-09337.

[82] The clause stated that 'ne contenait aucun renvoi à une règle de compétence en vigueur dans un Etat membre ni aucun élément objectif suffisamment précis pour identifier la juridiction qui pourrait être saisie, de sorte qu'elle ne répondait pas à l'objectif de prévisibilité'.

[83] *Etihad Airways PJSC v Prof. Dr. Lucas Flöther* [2020] EWCA Civ 1707, [93] (Henderson LJ); *Etihad Airways PJSC v Prof. Dr. Lucas Flöther* [2019] EWHC 3107 (Comm), [2020] QB 793 (Jacobs J); In *Commerzbank Aktiengesellschaft v Pauline Shipping and Liquimar Tankers* [2017] EWHC 161 (Comm), [52], [64], Cranston J decided that Article 31(2) covered asymmetric choice of court clauses even though the clause was exclusive in relation to the defendant's claim only. In *Perella Weinberg Partners UK LLP, Perella Weinberg Partners (Europe) LP v Codere SA* [2016] EWHC 1182 (Comm), [18], Walker J had also made an *obiter* remark that Article 31(2)'s protective cover extends to asymmetric choice of court clauses. For a critique of the view that Article 31(2) applies to exclusive choice of court agreements, see Ahmed, *Asymmetric Jurisdiction Agreements* (n 74).

[84] See *Continental Bank NA v Aeakos Compania Naviera SA* [1994] 1 WLR 588, 592F-594G (CA) (Steyn LJ); *Mauritius Commercial Bank Limited v Hestia Holdings Limited and Sujana Universal Industries Limited* [2013] EWHC 1328 (Comm), [2013] 2 Lloyds Rep 121, [37] (Popplewell J); *Bank of New York Mellon v GV Films* [2009] EWHC 2338, [14]; *Credit Suisse First Boston (Europe) Ltd v MLC (Bermuda) Ltd* [1999] 1 All ER 237, 249G-250A.

clause, but that is in any event a matter of some uncertainty until finally resolved by the CJEU.[85]

The Court of Appeal's view in *Etihad Airways PJSC v Prof. Dr. Lucas Flöther*, however, was that there were strong indications that the intention was to exclude asymmetric choice of court clauses from the Hague Convention.[86] Article 3(a) of the Hague Convention defines an exclusive choice of court agreement as:

> an agreement concluded by two or more parties that meets the requirements of paragraph c) and designates, for the purpose of deciding disputes which have arisen or may arise in connection with a particular legal relationship, *the courts of one Contracting State or one or more specific courts of one Contracting State to the exclusion of the jurisdiction of any other courts*[87]

The exclusion of asymmetric choice of court clauses from the Hague Convention is evident from the Explanatory Report of Professors Hartley and Dogauchi:[88]

> It was agreed by the Diplomatic Session that, in order to be covered by the Convention, the agreement must be exclusive irrespective of the party bringing the proceedings.

The rejection of an amendment expressly to include asymmetric choice of court clauses in the Hague Convention's definition of an exclusive choice of court clause supports this conclusion.[89] It should be observed that the Court of Appeal's view on the Hague Convention's applicability to asymmetric choice of court clauses was *obiter* as it was not necessary to adjudicate on the merits of the issue to resolve the dispute. As a consequence, it is likely that the issue of the compatibility of asymmetric choice of court clauses with the Hague Convention will be brought

[85] The CJEU's position on this matter is unclear and the Brussels Ia Regulation has not endeavoured to clarify the status of these clauses in the EU law of international civil procedure.

[86] The Court of Appeal in *Etihad Airways PJSC v Prof. Dr. Lucas Flöther* [2020] EWCA Civ 1707, [85] (Henderson LJ) referred in *obiter* comments to [106] of the Explanatory Report by Professors T Hartley and M Dogauchi as 'a strong indication' that asymmetric clauses fall outside the Hague Convention. cf In *Etihad Airways PJSC v Prof. Dr. Lucas Flöther* [2019] EWHC 3107 (Comm), [2020] QB 793, [215]-[217] (Jacobs J) and *Commerzbank Aktiengesellschaft v Pauline Shipping and Liquimar Tankers* [2017] EWHC 161 (Comm), [71]–[74] (Cranston J) it was noted that there are 'good arguments' that the definition of exclusive choice of court clauses in Article 3(a) of the Hague Convention covers asymmetric choice of court clauses. However, it should be observed that these *obiter* remarks are not supported by either the text of the Official Explanatory Report or the minutes of the Diplomatic Session.

[87] Emphasis added.

[88] Explanatory Report by Professors T Hartley and M Dogauchi (n 53) [105]–[106]; *Etihad Airways PJSC v Prof. Dr. Lucas Flöther* [2020] EWCA Civ 1707, [85].

[89] The Diplomatic Minutes of the Meeting of Wednesday 15 June 2005. The minutes show that a proposal by the Swiss delegate to amend the proposed definition of an 'exclusive choice of court agreement' so as to make it clear that it included asymmetric choice of court agreement (by inserting the words 'for some or all of the parties to the agreement') was debated but found no support. The amendment was then withdrawn. *Etihad Airways PJSC v Prof. Dr. Lucas Flöther* [2020] EWCA Civ 1707, [86].

before the English courts in the near future. If it is held that such clauses are excluded from the Hague Convention, pre-emptive proceedings in an EU Member State court may be commenced on a cause of action within the scope of an English asymmetric choice of court agreement. The EU Member State court will not be able to stay proceedings under Article 6 of the Hague Convention. However, such incursions by reincarnations of the torpedo may now be dealt with swiftly and effectively by an armoury consisting of anti-suit injunctions, damages, and anti-enforcement injunctions.

Third, arbitration is a possibility. Arbitration is already commonly used if enforcement is important and the counterparty has assets in a location where an English judgment is not enforceable because of the extensive reach of the 1958 New York Convention on the Recognition and Enforcement of Foreign Arbitral Awards.[90] All EU Member States are parties to the New York Convention, which provides for the enforcement in participating states of an arbitral award given in another participating state. An arbitration seated in a participating state, whether the UK, an EU Member State, or elsewhere, should therefore be able to produce an award enforceable throughout the EU. The post-Brexit English courts will also be able to grant anti-suit injunctions against proceedings in an EU Member State court in breach of an English arbitration agreement. Under the Brussels Ia Regulation, the principle of mutual trust and the principle of effectiveness of EU law (*effet utile*) prevent the courts of one Member State from restraining pre-emptive proceedings brought before the courts of another Member State in breach of an arbitration agreement.[91]

F. Intra-UK Recognition and Enforcement of Judgments

The CJJA provides for the recognition and enforcement of judgments from one part of the UK to another.[92] A judgment obtained in Scotland or Northern Ireland can be registered and enforced in England. No jurisdictional requirements need to be satisfied in relation to the proceedings in the court of origin. It is sufficient that the judgment was granted and that the time for an appeal has expired or any appeal has been disposed of. Enforcement is not confined to money judgments. Decrees of specific performance and injunctions are also enforceable.

It would seem that the common law defences of fraud, natural justice, and public policy do not apply to judgments given by the courts of other parts of the UK.[93] The

[90] United Nations Convention on the Recognition and Enforcement of Foreign Arbitral Awards, 10 June 1958, 330 UNTS 4739.

[91] Case C-185/07 *Allianz SpA v West Tankers Inc* [2009] ECR I-00663; Case C-536/13 *'Gazprom' OAO v Lietuvos Respublika* ECLI:EU:C:2015:316; *Nori Holdings v Bank Otkritie* [2018] EWHC 1343 (Comm), [2018] 2 Lloyd's Rep 80 (Males J).

[92] Sections 18 and 19; Schedules 6 and 7 of the CJJA.

[93] *Clarke v Fennoscandia Ltd* 1998 SC 464.

aggrieved party must seek the appropriate relief in the court of origin. Section 32 of the CJJA Act 1982 also does not apply to judgments originating from another part of the UK.[94] However, a judgment of the courts of Scotland and Northern Ireland cannot be enforced in England if it conflicts with a prior English judgment.[95]

G. Interim Conclusion

The loss of EU private international law and the Brussels Ia Regulation, in particular, will impact the mobility of English judgments in Europe and vice versa. Moreover, the effect of English judgments in Europe will be less than would be the case if the UK was allowed to join the Lugano II Convention. The revival of the pre-Brussels Convention bilateral treaties offers a glimmer of hope but the conclusion of agreements on the continued application of the bilateral conventions on reciprocal recognition and enforcement between the UK and the Member States should be able to guarantee access to this route.

The Hague Choice of Court Convention provides for the recognition and enforcement of judgments in the courts of Member States where the judgment originated from an English court designated in an exclusive choice of court clause. In the future, the recognition and enforcement of judgments regime between the UK and the EU will be the Hague Judgments Convention 2019 which will complement the Hague Choice of Court Convention. A judgment based on proceedings pursuant to a unilateral or asymmetric choice of court agreement is eligible for recognition and enforcement under the Hague Judgments Convention.[96] The Convention will also reduce the venue and enforcement risk arising from pre-emptive torpedo proceedings by refusing to recognise or enforce any judgment given in breach of a choice of court agreement.[97]

[94] Section 32(4) CJJA.
[95] Para 10(b) of Schedule 6 and para 9(b) of Schedule 7.
[96] Article 5(1)(m) of the Hague Judgments Convention 2019.
[97] Article 7(1)(d) of the Hague Judgments Convention 2019.

4
The Applicable Law

A. Introduction

This chapter will discuss the issues arising from the UK's decision to incorporate the Rome I Regulation[1] and the Rome II Regulation[2] into domestic law at the end of the post-Brexit transition period.[3] Unlike the Brussels Ia Regulation, the Rome I and II Regulations do not require reciprocity and have an *erga omnes* effect. This means that EU Member State courts will apply the Rome I and II Regulations after Brexit to cases with a connection to the UK according to the principle of universal application.[4] The Rome I and II Regulations ensure legal certainty, deter forum shopping, and promote decisional harmony in cross-border civil and commercial relations in the European Union. The incorporation of the Rome I and II Regulations into English domestic law ensures continued uniformity with the EU Member States in the significant area of the applicable law for cross-border contractual and non-contractual obligations.

The UK government set out its legislative plan to deliver Brexit in its White Paper, *Legislating for the United Kingdom's Withdrawal from the European Union*, published in March 2017.[5] The White Paper noted that converting EU law into UK law would not be sufficient to provide 'a smooth and orderly exit' because a large proportion of the converted law would not function properly when transplanted from the EU context to the new domestic context.[6] The EU Withdrawal Act 2018 (EUWA 2018) therefore contains powers to enable corrections to be made to the new body of law to overcome this issue. The EUWA 2018 is a statute of constitutional significance. It repeals the European Communities Act 1972 and fills the void left by EU law across a huge swathe of the UK statute book by creating a new and unique legal category termed retained EU law in the domestic law of the UK. The concept of retained EU law ensures continuity and legal certainty in the legal

[1] Regulation (EC) No 593/2008 on the law applicable to contractual obligations (Rome I), [2008] OJ L177/6 (hereafter Rome I Regulation).

[2] Regulation (EC) No 864/2007 on the law applicable to non-contractual obligations (Rome II), [2007] OJ L199/40 (hereafter Rome II Regulation).

[3] The Law Applicable to Contractual Obligations and Non-Contractual Obligations (Amendment etc) (EU Exit) Regulations 2019, SI 2019 No 834.

[4] Article 2 of the Rome I Regulation and Article 3 of the Rome II Regulation.

[5] Department for Exiting the European Union, *Legislating for the United Kingdom's Withdrawal from the European Union* (White Paper, Cm 9446, 2017).

[6] E Duhs and I Rao, *Retained EU Law: A Practical Guide* (The Law Society 2021) 2.

Brexit and the Future of Private International Law in English Courts. Mukarrum Ahmed, Oxford University Press.
 DOI: 10.1093/oso/9780192848116.003.0004

systems of the UK whilst also making provision for change where necessary. The Rome I Regulation and the Rome II Regulation remain part of UK domestic law as retained EU law.

The methodologically pluralist Rome I and Rome II Regulations offer a codified taxonomy that represents a significant improvement to the common law's piecemeal rules for determining the law applicable to contractual and non-contractual obligations.[7] Notably, the Rome II Regulation acknowledges that there are certain types of tort for which a modified, and more complex, rule is required because the basic architecture of these torts is distinct from the ordinary tort.[8] Provision is also made for the applicable law for restitution and unjust enrichment claims.[9] The Rome I Regulation regulates asymmetrical contracts such as consumer contracts or employment contracts.[10]

The dominant feature of modern choice of law codifications such as the Rome I and II Regulations has been defined as 'eclecticism'[11] where the drafters have had no qualms about combining ideas such as multilateralism with unilateralism and conflicts justice with material justice. The more traditional *Savigny*-inspired multilateral approach to the choice of law process which continues to prevail in Europe and most other parts of the world leans towards the goal of multilateral 'conflicts justice' but has made concessions to 'material justice' with the inclusion of unilateral choice of law rules.[12] The 'dichotomy' between 'conflicts justice' and 'material justice' should not be perceived as a dilemma and a focus on the question of when,

[7] A Briggs, 'Secession from the European Union and Private International Law: The Cloud with a Silver Lining' (Commercial Bar Association Brexit Lecture, 24 January 2017) <https://www.law.ox.ac.uk/sites/files/oxlaw/adrian_briggs_brexit_lecture.pdf> accessed 31 August 2021.

[8] Articles 5–9 of the Rome II Regulation.

[9] Articles 10–12 of the Rome II Regulation. See *Banque Cantonale de Geneve v Polevent Ltd and others* [2015] EWHC 1968 (Comm). cf for the common law rules, See *Barros Mattos (Jr) v MacDaniels Ltd* [2005] EWHC 1323 (Ch), [119]: 'an uncertain and developing area of the law'; *Dexia Crediop SpA v Comune di Prato* [2016] EWHC 2824 (Comm), [161]: 'I do not accept that Rule 230(2), as it appears in the 14th edition, gives a clear statement applicable to the restitution counterclaim. The sub-paragraphs of paragraph (2) of Rule 230 are introduced by the term "(semble)"'.

[10] Articles 6–8 of the Rome I Regulation.

[11] SC Symeonides, *Codifying Choice of Law Around the World* (OUP 2014) 348–49 (hereafter Symeonides, *Codifying Choice of Law*); H Batiffol, 'Le pluralisme des méthodes en droit international privé' (1973) 139 Recueil des Cours 75, 106; B Audit, 'Rapport Français' in S Symeonides (ed), *Private International Law at the End of the 20th Century: Progress or Regress?* (Kluwer Law International 1999) 191, 210; A Bucher, La dimension sociale du droit international privé (Cours general) (2009) Recueil des Cours 341; C Roodt, 'Reflections on Theory, Doctrine and Method in Choice of Law' (2007) 40 Comparative and International Law Journal of Southern Africa 76.

[12] PJ Borchers, 'Categorical Exceptions to Party Autonomy in Private International Law' (2008) 82 Tulane Law Review 1645, 1655 (hereafter Borchers, 'Categorical Exceptions'), notes that '[t]he European notion of mandatory rules is an intellectual cousin of Currie's interest analysis'; R Michaels, 'Post-critical Private International Law: From Politics to Technique' in H Muir Watt and DP Fernandez Arroyo (eds), *Private International Law and Global Governance* (OUP 2014) 54, favours the traditional continental private international rules and concludes that the next step for the existing European rules would be to show the extent to which they are already capable of integrating and formulating the political concerns that underlie the US conflict of laws revolution.

how, and how much considerations of material justice should temper the search for conflicts justice is apposite.[13]

The procedural law of the forum is immune from the effects of choice of law.[14] Significantly, the English common law's right–remedy approach to the substance–procedure distinction adopts a wide view of the proper and legitimate scope of the law of procedure.[15] However, the EU instruments on the applicable law in contractual and non-contractual matters have reduced the scope of the law of the forum, as compared to the English common law of conflict of laws.[16]

The English common law's treatment of foreign law may be pragmatic and cost-efficient but it lacks a conception of foreign law that is principled, multilateral, and does not discriminate based on the origin of the law.[17] Foreign law is a question of fact for the English courts.[18] Therefore, the foreign law has to be pleaded by the party seeking to rely on the law. Furthermore, the content of the foreign law has to be proved to the satisfaction of the court. If neither party pleads the applicability of foreign law, the court will apply English domestic law to the issues in dispute. The English court has neither power nor duty to apply foreign law *ex officio*. It may be observed that contract and tort cases litigated in the English courts will frequently be decided by application of English domestic law, even though choice of law rules might have indicated that a foreign law should be applied.[19] The difficulties in determining, understanding, and correctly applying foreign law cannot be understated.[20]

Even in the absence of an express choice of law agreement, the presence of an exclusive choice of court agreement may serve as evidence of an implied choice in favour of the law of the chosen court.[21] In this regard, Recital 12 of the Rome

13 SC Symeonides, *The American Choice-of-Law Revolution: Past, Present and Future* (Martinus Nijhoff 2006) 410; Symeonides, *Codifying Choice of Law* (n 11) 347–48.

14 *Lex fori regit processum*: 'the law of the forum governs procedure'. See n 71.

15 *Cox v Ergo Versicherung AG* [2014] UKSC 22, [2014] 1 AC 1379, [23] (Lord Sumption); Section 14 of the Private International Law (Miscellaneous Proceedings) Act 1995 as interpreted by *Harding v Wealands* [2006] UKHL 32, [2007] 2 AC 1; *Boys v Chaplin* [1971] AC 356; R Garnett, *Substance and Procedure in Private International Law* (OUP 2012), 7–10 (hereafter Garnett, *Substance and Procedure*); M Bogdan, *Private International Law as Component of the Law of the Forum* (Martinus Nijhoff 2012) ch VIII, 193 (Bogdan, *PIL as Law of the Forum*).

16 The Rome I and II Regulations adopt a direct approach, whereby certain issues are subjected to the applicable law of the obligation (for the existence, nature and assessment of damage, see, *Wall v Mutuelle De Poitiers Assurances* [2014] EWCA Civ 138; Article 15(c) Rome II; Article 12(1)(c) Rome I; for limitation of actions, see, Article 15(h) Rome II; Article 12(1)(d) Rome I) and others, for example formal validity, to the law of the obligation or the law of the country of performance of the act (*lex loci actus*), see, Article 21 Rome II; Article 11(1) Rome I. Garnett, *Substance and Procedure* (n 15) 37–39.

17 See S Geeroms, *Foreign Law in Civil Litigation* (OUP 2004) 30–34 (hereafter Geeroms, *Foreign Law*).

18 See generally, R Fentiman, *Foreign Law in English Courts* (OUP 1998) (hereafter Fentiman, *Foreign Law*); For a discussion on the *sua sponte* application of choice of law rules and foreign law: Bogdan, *PIL as Law of the Forum* (n 15) ch VI, 'Should Conflict Rules and Foreign Law Be Applied Ex Officio?'

19 A Briggs, *The Conflict of Laws* (OUP 2013), 9 (hereafter Briggs, *Conflict of Laws*).

20 Lord Mance, 'The Future of Private International Law' (2005) 1 Journal of Private International Law 185, 191.

21 The choice of a particular forum may indicate that the parties intend the contract to be governed by the law of that forum. For a discussion of the English common law presumption *Qui elegit judicem*

I Regulation prescribes an exclusive choice of court agreement as one of the factors to be taken into account in determining whether a choice of law has been clearly demonstrated.

In transaction planning and litigation strategy, choice of law considerations cannot be ignored as they may strongly influence where a party chooses to sue if the choice of law rules of that forum give a wide effect to the choice of law agreement in the absence of any countervailing factors such as overriding mandatory rules and the public policy of the forum. On the other hand, a party seeking to avoid the choice of law agreement may seek a forum, which limits the autonomy of the parties as to choice of law, restricts the scope of the applicable law or contains an anomalous public policy provision, which overrides the applicable law. The applicable law is a factor to consider in determining the natural forum for the purposes of the doctrine of *forum non conveniens*.[22] An English choice of law agreement also provides a jurisdictional gateway for service out of the jurisdiction with the permission of the English court.[23]

B. Applicable Law during the Transition Period

During the Brexit transition period, Articles 66 to 69 of the Agreement on the withdrawal of the United Kingdom of Great Britain and Northern Ireland from the European Union and the European Atomic Energy Community, 19 October 2019,[24] contains provisions on jurisdiction, recognition, and enforcement of judgments and the applicable law. The EU Withdrawal Agreement stipulates that, the Rome I Regulation shall apply in the UK in respect of contracts concluded before the end of the transition period.[25] The EU Withdrawal Agreement provides that the Rome II Regulation shall apply in the UK in respect of events giving rise to damage, where such events occurred before the end of the transition period.[26] The remaining EU Member States will of course continue to apply the Rome I and II Regulations in EU–UK relations during the transition period according to the principle of universal application.[27]

elegit jus, see BA Marshall, 'Reconsidering the Proper Law of the Contract' (2012) 13 Melbourne Journal of International Law 1, 15–17. See M Giuliano and P Lagarde, 'Report on the Convention on the Law Applicable to Contractual Obligations' [1980] OJ C282/1, 16.

22 *Spiliada Maritime Corporation v Cansulex Ltd* [1987] 1 AC 460, 478 (HL) (Lord Goff).
23 CPR PD 6B para 3.1(6)(c).
24 EU Withdrawal Agreement.
25 Article 66(a) of the EU Withdrawal Agreement.
26 Article 66(b) of the EU Withdrawal Agreement.
27 Article 2 of the Rome I Regulation and Article 3 of the Rome II Regulation.

C. Applicable Law in the Post-Brexit Landscape

The provisions of the Rome I Regulation, the Rome II Regulation, and the Rome Convention constitute retained EU law under the EU Withdrawal Act and are subject to the modifications laid down in the Law Applicable Exit Regulations.[28] These Regulations amend the existing EU legislation in order to convert them into the retained Rome instruments.[29] The EU Regulation on the negotiation of third country agreements with respect to contractual and non-contractual obligations is revoked.[30] On 29 January 2021, the UK government informed the European Council of its view that the Rome Convention has ceased to apply to the UK and Gibraltar with the expiry of the transition period on 1 January 2021.[31]

1. Contractual Obligations

The amendments that the Law Applicable Exit Regulations make to the text of the retained Rome I Regulation are mostly consequential and intelligible.[32] The reference in Article 2 (universal application) to the law of 'a Member State' is replaced by the law of 'the United Kingdom or a part of the United Kingdom'[33] and the application of Occam's razor omits Articles 22(2), 26, 27, and 29.[34] However, the legislator has chosen to retain the elements of Article 3(4) and Article 7 that treat situations connected with EU Member States differently from other situations.

Under Article 3(4), retained EU law, as defined by the Withdrawal Act, cannot be derogated from by agreement by selecting a law that is not the law of a 'relevant state'[35] if all other elements relevant to the situation at the time of choice are located in a relevant state.[36] Therefore, mandatory rules of retained EU law will be applied by an English court where apart from the law chosen by the parties all other relevant elements are located in an EU Member State or the UK.[37]

[28] The Law Applicable to Contractual Obligations and Non-Contractual Obligations (Amendment etc) (EU Exit) Regulations 2019, SI 2019 No 834.

[29] The Law Applicable to Contractual Obligations and Non-Contractual Obligations (Amendment etc) (EU Exit) Regulations 2019, SI 2019 No 834, regs 2–9.

[30] The Law Applicable to Contractual Obligations and Non-Contractual Obligations (Amendment etc) (EU Exit) Regulations 2019, SI 2019 No 834, reg 12. Regulation (EC) No 662/2009 is revoked.

[31] Letter of the UK Mission to the European Union dated 29 January 2021. <UK notifies that it considers the Brussels and Rome Convention to no longer apply to it – Conflict of Laws> accessed 31 August 2021.

[32] The Law Applicable to Contractual Obligations and Non-Contractual Obligations (Amendment etc) (EU Exit) Regulations 2019, SI 2019 No 834, reg 10.

[33] ibid reg 10(3).

[34] ibid regs 10(8), (12), (13).

[35] Relevant state is defined for this purpose as the UK and all EU Member States: ibid reg 10(2), restating Article 1(4) of the Rome I Regulation.

[36] ibid reg 10(4).

[37] See Case C-381/98 *Ingmar GB Ltd v Eaton Leonard Technologies Inc.* [2000] ECR I-09305.

Article 7 applies only to insurance contracts covering non-large risks situated inside the territory of a 'relevant state' and gives privileged status in certain respects to the law of the relevant states.[38] For instance, the parties to such a contract may choose, in accordance with Article 3, the law of any relevant state where the risk is situated but not the law of any other country.[39] The retained Rome I Regulation will apply to contracts concluded as from 1 January 2021.[40]

Where the subject-matter does not fall within the Rome I and II Regulations, contracts will be subject to the English common law doctrine of the 'proper law'.[41] The proper law is the concept used at common law to signify the law by which the validity of the contract is tested.[42] The proper law is the law expressly or impliedly chosen by the parties or, absent such a choice, the system of law with which the contract has the closest and most real connection.[43] Under the proper law doctrine, a court gives effect to an express choice of law, as long as it is bona fide, legal, and not contrary to public policy.[44] Hence, the entitlement of the parties to select the governing law is not absolute and there are limitations on it.[45]

Statutory rules regulating the law applicable to assignments and interests in securities need to be developed.[46] The UK had already chosen not to participate in the upcoming Regulation on the third-party effects of assignments but will need to track the result of the deliberations. Brexit presents an opportunity for developing a principled choice of law approach to the many questions that present themselves in securities transactions.[47] The way forward for England to retain its competitive

[38] The Law Applicable to Contractual Obligations and Non-Contractual Obligations (Amendment etc) (EU Exit) Regulations 2019, SI 2019 No 834, reg 10(7).

[39] Article 7(3)(a) of the Rome I Regulation, as amended by the Law Applicable to Contractual Obligations and Non-Contractual Obligations (Amendment etc) (EU Exit) Regulations 2019, SI 2019 No 834. The passage of Article 7 into the retained Rome I Regulation may be questioned, given its unnecessary complexity and inextricable links with the internal market in insurance services.

[40] Article 66(a) of the EU Withdrawal Agreement.

[41] This includes contracts for maritime carriage, arbitration agreements, choice of court agreements or other matters excluded from the Rome I Regulation's scope.

[42] For the proper law of an arbitration or choice of court agreement, see, L Collins and others (eds), *Dicey, Morris & Collins The Conflict of Laws* (Sweet & Maxwell 2012) ch 12, 603–04 (hereafter Collins and others, *Dicey, Morris & Collins*); D Joseph QC, *Jurisdiction and Arbitration Agreements and their Enforcement* (Sweet & Maxwell 2010) 182; see *Enka Insaat Ve Sanayi A.S. v OOO Insurance Company Chubb* [2020] UKSC 38; *Sulamerica CIA Nacional de Seguros SA and others v Enesa Engenharia SA and others* [2012] EWCA Civ 638, [2012] 1 All ER (Comm) 795.

[43] See the divergent approaches in *Amin Rasheed Shipping Corp v Kuwait Insurance Co* [1984] AC 50. See also, *Whitworth Street Estates (Manchester) Ltd v James Miller & Partners Ltd* [1970] AC 583; *Compagnie Tunisienne de Navigation SA v Compagnie d'Armament Maritime SA* [1971] AC 572

[44] *Vita Food Products Ltd v Unus Shipping Co Ltd* [1939] UKPC 7, [1939] AC 277 (Lord Wright). No English decision has rejected a choice of law which has been made by the parties by reference to this provision. See J Hill and M Ní Shúilleabháin, *Clarkson and Hill's Conflict of Laws* (5th edn, OUP 2016) 212.

[45] *Ace Insurance Ltd v Moose Enterprise Pty Ltd* [2009] NSWSC 724, [52] (Brereton J).

[46] See A Dickinson, 'Walking Solo—A New Path for the Conflict of Laws in England' Conflictoflaws.net, 4 January 2021 <> accessed 31 August 2021 (hereafter Dickinson, 'Walking Solo').

[47] M Ooi, 'Choice of Law in the Shifting Sands of Securities Trading' in A Dickinson and E Peel (eds), *A Conflict of Laws Companion: Essays in Honour of Adrian Briggs* (OUP 2021) ch 8, 224.

edge in attracting cross-border securities transactions is to ensure that it has clear and cogent choice of law rules that are flexible enough to accommodate the demands of new securities.[48] These matters are too important to be left to the ad hoc and piecemeal solutions of the common law.

2. Non-contractual Obligations

The amendments made by the Law Applicable Exit Regulations to the text of the retained Rome II Regulation reflect a similar approach.[49] Articles 25(2), 29, 30, and 32 are omitted[50] and most other provisions are amended by replacing references to 'Member State' with the 'United Kingdom'.

Article 6(3)(b) is amended to enable a party suing in a UK court to choose to apply the law of the forum to the claim if the UK market is amongst those directly and substantially affected by the restriction of competition, whether the defendant is domiciled in the UK or not. The law applicable under Article 6 may not be derogated from by an agreement pursuant to Article 14.

Article 8(2) is restricted to non-contractual obligations arising from infringements of pre-existing unitary Community intellectual property rights occurring before 1 January 2021 and to proceedings commenced before that date.[51] Read alongside the Withdrawal Agreement,[52] this change would seem to render Article 8(2) obsolete going forwards. Where the event giving rise to damage constitutes the infringement of a unitary Community intellectual property (IP) right, the 'country in which the act of infringement was committed' is located at the place of the initial act of infringement at the origin of the conduct complained of.[53] Before the exit date, the original Rome II Regulation will apply. For later events giving rise to damage, the law of the country for which the protection is claimed rule under Article 8(1) will apply to alleged infringements of unitary EU IP rights.[54] This will require the English court to identify the country, within a Member State, for which protection is claimed and to examine how the unitary right is given effect in that

[48] ibid.

[49] The Law Applicable to Contractual Obligations and Non-Contractual Obligations (Amendment etc) (EU Exit) Regulations 2019, SI 2019 No 834, reg 11.

[50] ibid regs 11(7), (10), (12). Oddly, reg 11(11) amends Art 31 to reflect the CJEU's decision in Case C-412/10 *Homawoo v GMF Assurances SA* [2011] I-11603, inserting 11 January 2009 as the reference date, even though the modified instrument will apply only to events giving rise to damage after 1 January 2021.

[51] ibid reg 11(5).

[52] Article 66(b) of the Withdrawal Agreement which ensures the continued application of the Rome II Regulation for events giving rise to damage up to 31 December 2020. See also, Article 54, concerning the continuing effect of unitary EU IP rights in the UK.

[53] Case C-24/16 *Nintendo Co Ltd v BigBen Interactive GmbH* EU:C:2017:724.

[54] See Case C-170/12 *Pinckney v KDG Mediatech AG* EU:C:2013:635, [2014] FSR 354.

country through its implementation of EU law. The law applicable under Article 8 may not be derogated from by a choice of law agreement pursuant to Article 14.

Article 14(3), like the corresponding provision in Article 3(4) of the retained Rome I Regulation, is amended to prevent parties from derogating from retained EU law by selecting the law of a country beyond the 'relevant states' (defined as including the UK and all EU Member States other than Denmark)[55] in situations that are otherwise entirely connected with the relevant states.[56]

Tort cases that fall outside the Rome II Regulation are governed by the Private International Law (Miscellaneous Provisions) Act 1995 which, generally, applies a *lex loci delicti commissi* test.[57] Defamation cases continue to apply the common law's double actionability rule.[58] This is an anomalous choice of law rule premised on insular policy-oriented grounds. The double actionability rule is problematic

[55] The Law Applicable to Contractual Obligations and Non-Contractual Obligations (Amendment etc) (EU Exit) Regulations 2019, SI 2019 No 834, reg 11(2), amending Art 1(4) of the Rome II Regulation.

[56] ibid reg 11(6).

[57] The Private International Law (Miscellaneous Provisions) Act 1995, Section 11(1) provides: 'The general rule is that the applicable law is the law of the country in which the events constituting the tort or delict in question occur.' The Private International Law (Miscellaneous Provisions) Act 1995, s 12(1) provides:

> If it appears, in all the circumstances, from a comparison of—
>
> (a) the significance of the factors which connect a tort or delict with the country whose law would be the applicable law under the general rule; and
>
> (b) the significance of any factors connecting the tort or delict with another country, that it is substantially more appropriate for the applicable law for determining the issues arising in the case, or any of those issues, to be the law of the other country, the general rule is displaced and the applicable law for determining those issues or that issue (as the case may be) is the law of that other country.

For the Private International Law (Miscellaneous Provisions) Act 1995, see A Dickinson, *The Rome II Regulation* (OUP 2008) ch 1, 9–12 (hereafter Dickinson, *Rome II Regulation*). It should be noted that the arguments in favour of displacing the applicable law under Articles 4(1) and (2) by virtue of Article 4(3) of the Rome II Regulation will have to cross a higher threshold as compared to Section 12 of the Private International Law (Miscellaneous Provisions) Act 1995. 'A comparison of the respective wording "*substantially more appropriate*" as opposed to "*manifestly more closely connected*" indicates that the burden imposed by the Rome II Regulation is probably heavier than that imposed by Section 12 of the 1995 Act' (emphasis added); R Plender and M Wilderspin, *The European Private International Law of Obligations* (Sweet & Maxwell 2015) 557.

[58] Among the common law countries which have been influenced by the English line of authority originating from *Phillips v Eyre* (1870) LR 6 QB 1 (Willes J), some have since rejected the double actionability rule (eg the Supreme Court of Canada in *Jensen v Tolofson* [1994] 3 SCR 1022; the Australian High Court in *Régie Nationale des Usines Renault SA v Zhang* (2002) 187 ALR 1) but there are other countries which still retain some variant of the rule. For example in Scots law an action for a delict committed outside Scotland will fail unless the pursuer can show that the specific *jus actionis* which he invokes is available to him both by Scots law and by the *lex loci delicti commissi*. The Scottish courts have failed to accept the 'flexible exception' employed in the persuasive authority of *Boys v Chaplin* [1971] AC 356 (Lord Wilberforce). This exception was furthered in *Red Sea Insurance Co Ltd v Bouygues SA* [1995] 1 AC 190 (Lord Slynn) which provided that the exception can displace either the law of the forum or the law of the place of tort such that a tort may be actionable even though it is not actionable under either the *lex fori* or the *lex loci delicti commissi*. However, the Scottish courts apply the Rome II Regulation and the common law rule is restricted to defamation cases; see PR Beaumont and PE McEleavy, *Anton's Private International Law* (3rd edn, SULI/W Green 2011) ch 14, 714–22.

where the facts of the claim do not disclose a cause of action in tort according to English law over and above the requirements of the law of the place of the tort.

D. Interpretation and Divergence from Retained EU Law in the Context of the Rome I and II Regulations

The Rome I and II Regulations under the guise of retained EU law constitute a new and unique category of law that is neither EU law nor English law *per se*. The interpretation of retained EU law will give rise to its own set of challenges. Ultimately, fidelity to EU law will have to be balanced with the ability of UK appellate courts to diverge from retained EU law and develop their own jurisprudence.[59] Courts at the level of the Court of Appeal in England and Wales and the UK Supreme Court may overturn binding pre-Brexit EU case law if they consider it 'right to do so'.[60] In practice, all UK courts are likely to be influenced by non-binding post-Brexit EU case law where they are interpreting the same piece of legislation. As a result of the extension of the power to amend binding pre-Brexit EU case law to the Court of Appeal, the category of retained EU law is more amenable to change than ordinary English domestic law.

Over the course of time, it seems likely that aspects of the UK's approach to the applicable law for cross-border contractual and non-contractual obligations will depart from the jurisprudence of the CJEU. A broader question is the extent to which the EU objectives of the Rome I and II Regulations should be applied when interpreting the retained EU Regulations. Should the approach to interpretation be different because the UK is outside the EU? Judges sometimes rely on viable consequentialist arguments and arguments of principle to interpret precedents very restrictively in order to 'explain' or 'distinguish' them from the point in issue in a given case.[61] It should be possible for an English court to distinguish or explain a binding CJEU decision.

In addition to questions about interpreting the EU objectives of the Rome I and II Regulations, the definitions of autonomous terms and concepts in the applicable law Regulations borrow from the Brussels regime and its case law. As the Brussels regime is revoked and its associated case law is redundant, will an English court

[59] From the perspective of a theory of adjudication, the tension between the category of 'fit' exemplified by retained EU law and the category of 'justification' based on principle or policy in hard cases will result in the indigenous development of the corpus of retained EU law. See generally, R Dworkin, *Taking Rights Seriously* (Harvard University Press 1977) ch 4 (hereafter Dworkin, *Taking Rights Seriously*).

[60] The European Union (Withdrawal) Act 2018 (Relevant Court) (Retained EU Case Law) Regulations (SI 2020/1525) allow the Court of Appeal of England and Wales (and equivalent courts across the UK) to depart from retained EU case law. Under the European Union (Withdrawal) Act 2018, it is only the UK Supreme Court (or High Court of Justiciary in Scotland) that has this power.

[61] N MacCormick, *Legal Reasoning and Legal Theory* (Clarendon Press, OUP 1978) 219–24; JW Harris, *Legal Philosophies* (2nd edn, Butterworths 1997) 183.

be able to rely on case law of the CJEU on the Brussels regime when interpreting a term or concept under the Rome I or Rome II Regulations? It is submitted that the case law on the Brussels regime should still be used as an aid to interpretation but without having any strict or binding legal authority. Otherwise, if this case law is deemed irrelevant, a void may emerge in the UK in the application of the Rome I and II Regulations without the lived experience of the Brussels regime. This approach will ensure continuity and certainty whilst permitting change to occur where appropriate.

The Rome I and II Regulations refer expressly to the internal market rationale for harmonised applicable law rules.[62] Notwithstanding, the Rome I and II Regulations are underpinned by sound private international law principles and can operate effectively outside the confines of the EU. The Rome I and II Regulations intend to:[63]

> improve the predictability of the outcome of litigation, certainty as to the law applicable and the free movement of judgments, for the conflict-of-law rules in the Member States to designate the same national law irrespective of the country of the court in which an action is brought.

It is the mandatory choice of law rules of the forum that characterise a given issue as procedural or substantive.[64] The Rome I and II Regulations adopt a direct approach by subjecting particular issues to the applicable law of the contractual or non-contractual obligation.[65] The instruments exclude matters relating to 'evidence and procedure'[66] from their scope and lack any autonomous definition for these terms. The result is that national law will have to be applied to determine both the meaning given to these terms and what law should be applied to an individual issue (assuming that the matter has not been directly subjected to the applicable law by the Regulations).

Considerable scope for operation is therefore left to national choice of law rules under the Regulations. Some commentators have criticised this position, stating that the application of national law to matters of evidence and procedure, where

[62] Recital 1 of the Rome I and II Regulations. cf It is not always clear how some of the EU's initiatives can be said to be 'necessary for the proper functioning of the internal market'. Prominent English commentators expressed their doubts about the Rome II Regulation being necessary for the proper functioning of the internal market. Article 81 of the Treaty of Lisbon extended the competence of the EU over matters of private international law. Article 81(2) refers to the adoption of measures by the EU '*particularly* when necessary for the proper functioning of the internal market' (emphasis added). The wording suggests that an EU initiative need not be incontrovertibly necessary for the furtherance of the internal market. See J Harris, 'Understanding the English Response to the Europeanisation of Private International Law' (2008) 4 Journal of Private International Law 347, 357–59.

[63] Recital 6 of the Rome I and II Regulations.

[64] M Ahmed, 'The Nature and Enforcement of Choice of Law Agreements' (2018) 14 Journal of Private International Law 500, 519–23 (hereafter Ahmed, 'Choice of Law Agreements').

[65] Article 12 of the Rome I Regulation; Article 15 of the Rome II Regulation.

[66] Article 1(3) of the Rome I Regulation; Article 1(3) of the Rome II Regulation.

the law of the cause of action falls under the Regulations, will lead to disharmony of court decisions and is incompatible with an EU system of private international law.[67] It has been argued that an autonomous conception of 'evidence and procedure' is required, based on the idea of 'neutrality',[68] which means that a national court must apply the law of the cause of action to any issue which is concerned with or directed at the decision on the merits and which requires the law of the forum to be applied to any matter which concerns the mode or conduct of court proceedings. Garnett argues that procedure should be based on the narrow mode or conduct of court proceedings view espoused by the Australian courts[69] rather than the traditional right–remedy test that adopts a wide view of the scope of the law of procedure and a correspondingly narrow view of the scope of the applicable law.[70] Following the *lex fori regit processum* rule,[71] the law of the forum applies to matters of procedure and the applicable law applies to matters of substance.

In the CJEU's jurisprudence on the Rome I Regulation and the Rome II Regulation, an autonomous pan-European approach is adopted to determine the meaning of particular terms and concepts.[72] Whether an obligation is classified as a contractual or non-contractual obligation for EU conflict of laws purposes is a matter for the statutory interpretation of the Rome I and II Regulations.[73] In deciding that issue, the court will not adopt any domestic law notion; rather the court will apply an autonomous EU meaning. For instance, the autonomous EU meaning of 'contract' is an obligation freely assumed[74] but it does not require that

[67] M Illmer, 'Neutrality Matters—Some Thoughts About the Rome Regulations and the so called Dichotomy of Substance and Procedure in European Private International Law' (2009) 28 Civil Justice Quarterly 237; Dickinson sees the concepts of evidence and procedure as 'matters that define the scope of the Regulation' which must therefore be given a uniform, autonomous meaning, independent of the forum's notions: Dickinson, *Rome II Regulation* (n 57) [14.57].

[68] ibid 246–47.

[69] *McKain v RW Miller and Co (South Australia) Pty Ltd* (1991) 174 CLR 1, 26–27 (Mason CJ); *John Pfeiffer Pty Ltd v Rogerson* (2000) 203 CLR 503, [192] (Callinan J); see also, *Tolofson v Jensen* [1994] 3 SCR 1022, 1071–72 (La Forest J) (Supreme Court of Canada): 'the purpose of substantive/procedural classification is to determine which rules will make the machinery of the forum court run smoothly as distinguished from those determinative of the rights of both parties'. cf AV Dicey, *Digest of the Law of England with Reference to the Conflict of Laws* (Stevens & Sons, 1896) 712: 'Any rule of law which solely affects, not the enforcement of a right but the nature of the right itself, does not come under the head of procedure.'

[70] *Cox v Ergo Versicherung AG* [2014] UKSC 22, [2014] 1 AC 1379, [23] (Lord Sumption); Section 14 of the Private International Law (Miscellaneous Proceedings) Act 1995 as interpreted by *Harding v Wealands* [2006] UKHL 32, [2007] 2 AC 1; *Boys v Chaplin* [1971] AC 356. Garnett, *Substance and Procedure* (n 15) 39; Dickinson, *Rome II Regulation* (n 57) [14.60] suggests the adoption of a test on similar lines; Briggs and Bogdan also express dissatisfaction with the traditional English approach that remedies are a matter of procedure to be governed by the law of the forum: Briggs, *Conflict of Laws* (n 19) 193; Bogdan, *PIL as Law of the Forum* (n 15) 194.

[71] 'the law of the forum governs procedure': See Garnett, *Substance and Procedure* (n 15) 1–4.

[72] R Plender and M Wilderspin, *The European Private International Law of Obligations* (5th edn, Sweet & Maxwell 2020) 36 (hereafter Plender and Wilderspin, *Private International Law of Obligations*).

[73] Article 1 of the Rome I Regulation and Article 1 of the Rome II Regulation.

[74] Case C-26/91 *Handte* EU:C:1992:268; Case 38/81 *Effer SpA v Hans-Joachim Kantner* EU:C:1982:79 . cf For the purposes of the English common law of conflict of laws, a 'contract' may acquire a different meaning from that used in English domestic law. Thus in *Re Bonacina* [1912] 2 Ch 394, an agreement

the parties in the proceedings are direct parties to the contract.[75] Characterisation under the Rome I and II Regulations is better understood as an entirely distinct, self-contained exercise, and not one whose end product results from any prefabricated common law legal structure.[76]

At common law, questions of characterisation resulted in a three-stage analysis.[77] The first stage involved allocating the issue in dispute to a legal category. At the second stage, the court applied what it considered to be the appropriate conflict of laws rule to lay down the relevant connecting factor to the issue in dispute. The third stage involved the identification of the system of law selected by the court's application of the rule selected in the second stage.[78] The choice of law process falls to be undertaken in a broad internationalist spirit in accordance with the principles of conflict of laws of the forum.[79]

In terms of areas for law reform, in the context of the Rome I Regulation, is whether to amend the current rules in relation to provisions where there was an opt out in the Rome Convention.[80] There has always been controversy about the role and application of third country mandatory rules.[81] This resulted in Member States being allowed to opt out of the relevant provision in the Rome Convention.[82] The UK's influence helped shape the attenuated provision on third country mandatory rules in the Rome I Regulation that reflected existing English case law.[83]

made in Italy and unsupported by consideration was regarded as a contract. Kennedy LJ (at ibid 403) noted that the doctrine of consideration as it exists in English law is peculiar to the common law.

[75] Case C-337/17 *Feniks* EU:C:2018:805; Joined Cases C-274/16, C-447/16, and C-448/16 *flightright* EU:C:2018:160. See G van Calster, *European Private International Law* (Hart Publishing 2020) 162–68.

[76] M McParland, *The Rome I Regulation on the Law Applicable to Contractual Obligations* (OUP 2015) 109 (hereafter McParland, *Rome I Regulation*).

[77] ibid.

[78] *Macmillan Inc. v Bishopsgate Investment Trust Plc* [1996] 1 WLR 387, 397D-405F (Staughton LJ); *Raifeisen Zentralbank Österreich AG v Five Star Trading* [2001] EWCA Civ 68, [2001] QB 825, [25]–[33] (Mance LJ).

[79] *Raifeisen Zentralbank Österreich AG v Five Star Trading* [2001] EWCA Civ 68, [2001] QB 825, [26] (Mance LJ); *Macmillan Inc. v Bishopsgate Investment Trust Plc* [1996] 1 WLR 387, 391–92 (Staughton LJ).

[80] According to Section 2(2) of the Contracts (Applicable Law) Act 1990, Article 7(1) (third country mandatory rules) and Article 10(1)(e) (the consequences of nullity of the contract) of the Rome Convention shall not have the force of law in the UK.

[81] McParland, *Rome I Regulation* (n 76) 698.

[82] Germany, Ireland, Latvia, Luxembourg, Portugal, Slovenia, and the UK entered a reservation under Article 22 of the Rome Convention in relation to Article 7(1) of the Rome Convention. See Beaumont and McEleavy, *Anton* (n 58) 514.

[83] Article 9(3) of the Rome I Regulation. *Foster v Driscoll* [1929] 1 KB 470; *Regazzoni v KC Sethia* [1958] AC 301; *Ralli Bros v Cia Naviera Sota y Aznar* [1920] 2 KB 287; *Mackender v Feldia A.G.* [1967] 2 QB 590 (CA) (Diplock LJ): 'the English courts will not enforce performance or give damages for non-performance of an act required to be done under a contract, whatever be the proper laws of the contract, if the act would be illegal in the country in which it is required to be performed'. cf *Howard v Shirlstar Container Transport Ltd* [1990] 3 All ER 366, [1990]1 WLR 1292 (CA).

The choice of law rules set out in the Rome I Regulation will be applied to determine whether a contract is governed by English law. However, the Rome I Regulation recognises that there are some rules of national law which, for important policy reasons, a court applies regardless the otherwise applicable law.[84] Therefore, Article 9(2) of the Rome I Regulation provides that 'nothing in this Regulation shall restrict the application of the overriding mandatory provisions of the law of the forum'.[85] The mandatory rules of the forum cannot be derogated from or evaded by a choice of law agreement.[86]

Article 9(1) of the Rome I Regulation defines overriding mandatory provisions as:[87]

> provisions the respect for which is regarded as crucial by a country for safeguarding its public interests, such as its political, social or economic organization, to such an extent that they are applicable to any situation falling within their scope, irrespective of the law otherwise applicable to the contract under this Regulation.

This definition is inspired by the CJEU's decision in *Arblade* where the Court applied an attenuated definition of overriding mandatory rules to the relevant national legislation.[88] In the Rome I Regulation Proposal, the Commission referred to *Arblade* and, in particular, that the judgment made it clear that the fact that national rules are categorised as mandatory rules does not mean that they are exempt from compliance with the provisions of the Treaties.[89] It is accordingly arguable that this definition was intended to be restrictive, meaning that the rules can only be applied as overriding mandatory rules if they meet the definition and are crucial for safeguarding one of the public interests identified.[90] The CJEU has jurisdiction to consider whether this definition has been met, and presumably could decide that a national rule's express scope should be ignored.

[84] For a discussion on the application of mandatory rules post Brexit, see L Merrett, 'International Employment Cases Post-Brexit: Choice of Law, Territorial Scope, Jurisdiction and Enforcement' (2021) 50 Industrial Law Journal 343, 352–54.

[85] Case C-184/12 *United Antwerp Maritime Agencies (Unamar) NV v Navigation Maritime Bulgare* [2014] 1 Lloyd's Rep 161.

[86] See Sections 27(2) and 27(3) of the Unfair Contract Terms Act 1977 which apply regardless of the applicable law of the contract where the choice of law agreement appears to the court, or arbitrator to have been imposed wholly or mainly for the purpose of enabling the party imposing it to evade the operation of the Act or in the making of the contract one of the parties dealt as consumer, and he was then habitually resident in the UK, and the essential steps necessary for the making of the contract were taken there, whether by him or by others on his behalf.

[87] A rule with similar effect is found in Article 16 of the Rome II Regulation, although the term 'overriding mandatory provisions' is not defined therein.

[88] Joined Cases C-369/96 and C-376/96 *Arblade* [1999] ECR I-8453, [31].

[89] Proposal for a Regulation of the European Parliament and the Council on the law applicable to contractual obligations (Rome I), Brussels 15.12.2005, COM(2005) 650 final, [4.2].

[90] Recital 37 to the Rome I Regulation.

These issues remain controversial as a matter of EU private international law. The question addressed here is the effect of Brexit on Article 9(1) of the Rome I Regulation when it is applied as retained EU law.

If an English Act expressly says a provision has overriding mandatory effect is an English court required to consider the legality of this provision by testing its compliance with the definition in Article 9(1)? The CJEU will no longer have power to adjudicate on this issue under the preliminary reference procedure.[91] The supremacy of EU law applies to any enactment or rule of EU law 'so far as relevant to the interpretation, disapplication or quashing of any enactment or rule of law passed or made before exit day'.[92] However, one of the reasons for the restrictive definition in *Arblade* was the need to balance domestic law with other Treaty obligations. It is arguable that a restrictive definition of overriding mandatory rules is rendered obsolete after Brexit. At common law, mandatory rules have a narrow application and a court gives effect to an express choice of law, as long as it is bona fide, legal, and not contrary to public policy.[93]

Another area where there is scope for a divergence in approach is the statutory construction of the escape clause in the retained Article 4(3) of the Rome I Regulation and the retained Article 4(3) of the Rome II Regulation.

The escape clause in Article 4(3) of the Rome I Regulation is designed to address one of the most controversial features of the Rome Convention.[94] Article 4 of the Rome Convention sought to determine the applicable law in the absence of choice through a number of presumptions.[95] However, these presumptions could be avoided if the contract was more closely connected with a country other than the country identified by the relevant presumption.[96] Article 4 of the Rome I Regulation seeks to resolve the difficulties, under the Rome Convention, surrounding the relationship between the presumptions and the possibility of the presumptions being avoided if the contract was more closely connected with another country. Notwithstanding, many of the same difficulties exist under Article 4 of the Regulation in the relationship between the rules in Article 4(1) and Article 4(2) and the escape clause in Article 4(3).[97] *Prima facie*, the Rome I Regulation's use of the word 'manifestly' in the escape clause does not bring about a radical change. However, arguably Article 4(3) of the Regulation sets the bar higher than Article 4(5) of the Convention.

91 Article 267 TFEU.

92 Section 5(2) EUWA 2018.

93 *Vita Food Products Ltd v Unus Shipping Co Ltd* [1939] UKPC 7, [1939] AC 277 (Lord Wright). No English decision has rejected a choice of law which has been made by the parties by reference to this provision.

94 The Rome Convention 1980 on the law applicable to contractual obligations (OJ C 27, 26.1.1998, 36–53) was brought into force in the UK on 1 April 1991 by the Contracts (Applicable Law) Act 1990.

95 Article 4(2)–(4) of the Rome Convention.

96 Article 4(5) of the Rome Convention.

97 Recital 20 of the Rome I Regulation describes Article 4(3) of the Regulation as the 'escape clause'.

In broad outline, there are two possible approaches to Article 4.[98] The first is to treat the application of the rules in Article 4(1) and Article 4(2) as usual, with the escape clause being applicable only in exceptional cases. This approach is supported by the fact that Article 4(3) can be applied only if the contract is manifestly more closely connected with another country. Further support may be drawn from the *travaux préparatoires* of the Rome II Regulation which contains a similar escape clause. In order to prevent EU Member State courts from abusing the escape clause by using it as a surrogate for the application of the law of the forum, the EU legislature refused to establish Article 4(3) as a general rule and instead structured it as an exception.[99]

The alternative is to adopt a more liberal approach to the escape clause and not to make the condition for its application too difficult to satisfy. The stipulation that for the application of Article 4(3), a contract must be manifestly closely connected with another country requires only that it is clear that the contract is more closely connected with one country than with another without it being necessarily being overwhelmingly more closely connected with it.

Under the Rome Convention there was a strand of judicial authority which took a very restrictive view of the exception in Article 4(5). An extreme example of this line of case law is the decision of the Supreme Court of the Netherlands in *Société Nouvelle des Papéteries de l'Aa v Machinefabriek BOA*.[100] The Dutch claimant sold a paper press to the French defendant. The contract was made and negotiated in France with payment in French currency. The machine was delivered and assembled in France. When the defendant failed to pay the price, the claimant commenced proceedings in the Netherlands. One of the issues before the Netherlands court was whether the applicable law of the contract was Dutch law (as the seller was a Dutch company) or French law (as the contract was more closely connected with France). The Netherlands court deemed that Dutch law was the applicable law. It reasoned that the law of closest connection should be applied restrictively and only if the seller's place of business has no real significance as a connecting factor.

In the English decisions under the Rome Convention, the courts tended to favour the application of the law with which the contract was most closely connected, rather than the characteristic performer's law at least where the characteristic performance occurred in a single state.[101] These authorities must be used with caution under the Rome I Regulation.

[98] Hill and Shúilleabháin, *Clarkson & Hill* (n 44) 231.

[99] Explanatory Memorandum of the Proposal for a Regulation of the European Parliament and the Council on the Law Applicable to Non-Contractual Obligations ('Rome II') COM (2003) 427 final, 12.

[100] 1992 Netherlands Jurisprudentie 750. See also, *Caledonia Subsea Ltd v Micoperi Srl* 2003 SC 70.

[101] See, for instance, *Definitely Maybe (Touring) Ltd v Marek Lieberberg Konzertagentur GmbH* [2001] 1 WLR 1745; *Kenburn Waste Management Ltd v Bergmann* [2002] CLC 644; *PT Pan Indonesia Bank Ltd Tbk v Marconi Communications International Ltd* [2005] EWCA Civ 235, [2007] 2 Lloyd's Rep 72.

The CJEU adjudicated that Article 4(5) of the Rome Convention must be construed as, where it is clear from the circumstances as a whole that the contract is more closely connected with a country other than that determined on the basis of one of the criteria set out in Article 4(2) to (4) of the Convention, it is for the court to disregard those criteria and apply the law of the country with which the contract is most closely connected.[102]

The language and structure of the Rome I Regulation suggests a higher threshold, which requires that the cumulative weight of the factors connecting the contract to another country must clearly and decisively outweigh the need for certainty in applying the test in Articles 4(1) and 4(2).[103] If an appropriate balance is achieved between Articles 4(1) and 4(2) and the escape clause in Article 4(3), Article 4 can promote certainty and predictability. To justify the application of the escape clause, there must be a preponderance of connecting factors that clearly favours a law other than the characteristic performer's law.

The interpretation of the retained Article 4 of the Rome I Regulation will give rise to the same issues that were prevalent under Article 4 of the Rome Convention and the Rome I Regulation. The only difference will be the ability of the English appellate courts to depart from a previous approach to interpretation. The English courts tendency under the Rome Convention to favour the application of the law with which the contract was most closely connected, rather than the characteristic performer's law might resurface. Eventually, the influence of the proper law of the contract may make itself more apparent in the Article 4 balancing act.

Human rights and environmental damage litigation by foreign claimants against multinational companies in the English courts may necessitate the application of the escape clause in Article 4(3) of the retained Rome II Regulation.[104] Where a parent company is sued in relation to the activities of a foreign subsidiary and the parties have not entered into a choice of law agreement,[105] the applicable law under Article 4(1) of the Rome II Regulation is the law of the country where the damage occurred, that is usually the law of the foreign country.[106] This could be a law that is either undeveloped or otherwise ill-suited for the claimant's proceedings in the English courts. However, the parties may instead rely on English tort law as the

[102] Case C-133/08 *Intercontainer Interfrigo SC (ICF) v Balkenende Oosthuizen BV and MIC Operations BV* [2009] ECR I-9710, [62]–[64], operative part 3 (Grand Chamber). See A Briggs, *The Conflict of Laws* (4th edn, OUP 2019) 223 (hereafter Briggs, *Conflict of Laws 2019*).

[103] *Molton Street Capital LLP v Shooters Hill Capital Partners LLP* [2015] EWHC 3419 (Comm), [94] (Popplewell J).

[104] The Law Applicable to Contractual Obligations and Non-Contractual Obligations (Amendment etc) (EU Exit) Regulations 2019, SI 2019 No 834.

[105] Article 14 of the Rome II Regulation. See generally, Ahmed, *Choice of Law Agreements* (n 898).

[106] If the claim is framed in terms of the alleged violation of human rights, the general choice of law rule under Article 4 would apply and point towards the application of the law of the country of 'direct damage'. Case C-350/14 *Florin Lazar v Allianz SpA* EU:C:2015:802 [30], confirms that it is only the place where the direct victim suffers direct damage that is relevant for the purposes of Article 4(1) of the Rome II Regulation.

default applicable law by choosing not to plead or prove the content of foreign law.[107]

Post Brexit, it remains to be seen whether the English courts would be more willing to displace the applicable law under Article 4(1) by applying Article 4(3) of the Rome II Regulation more liberally.[108] The territorial limitations of the *lex loci damni* might be overcome by applying the principle of closest connection to select a more favourable law.[109] Article 4(3) could ensure that the law manifestly more closely connected to the tort such as the law of the country in which the event giving rise to the damage occurred or the law of the country in which the parent company is domiciled applies. However, it should be noted that this methodologically pluralist and liberal application of the exception in Article 4(3) will depart from Article 4's preference for objective choice of law rules by rendering the provision susceptible to being used as a surrogate for the discretionary closest connection principle.

Article 7 of the Rome II Regulation applies to a non-contractual obligation arising out of environmental damage or damage sustained by persons or property as a result of such damage.[110] According to Article 7, the law applicable to environmental damage is the *lex loci damni* as per Article 4(1), but the victim can choose to base his or her claim on the law of the country in which the event giving rise to the damage occurred.[111] It should be noted that Article 7 only refers to Article 4(1) and does not

[107] See generally, Fentiman, *Foreign Law* (n 18).

[108] Briggs, *Conflict of Laws 2019* (n 102) 264, argues that the abstract debate about Article 4(3)'s strict or restrictive interpretation is not illuminating and every case will turn on its own set of facts. In the context of cross-border personal injury disputes, there is English precedent for Article 4(3) of the Rome II Regulation displacing the applicable law in *Gary Owen v Galgey & Ors* [2020] EWHC 3546 (QB) (Linden J) and *Marshall v Motor Insurers' Bureau & Ors* [2015] EWHC 3421 (QB) (Dingemans J). cf *Winrow v Hemphill* [2014] EWHC 3164 (QB) [63] (Slade J); *Stylianou v Toyoshima and Suncorp Metway Insurance Limited* [2013] EWHC 2188 (QB) (Sir Robert Nelson J); Collins and others, *Dicey, Morris & Collins* (n 42) ch 35, 2214–15 ('the court must be satisfied that the threshold of closer connection has been clearly demonstrated'); Dickinson, *Rome II Regulation* (n 57) ch 4, 340–41 ('Article 4(3) must, therefore, be considered exceptional, requiring strong and clear reasons for displacing the law otherwise applicable under Arts 4(1) and (2)'); P Torremans (ed), *Cheshire, North & Fawcett: Private International Law* (15th edn, OUP 2017) 814.

[109] The result-selectivism inherent in the idea of a favourable law is reminiscent of the regulatory approach of governmental interest analysis. See Symeonides, *Codifying Choice of Law* (n 11) 287; M Lehmann, 'Regulation, Global Governance and Private International Law: Squaring the Triangle' (2020) 16 Journal of Private International Law, 1, 10–13 (hereafter Lehmann, 'Regulation').

[110] If the claim is framed in terms of environmental damage, Article 7 of the Rome II Regulation provides a special choice of law rule for environmental damage. Recital 24 of the Rome II Regulation adopts a definition of 'environmental damage'.

[111] Recital 25 of the Rome II Regulation. In its recent CO_2 emission reduction ruling against Shell, the Hague District Court in *Milieudefensie et al. v Royal Dutch Shell Plc,* [C/09/571932 / HA ZA 19-379], (English version) see <ECLI:NL:RBDHA:2021:5339, Rechtbank Den Haag, C/09/571932 / HA ZA 19-379 (engelse versie) (rechtspraak.nl)> accessed 9 June 2021, considered that Dutch law applies on the basis of Article 7 of the Rome II Regulation and that, in so far as the action seeks to protect the interests of Dutch residents, this also leads to the application of Dutch law on the basis of Article 4 of the Rome II Regulation. For a discussion of whether the decisions concerning the subsidiary company's operations taken by the parent company that start the chain of events resulting in the environmental damage are to be considered as the event giving rise to the damage under Article 7, see, U Grusic, 'International

refer to the other sub-provisions in Article 4. Thus, in the absence of agreement by the parties as to choice of law,[112] Article 7 prevents the designation of the law of the parties' common habitual residence or another, manifestly more appropriate law.[113]

Alternatively, any regulatory provisions in English law may be classified as overriding mandatory provisions of the law of the forum under Article 16 of the Rome II Regulation.[114] Such provisions of English law will then apply regardless of the otherwise applicable law in an English court.[115] Overriding mandatory rules may be identified expressly in statute law or the courts may determine whether it was the legislator's intention that they should be given that effect.[116]

Notwithstanding the technicalities in the application of Articles 4, 7, and overriding mandatory provisions, the Rome II Regulation under the guise of retained EU law constitutes a new and unique category of law that is neither EU law nor English law *per se*. The interpretation of retained EU law will give rise to its own set of challenges. Ultimately, fidelity to EU law will have to be balanced with the ability of UK appellate courts to diverge from retained EU law and develop their own jurisprudence.[117] Courts at the level of the Court of Appeal in England and Wales and the UK Supreme Court may overturn binding pre-Brexit EU case law if they consider it 'right to do so'.[118] In practice, all UK courts are likely to be influenced by non-binding post-Brexit EU case law where they are interpreting the same piece of legislation. A flexible interpretation of the retained Article 4(3) and the concept of overriding mandatory provisions might enable English law to achieve parity with any future amendments to EU private international law through the backdoor.[119]

Environmental Litigation in EU Courts: A Regulatory Perspective' (2016) 35 Yearbook of European Law 180, 221–25.

[112] Article 14 of the Rome II Regulation.

[113] Plender and Wilderspin, *Private International Law of Obligations* (n 72) 694.

[114] See G Rühl, 'Human Rights in Global Supply Chains: Do We Need to Amend the Rome II-Regulation?' (*Conflictoflaws.net*, 9 October 2020) <https://conflictoflaws.net/2020/human-rights-in-global-supply-chains-do-we-need-to-amend-the-rome-ii-regulation/> accessed 31 August 2021. cf J von Hein, 'Back to the Future—(Re-)Introducing the Principle of Ubiquity for Business-related Human Rights Claims' (*Conflictoflaws.net*, 12 October 2020) <https://conflictoflaws.net/2020/back-to-the-future-re-introducing-the-principle-of-ubiquity-for-business-related-human-rights-claims/> accessed 31 August 2021.

[115] Borchers, 'Categorical Exceptions' (n 12) 1655. For the regulatory function of overriding mandatory rules and public policy, see, Lehmann, 'Regulation' (n 109) 15–17.

[116] Plender and Wilderspin, *Private International Law of Obligations* (n 72) 806.

[117] See Dworkin, *Taking Rights Seriously* (n 59).

[118] The European Union (Withdrawal) Act 2018 (Relevant Court) (Retained EU Case Law) Regulations (SI 2020/1525) allow the Court of Appeal of England and Wales (and equivalent UK courts) to depart from retained EU case law.

[119] The European Parliament resolution of 10 March 2021 with recommendations to the Commission on corporate due diligence and corporate accountability does not include the proposed amendments to the EU private international law instruments. Article 20 of the proposed Directive of the European Parliament and of the Council on Corporate Due Diligence and Corporate Accountability provides that Member States shall ensure that relevant provisions of the Directive are considered overriding mandatory provisions in line with Article 16 of the Rome II Regulation: See <https://www.europarl.europa.eu/doceo/document/TA-9-2021-0073_EN.html#title1> accessed 31 August 2021.

E. Interim Conclusion

In relation to the law applicable to cross-border contractual and non-contractual obligations, the law is practically the same with some minor consequentialist amendments. Over the course of time, it seems likely that the UK approach will diverge from the EU Member States through judicial precedent and legislative reform.

There is a need to address the cost and inconvenience of pleading and proving the content of foreign law in English courts.[120] The English 'dispute resolution' paradigm[121] relegates foreign law by characterising it as a question of fact rather than a question of law.[122] Therefore, the party relying on foreign law is required to plead and prove the content of foreign law.[123] An inherent advantage of the English common law treating issues of proof of foreign law as questions of fact is that the parties can choose not to rely on the foreign law by not pleading it.[124] English law as the law of the forum is applied instead.[125] Secondly, the English courts usually apply English law as a fallback where the content of the foreign law is not proved.[126] An analogy can be drawn between the parties not relying on the foreign law and a delayed choice of English law to govern the dispute.[127] In the different context of public international law, dualists frequently make the argument that international courts only apply sources of international law and characterise municipal law as a question of fact.[128]

The effective use of foreign law in English courts faces obstacles. The litigating parties are the masters of the suit. The judge acts 'as an umpire'[129] and is led by the imperative of achieving material injustice *inter partes* in the individual instance when passively deciding on the private interests of the parties.[130] A shift in approach towards more active judicial case management is needed.[131]

[120] See Dickinson, 'Walking Solo' (n 46).

[121] See M Ahmed, 'Private International Law, Party Autonomy and the English "Dispute Resolution" Paradigm' in M Ahmed, *The Nature and Enforcement of Choice of Court Agreements* (Hart Publishing 2017) ch 2

[122] cf Civil law legal systems characterise foreign law as a question of law and the principle of *iura novit curia* ('the court knows the laws') applies. Geeroms, *Foreign Law* (n 17). See *iura novit curia* in AX Fellmeth and M Horwitz, *Guide to Latin in International Law* (OUP 2011).

[123] Briggs, *Conflict of Laws* (n 19) ch 1, 7–13.

[124] ibid.

[125] ibid.

[126] ibid.

[127] Article 3(2) of the Rome I Regulation and the Rome Convention; Collins and others, *Dicey, Morris & Collins* (n 42) ch 32, 1805–06; Beaumont and McEleavy, *Anton* (n 58) ch 10, 455–56.

[128] English private international lawyers often justify the treatment of foreign law as pragmatic, efficient and in accordance with party autonomy but the relegation of foreign law in English courts might also be explained with the idea of dualism and a legal positivist notion of state sovereignty, where the applicable foreign law of another state exists separately and independently of English law.

[129] A Briggs, *Agreements on Jurisdiction and Choice of Law* (OUP 2008) 532.

[130] H Muir Watt, 'Party Autonomy in International Contracts: From the Makings of a Myth to the Requirements of Global Governance' (2010) 3 European Review of Contract Law 1, 30–31.

[131] Dickinson, 'Walking Solo' (n 46).

A move away from expensive and often unreliable expert evidence towards allowing issues of foreign law to be dealt with by submissions in the same way as issues of English law[132] will ensure that an international approach, driven by concerns about objective connecting factors, comity, and conflicts justice prevails.[133]

[132] Especially in straightforward as opposed to hard cases.

[133] See G Cuniberti, 'Ex Officio Application of EU Choice of Law Rules: Should the Interests of the Parties Matter?' (*EAPIL Blog*, 9 August 2021) <Ex Officio Application of EU Choice of Law Rules: Should the Interests of the Parties Matter? – EAPIL> accessed 31 August 2021.

5

Reflections on the Post-Brexit Private International Law Regime in England

This chapter will contemplate the state of English private international law and pre-empt its future development by introducing the Hague Judgments Convention 2019.

> Common law: If service is made, there is jurisdiction—Regulation: If there is jurisdiction, service may be made.[1]

The loss of EU private international law and the Brussels Ia Regulation, in particular, will impact the mobility of English judgments in Europe and vice versa. Moreover, the effect of English judgments in Europe will be less than would be the case if the UK was allowed to join the Lugano II Convention. However, focusing attention solely on English judgments losing their European mobility is just one ramification of the demise of the Brussels–Lugano regime. The loss in terms of the free movement of English judgments in Europe may be offset by a gain in judicial jurisdiction and more effective measures for English enforcement. The common law jurisdictional rules are wider, discretionary and the ancillary powers of English courts are greater. The common law regime provides flexible and fine-tuned techniques for the exercise of discretion in controlling and managing judicial jurisdiction and *lis pendens*. Anti-suit injunctions are available in cases involving the EU Member States and the Lugano II Convention Contracting States and the injunction may be justified in the 'jungle of separate, broadly based, jurisdictions all over the world'.[2] The applicable law rules for cross-border contractual and non-contractual obligations that apply to the merits of a dispute will be practically the same as before Brexit. If the Lugano II Convention or a bespoke deal on civil and commercial judicial cooperation was agreed between the UK and the EU, the UK would have found itself bound by a regime which controlled the judicial jurisdiction of English courts yet provided for the free recognition and enforcement of English court judgments in Europe and vice versa.

[1] A Briggs, 'The Hidden Depths of the Law of Jurisdiction' [2016] Lloyd's Maritime and Commercial Law Quarterly 236, 237.
[2] *Airbus Industrie GIE v. Patel and Others* [1998] UKHL 12; [1999] 1 AC 119 (Lord Goff).

Brexit and the Future of Private International Law in English Courts. Mukarrum Ahmed, Oxford University Press.
 DOI: 10.1093/oso/9780192848116.003.0005

The fact that the common law jurisdictional rules *are* wide and discretionary does not mean that they *ought* to be so. There is a core of good sense in Lord Diplock's description of exorbitant jurisdiction as that 'which, under general English conflict rules, an English court would not recognise as possessed by any foreign court in the absence of some treaty providing for such recognition'.[3] The wide, discretionary, service-based common law jurisdictional rules can be described as exorbitant.[4] English courts display a willingness to grant anti-suit injunctions to counter interferences with their own exercise of jurisdiction whilst adopting a complacent attitude towards the interferences of English court orders with foreign legal systems.[5]

On the other hand, the direct rules of jurisdiction of the Brussels–Lugano regime are based on an objective territorial connection between the dispute and the forum. These jurisdictional rules promote legal certainty and predictability in relation to where a claimant may sue and where a defendant may be sued.[6] Writing extrajudicially, Lord Bingham observed that '[t]he law must be accessible and so far as possible intelligible, clear and predictable'.[7] These are characteristics which have been described as the very essence of certainty.[8] Lord Bingham then proceeds to state that '[q]uestions of legal right and liability should ordinarily be resolved by the application of the law and not the exercise of discretion'.[9] The jurisdictional rules of the Brussels–Lugano regime largely abide by the characteristics of *ex ante* legal certainty with a modicum of discretion whilst the same cannot be said about the common law rules.

According to the 'declaratory' theory of the common law, in its most traditional guise the common law has never changed.[10] The judges have merely revealed the law from time to time.[11] The declaratory theory of the common law may be viewed

[3] *Amin Rasheed Shipping Corp v Kuwait Insurance Co* [1984] AC 50, 65.

[4] P Herrup and RA Brand, 'A Hague Convention on Parallel Proceedings' (2021) University of Pittsburgh School of Law Working Paper No 23, 4.

[5] A Dickinson, 'The Interference Paradox' (2020) 136 Law Quarterly Review 569.

[6] Recital 16 of the Brussels Ia Regulation.

[7] Lord Bingham, *The Rule of Law* (Allen Lane 2010) ch 3 (hereafter Bingham, *Rule of Law*). In *Vallejo v Wheeler* (1774) 1 Cowp 143, 153, Lord Mansfield said that 'in all mercantile transactions the great object should be certainty. And therefore it is of more consequence that a rule should be certain than whether the rule is established one way or the other: because speculators in trade then know which ground to go upon'. In *Golden Straight Corporation v Nippon YKK (The 'Golden Victory')* [2007] UKHL 12, [1], Lord Bingham said that 'the quality of certainty [is] a traditional strength and major selling point of English commercial law'.

[8] Lord Mance, 'Should the Law Be Certain?' The Oxford Shrieval Lecture given in the University Church of St Mary The Virgin, Oxford 11 October 2011.

[9] Bingham, *Rule of Law* (n 7) ch 3.

[10] The view associated with Sir William Blackstone and grounded in legal positivism, that judges do not make the common law, but merely find, declare, and apply it.

[11] Lord Esher MR subscribed to a similar view to Blackstone's in *Willis & Co v Baddeley* [1892] 2 QB 324, 326: 'This is not a case, as has been suggested, of what is sometimes called judge-made law. There is, in fact, no such thing as judge-made law, for the judges do not make the law, though they frequently have to apply existing law to circumstances as to which it has not been authoritatively laid down that such law is applicable.'

simultaneously as a façade for legal certainty and as a protective cover for the discretion inherent in the common law.

Lord Sumption in *Abela v Baadarani* stated that, '[i]t should no longer be necessary to resort to the kind of muscular presumptions against service out which are implicit in adjectives like "exorbitant". The decision is generally a pragmatic one in the interests of the efficient conduct of the litigation in an appropriate forum.'[12] However, the pragmatism inherent in the idea of litigation in an appropriate forum is arguably less principled than the accessible, clearly articulated, and predictable rules of jurisdiction that represent a significant connection between the dispute and the forum.[13] The codified and mandatory direct rules of jurisdiction of the Brussels–Lugano regime adopt an internationalist approach, driven by concerns about jurisdictional connection, comity, and conflicts justice.

The emphasis placed on the private law perspective to choice of court agreements in the English common law of conflict of laws is 'clearly culturally conditioned'.[14] The position of the English courts in relation to the bifurcated conception of choice of court agreements stands in stark contrast to that of the courts of the continental tradition, for whom the obligational content of a contract (effects *in personam*) cannot be dissociated from the effects it can produce under a public law rule (effects *in rem*).[15] The 'privatisation of court access'[16] resulting from courts willing to enforce choice of court agreements *inter partes* despite a rule allocating exclusive jurisdiction to another court appears to perpetuate the notion that the courts are only there to serve the 'dispute resolution' needs of the business community.[17] Whether the interests of third parties and wider societal concerns are adequately factored into a model of adjudication focused on 'dispute resolution'[18] where the English Commercial Court acts 'as an umpire'[19] when passively deciding on the private interests as between the parties can be questioned.[20]

[12] *Abela v Baadarani* [2013] UKSC 44, [2013] 1 WLR 2403, [53]. Briggs developed Lord Sumption's observations in *Abela* to suggest that *forum conveniens* could become the sole criteria for service outside jurisdiction. See A Briggs, *Civil Jurisdiction and Judgments* (7th edn, Informa Law from Routledge 2021) 23; A Briggs, *The Conflict of Laws* (4th edn, OUP 2019) 110; A Briggs, 'Service Out in a Shrinking World' [2013] Lloyd's Maritime and Commercial Law Quarterly 415. Lord Sumption dismissed Briggs' inference in *Brownlie v Four Seasons Holdings Inc* [2017] UKSC 80, [2018] 1 WLR 192, [31].

[13] 'Far from advancing comity, ironically [the natural forum] has contributed to its infraction and exposed the judiciary to the most invidious of tasks, all the while representing a massive 'own goal' as far as the English legal profession is concerned.' A Bell, 'The Natural Forum Revisited' in A Dickinson and E Peel (eds), *A Conflict of Laws Companion: Essays in Honour of Adrian Briggs* (OUP 2021) ch 1, 30.

[14] H Muir Watt, 'Party Autonomy in International Contracts: From the Makings of a Myth to the Requirements of Global Governance' (2010) 3 European Review of Contract Law 1, 30 (hereafter Muir Watt, 'Party Autonomy').

[15] ibid.

[16] M Ahmed, *The Nature and Enforcement of Choice of Court Agreements* (Hart Publishing 2017) 263 (hereafter Ahmed, *Choice of Court Agreements*).

[17] *Pan Foods Co Importers and Distributors Pty Ltd v Australia and New Zealand Banking Group Ltd* (2000) 170 ALR 579, [24] (Kirby J) (High Court of Australia) discussed in A Briggs, *Agreements on Jurisdiction and Choice of Law* (OUP 2008) 527 (hereafter Briggs, *Agreements*).

[18] See Muir Watt, 'Party Autonomy' (n 14) 29–32.

[19] Briggs, *Agreements* (n 17) 532.

[20] See Muir Watt, 'Party Autonomy' (n 14) 30–31.

Under the Brussels Ia Regulation, choice of court agreements serve an international allocative function and do not give rise to an enforceable obligation not to sue in a non-contractual forum. However, what counts as a 'contract' is a matter of perspective or legal culture and it would be unfair to classify the operation of a 'procedural contract' as a 'formal waiver of jurisdictional privilege' which does 'not depend upon the existence of a private contract'.[21] If consent or agreement rather than the mutual exchange of promises is considered to be the theoretical basis of a contract then there is no reason to deny a procedural contract the status of a contract.[22]

The private law enforcement of foreign (non-English) choice of court agreements premised on pure contractual principles and lacking any jurisdictional connection with the English forum is tantamount to enforcing an international contract between the parties (*in personam*) without any regard for the specific international allocative relationship between the foreign courts (*in rem*).[23] The author identifies this phenomenon as another manifestation of the *substantive law* paradigm which subordinates the interests of states to the dispute resolution needs of the litigating parties. Moreover, the prospects of English courts policing foreign choice of court agreements by treating them as ordinary contracts is bound to provoke resentment from other states.

The revival of the pre-Brussels Convention bilateral treaties offers a glimmer of hope but the conclusion of agreements on the continued application of the bilateral conventions on reciprocal recognition and enforcement between the UK and the Member States should be able to guarantee access to this route. The nineteenth-century common law rules for the recognition and enforcement of judgments need to be reviewed. The rules allow the enforcement of foreign default judgments based only on the defendant's transient presence in the foreign jurisdiction at the time of service. However, a 'real and substantial connection' which could serve as an indirect jurisdictional rule such as the place of performance of a contract or the place where a tort occurred is deemed irrelevant for the purposes of recognition and enforcement. The jurisdictional filters in the Hague Judgments Convention 2019 resemble the connecting factors which justify exorbitant jurisdiction in some legal systems. As a result, the grounds for recognition and enforcement under the Convention are wider than the traditional requirement of a court of competent

[21] Briggs, *Agreements* (n 17) 524.

[22] RE Jones and G MacCormack, 'Obligations' in E Metzger (ed), *A Companion to Justinian's Institutions* (Duckworth 1998) 127, 150. cf C Fried, *Contract as Promise: A Theory of Contractual Obligation* (Harvard University Press 1981).

[23] *People's Insurance Co v Akai Pty Ltd* [1998] 1 SLR 206 (Singapore High Court), quoted with apparent approval in *Akai Pty Ltd v People's Insurance Co Ltd* [1998] 1 Lloyd's Rep 90, 108; Ahmed, *Choice of Court Agreements* (n 16) 91–98. cf *IPOC International Growth Fund Ltd v OAO CT Mobile* [2007] Bermuda LR 43; L Collins and others (eds), *Dicey, Morris & Collins on the Conflict of Laws* (15th edn, Sweet and Maxwell 2012) ch 12, 600 (r 39(4)): The use of the word *semble* in relation to the English enforcement of a breach of foreign choice of court agreement via an anti-suit injunction indicates that the point is undecided or doubtful.

jurisdiction according to English private international law rules. Legislation is likely to be needed if a better set of rules is to be formulated.

A weaker conception of comity is characteristic of the English *substantive law* paradigm which focuses on the vertical relationship between the court and the parties.[24] As a result, the notion of comity is nearly irrelevant in the enforcement of choice of court and arbitration agreements with anti-suit injunctions and damages. The author has dismissed the use of a 'system-transcendent' rationale such as freedom of contract or *pacta sunt servanda* to justify the enforcement of choice of court and arbitration agreements because such a concept cannot justify the unilateral nature of the English court's interpretation of the rights of the parties and their enforcement without regard to the rights of other states. In similar vein, a 'system-transcendent' rationale of comity cannot be applied to the unilateral *Spiliada forum non conveniens* unless other states adopt the doctrine and ideally belong to the same legal tradition. A better role for *forum non conveniens* may be based on a 'manifestly more appropriate forum' or a 'clearly inappropriate' forum test. The methodologically pluralist parameters of these tests are more predictable than the wide-ranging evaluative enquiry required in the quest for the natural forum. The proposed stricter variants of the *forum non conveniens* test will help structure the judge's evaluative process and allocation of time and resources in hard cases where there may be no easy answers as to the natural forum especially at the interim stage of proceedings.

It is evident that the advantages of a double convention jurisdiction and judgments regime of the Brussels Ia Regulation cannot be achieved through the unilateral common law regime. Although the EU has refused the UK's application for accession to the Lugano II Convention, the Convention itself does not replicate the improvements of the Brussels Ia Regulation. However, it does offer an acceptable double convention regime, at least until the Convention is reformed to incorporate the state-of-the-art provisions.

The Hague Choice of Court Convention 2005 has become a far more significant instrument after Brexit because it regulates the civil judicial cooperation relationship between the UK and the EU for matters within its scope. The Hague Choice of Court Convention provides legal certainty and substantial protection to exclusive choice of court agreements. It obliges the Contracting States (including Member States) to decline jurisdiction in the face of a relevant English exclusive choice of court clause, and to recognise and enforce judgments from the chosen court in a Contracting State (including Member States). It has been observed that the Hague Choice of Court Convention complemented by the common law's remedies

[24] Ahmed, *Choice of Court Agreements* (n 16) 266; L Collins, 'Comity in Modern Private International Law' in J Fawcett (ed), *Reform and Development of Private International Law: Essays in Honour of Sir Peter North* (OUP 2002) 89; Briggs, *Agreements* (n 17) 538; A Briggs, 'The Principle of Comity in Private International Law' (2012) 354 Recueil des Cours 65.

for breach of exclusive choice of court agreements synergises the enforcement of exclusive choice of court clauses in English courts. However, Article 31(2) of the Brussels Ia Regulation went beyond the solution adopted by the Hague Choice of Court Convention because it created a rule on *lis pendens* which accorded priority to the chosen court.

Post Brexit, the UK has decided to replicate the EU's declaration limiting the application of the Hague Convention in relation to a significant class of insurance contracts. It has been argued that the UK should withdraw this declaration and enable the UK insurance services market to effectively utilise choice of court agreements in commercial cases.[25]

The Hague Convention provides that Contracting States may make reciprocal declarations for the recognition and enforcement of judgments based on non-exclusive choice of court agreements.[26] It is recommended that the UK and the EU (as a Regional Economic Integration Organisation)[27] should make a reciprocal declaration under Article 22 of the Convention to enable enhanced judicial co-operation in civil and commercial matters between the UK and the EU within the minimum mandatory framework of the Hague Convention. There has been no positive indication of any reciprocal declarations to date.

The post-Brexit application of the Hague Choice of Court Convention is likely to give rise to the issue whether asymmetric choice of court agreements are exclusive choice of court agreements for the purposes of the Convention. There is no definitive English ruling on the point and the issue may be brought before the Court of Justice of the European Union (CJEU) on a preliminary reference from a Member State court after Brexit. The other contentious issue that could be addressed by the CJEU on a preliminary reference from the courts of a Member State is the date the Hague Convention entered into force in the UK. The CJEU could either vindicate the stance of the UK government that 1 October 2015 is when the UK joined the Convention by virtue of its EU membership or confirm the position adopted by the European Commission that 1 January 2021 is when the UK joined the Convention as an independent Contracting State.

The UK should persuade other states to accede to the Hague Choice of Court Convention. In order to cast the net of the Hague Choice of Court Convention as far and wide as possible, it is recommended that Switzerland, Norway, and Iceland (the non-EU Lugano II Convention Contracting States) should become parties to the Hague Choice of Court Convention at the earliest opportunity.

The Rome I and II Regulations under the guise of retained EU law constitute a new and unique category of law that is neither EU law nor English law *per se*. The

[25] P Beaumont, 'Some Reflections on the Way Ahead for UK Private International Law after Brexit' (2021) 17 Journal of Private International Law 1, 7.

[26] Article 22 of the Hague Convention.

[27] Article 29 of the Hague Convention.

identification and interpretation of retained EU law will give rise to its own set of challenges. Ultimately, fidelity to EU law will have to be balanced with the ability of UK appellate courts to diverge from retained EU law and develop their own jurisprudence.[28] Courts at the level of the Court of Appeal in England and Wales and the UK Supreme Court may overturn binding pre-Brexit EU case law if they consider it 'right to do so'.[29] In practice, all UK courts are likely to be influenced by non-binding post-Brexit EU case law where they are interpreting the same piece of legislation. As a result of the extension of the power to amend binding pre-Brexit EU case law to the Court of Appeal, the category of retained EU law is more amenable to change than ordinary English domestic law.

Any future amendments to the EU private international law of obligations will not affect the course of international civil litigation before English courts. Notwithstanding, it is suggested that the EU's reviews of the Rome I and II Regulations will provide a useful opportunity for the UK to re-evaluate its own choice of law rules with a view to making appropriate changes.

The UK should seize the initiative by taking the lead in ratifying the Hague Judgments Convention 2019. It is hoped that accessions by some of the world's major trading nations to the Hague Judgments Convention will encourage other states to follow suit. The next section will briefly survey the Hague Judgments Convention and whether it can act as a post-Brexit substitute for the EU's civil judicial cooperation instruments in the UK.

A. The Hague Judgments Convention 2019: A Panacea for Brexit?

The European Commission has adopted a proposal for the EU to accede to the Hague Judgments Convention 2019, an international treaty which is aimed at facilitating the mutual recognition and enforcement of judgments in civil and commercial matters.[30] In order for the EU to join the Convention, the Commission's

[28] From the perspective of a theory of adjudication, the tension between the category of 'fit' exemplified by retained EU law and the category of 'justification' based on principle or policy in hard cases will result in the indigenous development of the corpus of retained EU law. See generally, R Dworkin, *Taking Rights Seriously* (Harvard University Press 1977) ch 4.

[29] The European Union (Withdrawal) Act 2018 (Relevant Court) (Retained EU Case Law) Regulations (SI 2020/1525) allow the Court of Appeal of England and Wales (and equivalent courts across the UK) to depart from retained EU case law. Under the European Union (Withdrawal) Act 2018, it is only the UK Supreme Court (or High Court of Justiciary in Scotland) that has this power.

[30] Proposal for a Council Decision on the accession by the European Union to the Convention on the Recognition and Enforcement of Foreign Judgments in Civil or Commercial Matters COM (2021) 388 final. On 2 July 2019, the Hague Conference on Private International Law finalised a new treaty on the recognition and enforcement of judgments: the Convention on the Recognition and Enforcement of Foreign Judgments in Civil or Commercial Matters, or the Hague Judgments Convention 2019.

proposal will have to be adopted by the European Council, with the European Parliament's consent.

The 2019 Convention has been described as a game changer in international dispute resolution. It is a single global framework, enabling the free circulation of judgments in civil or commercial matters, which will provide better, more effective, and cheaper justice for individuals and businesses alike.

In essence, it complements the Hague Choice of Court Agreements Convention 2005 by allowing enforcement of judgments in much broader circumstances—in particular, in contrast to the 2005 Convention, it does not require an exclusive choice of court clause in favour of a Contracting State, and employment and consumer contracts are within scope.

The Hague Conventions of 2005 and 2019 resulted from a broader project begun in the early 1990s considering issues of jurisdiction as well as the recognition and enforcement of judgments.[31] A consensus determination in 2001 that a comprehensive treaty on jurisdiction and judgments was not possible allowed the Hague Conference on Private International Law to focus on specific pieces of that broader project and led to the two existing Conventions.[32]

If the EU accedes to the Convention, and assuming the UK also signs up in due course, it could significantly streamline the recognition and enforcement of judgments between the UK and the EU. Currently, while the UK has been refused accession to the Lugano II Convention,[33] recognition and enforcement in most cases relies on national rules in each country, unless there is an exclusive choice of court clause falling within the 2005 Convention.

The 2019 Convention will not, however, come into force for any state until (approximately) twelve months after ratification.[34] Even then, it won't apply unless the proceedings were started (as opposed to the judgment being issued) when the Convention was in force for both the state of origin and the state of enforcement.[35] This means that it will be some considerable time before it has any impact in practice. It is also worth noting that it is not a complete replacement for the Lugano

[31] See, Preparatory Work on the Judgments Convention, available at <https://www.hcch.net/en/instruments/conventions/publications1/?dtid=61&cid=137> accessed 31 August 2021.

[32] See, Response to the preliminary draft convention (2000-2001) by the Hague Conference Special Commission on General Affairs and Policy, available at <https://www.hcch.net/en/publications-and-studies/details4/?pid=6840&dtid=61> accessed 31 August 2021.

[33] An advantage of the UK and EU ratifying the Hague Judgments Convention 2019 prior to the UK acceding to the Lugano II Convention would be that judgments emanating from pre-emptive torpedo proceedings in Europe in breach of an English choice of court agreement could be refused recognition and enforcement in the UK courts by virtue of Article 7(1)(d) of the Hague Judgments Convention.

[34] Under Article 29 of the Hague Judgments Convention, there is a delay of approximately twelve months post ratification before the convention can have effect between Contracting States.

[35] Under Article 16 of the Hague Judgments Convention, it will only apply to the recognition and enforcement of judgments if, at the time the proceedings were instituted in the State of origin, the Convention had effect between that State and the requested State.

II Convention because recognition and enforcement can be refused on broader grounds than under the Lugano II Convention.

Unlike the Brussels–Lugano regime as well as the Hague Choice of Court Convention 2005, the Hague Judgments Convention 2019 is not a double convention. Whilst the Hague Judgments Convention deals with the recognition and enforcement of judgments, it does not address the jurisdiction of a court to hear a dispute in the first place. The recognition and enforcement of judgments is subject to exequatur and unless defined by the Hague Judgments Convention, is governed by the law of the requested state.[36] Ratification by both the EU and the UK would be a positive step in facilitating mutual recognition and enforcement of judgments in the longer term.

B. Introducing the Hague Judgments Convention 2019

The Convention is a private international law instrument in civil or commercial matters.[37] It deals with one of the three classical areas of private international law, namely the recognition and enforcement of foreign judgments. In so doing, it furthers one of the main goals of private international law: international judicial cooperation, with a view to enhancing predictability and justice in cross-border legal relations in civil or commercial matters. The Convention does not deal with the other two traditional areas of private international law, relating to court jurisdiction to adjudicate disputes in cross-border cases and rules determining the law applicable to such cases. Those matters are not affected by the Convention.

1. Objective

This Convention seeks to promote access to justice globally through enhanced judicial cooperation, which will reduce risks and costs associated with cross-border legal relations and dispute resolution. As a result, implementation of the Convention should facilitate rule-based multilateral trade and investment and mobility.

These goals will be advanced in a number of ways.

First and most importantly, the Convention provides a framework for the recognition and enforcement of foreign judgments in all Contracting States('States'), thereby enhancing the practical effectiveness of those judgments. Access to justice is frustrated if a wronged party obtains a judgment that cannot be enforced in

[36] Article 13 of the Hague Judgments Convention.

[37] This section is adapted from the Explanatory Report by Professor Francisco Garcimartín and Professor Geneviève Saumier.

practice because the other party or the other party's assets are in a State where the judgment is not readily enforceable.

Second, the Convention will reduce the need for duplicative proceedings in two or more States; a judgment determining the claim in one State will be effective in other States, without the need to re-litigate the merits of the claim.

Third, the Convention will reduce the cost and time frame of obtaining recognition and enforcement of judgments; access to practical justice will be faster and at lower cost.

Fourth, the Convention will improve the predictability of the law; individuals and businesses will be able to more readily ascertain the circumstances in which judgments will circulate among States.

Fifth, it will enable claimants to make informed choices about where to bring proceedings, taking into account the ability to enforce the resulting judgment in other States and the need to ensure fairness to defendants.

In a globalised and interconnected world, with ever-increasing movement of people, information and assets across borders, the practical importance of achieving these goals is self-evident. The Convention's potential to reach these goals is significant.

2. Relationship with the Hague Choice of Court Convention

The Hague Choice of Court Convention pursues the same objectives by enabling parties to agree on the court that will hear a claim and providing for the recognition and enforcement of a judgment given by the chosen court. However, in many cases there is no exclusive choice of court agreement between the parties to a dispute.[38] This Convention seeks to extend the benefits of enhanced access to justice and reduced costs and risks of cross-border dealings to a broader range of cases. It is intended to complement the Hague Choice of Court Convention.[39]

3. Outline of Provisions

The Convention is designed to provide an efficient and effective system for recognising and enforcing foreign judgments in civil or commercial matters in largely uncontroversial circumstances. The Convention provides for the recognition

[38] According to Article 5(1)(m) of the Hague Judgments Convention 2019, a judgment based on proceedings pursuant to a unilateral or asymmetric choice of court agreement is eligible for recognition and enforcement under the Convention.

[39] Article 7(1)(d) of the Hague Judgments Convention 2019 will ameliorate the venue and enforcement risk arising from pre-emptive torpedo proceedings by refusing to recognise or enforce any judgment given in breach of a choice of court agreement.

and enforcement of judgments that meet certain requirements[40] and sets out the grounds on which recognition or enforcement of such judgments may be refused.[41] To facilitate the circulation of judgments, the text does not prevent States from recognising or enforcing judgments under national law or under other treaties,[42] subject to one exclusive basis for recognition and enforcement.[43]

4. Looking Forward: The Regulation of International Parallel Proceedings

This proliferation of cross-border activity results in an increase in the number of states with a legal or factual connection to a transaction or relationship.[44] For instance, in a sale of goods contract, there are a number of localising elements that could justify a jurisdictional connection, such as the location of the advertisement for sale, the contract offer, the contract acceptance, the initial packaging of the goods, the loading of the first carrier for transit, the export customs territory, the import customs territory, the storage upon arrival in the import customs territory, the unloading from the final carrier for transit, the purchaser's facility at destination, the bank through which payment is made or financing is arranged, the office where payment is received, or other geographic activity of one or more of the parties to the transaction. Each of these connecting factors could be considered important by national rules determining judicial jurisdiction, resulting in there being courts in multiple states where a legal action may be commenced when a dispute arises.[45]

The question facing the Hague Conference on Private International Law is whether further international legal instruments may resolve other significant problems raised by cross-border litigation. There is a growing need for rules that address questions of parallel proceedings when courts in more than one State are seised of the same or related causes of action under their own jurisdictional rules.

[40] Articles 5 and 6 of the Hague Judgments Convention.

[41] Article 7 of the Hague Judgments Convention. The grounds on which courts may refuse to recognise or enforce judgments include that the judgment is 'manifestly incompatible with public policy of the requested State'. Refusal is justified if the foreign judgment was obtained by fraud or is inconsistent with a judgment of a court of the requested state between the same parties. Recognition or enforcement may also be refused if, and to the extent that, the judgment awards non-compensatory damages, including exemplary damages.

[42] Articles 15 and 23 of the Hague Judgments Convention.

[43] Article 6 of the Hague Judgments Convention. Rights *in rem* in immovable property are subject to an exclusive basis for recognition and enforcement. A judgment that ruled on rights *in rem* in immovable property shall be recognised and enforced if and only if the property is situated in the state of origin.

[44] The Hague Jurisdiction Project <HCCH | Jurisdiction Project> accessed 31 August 2021.

[45] P Herrup and RA Brand, 'A Hague Convention on Parallel Proceedings' (2021) University of Pittsburgh School of Law Working Paper No 23, 3.

It has been suggested that a new solution to *lis pendens* driven by the imperatives of globalisation and developed by cooperative law reform between civil law and common law is already upon us.[46] Articles 21 and 22 of the Preliminary Draft Convention on Jurisdiction and Foreign Judgments in Civil and Commercial Matters (30 October 1999) could become the basis for a global solution to the conflicts of jurisdiction by balancing the EU *lis pendens* rule with a clearly circumscribed and exceptionally applicable *forum non conveniens*.[47] This diminished, but acceptable, global role for *forum non conveniens* is based on a 'clearly inappropriate' forum test.[48]

[46] C McLachlan, *Lis Pendens in International Litigation* (Martinus Nijhoff 2009) 438–39.

[47] Articles 21 and 22 and the Nygh/Pocar Report on the Preliminary Draft Convention on Jurisdiction and Foreign Judgments in Civil and Commercial Matters adopted by the Special Commission on 30 October 1999, 89–98.

[48] P Beaumont, 'Forum Non Conveniens and the EU Rules on Conflicts of Jurisdiction: A Possible Global Solution' [2018] Revue critique de droit international privé 447.

Bibliography

Ahmed M, 'The Enforcement of Settlement and Jurisdiction Agreements and Parallel Proceedings in the European Union: *The Alexandros T* Litigation in the English Courts' (2015) 11 Journal of Private International Law 406

——'BREXIT and English Jurisdiction Agreements: The Post-Referendum Legal Landscape' (2016) 27 European Business Law Review 989

——'The Legal Regulation and Enforcement of Asymmetric Jurisdiction Agreements in the European Union' (2017) 28 European Business Law Review 403

——*The Nature and Enforcement of Choice of Court Agreements: A Comparative Study* (Hart Publishing 2017)

——'The Nature and Enforcement of Choice of Law Agreements' (2018) 14 Journal of Private International Law 500

——'A Dangerous Chimera: Anti-Suit Injunctions Based on a "Right to Be Sued" at the Place of Domicile under the Brussels Ia Regulation?' (2020) 136 Law Quarterly Review 379

——'The Validity of Choice of Court Agreements in International Commercial Contracts under the Hague Choice of Court Convention and the Brussels Ia Regulation' in M Furmston (ed), *The Future of the Law of Contract* (Informa Law from Routledge 2020) ch 11, 217–36

——'Private International Law and Substantive Liability Issues in Tort Litigation against Multinational Companies in the English Courts: Recent UK Supreme Court Decisions and Post-Brexit Implications' (2022) 18 Journal of Private International Law

——and Beaumont P, 'Exclusive Choice of Court Agreements: Some Issues on the Hague Convention on Choice of Court Agreements and its Relationship with the Brussels I Recast Especially Anti-suit Injunctions, Concurrent Proceedings and the Implications of BREXIT' (2017) 13 Journal of Private International Law 386

——and Beaumont P, 'I Thought We Were Exclusive? Some Issues with the Hague Convention on Choice of Court, Brussels Ia and Brexit' (24 September 2017, *Conflictoflaws.net*) <I thought we were exclusive? Some issues with the Hague Convention on Choice of Court, Brussels Ia and Brexit – Conflict of Laws> accessed 31 August 2021

Antomo J, 'Anmerkung zu BGH III ZR 42/19' [2020] Europäische Zeitschrift für Wirtschaftsrecht 143

Arzandeh A, 'Should the *Spiliada* Test Be Revised?' (2014) 10 Journal of Private International Law 89

——' "Gateways" within the Civil Procedure Rules and the Future of Service-out Jurisdiction in England' (2019) 15 Journal of Private International Law 516

——'Reformulating the Common Law Rules on the Recognition and Enforcement of Foreign Judgments' (2019) 39 Legal Studies 56

Audit B, 'Rapport Français' in S Symeonides (ed), *Private International Law at the End of the 20th Century: Progress or Regress?* (Kluwer Law International 1999) 191

Barnard C, 'Law and Brexit' (2017) 33 Oxford Review of Economic Policy S4

——'Law and the Courts' in A Menon (ed), *Brexit: What Next?* (The UK in a Changing Europe, 13 February 2020) <Brexit-what-next-report.pdf (ukandeu.ac.uk)> accessed 31 August 2021

Barnett P, *Res Judicata, Estoppel, and Foreign Judgments: The Preclusive Effects of Foreign Judgments in Private International Law* (OUP 2001)

Basedow J, 'Brexit und das Privat- und Wirtschaftsrecht' (2016) 24 Zeitschrift für EuropäischesPrivatrecht (ZEuP) 567

——and others (eds), *Elgar Encyclopedia of Private International Law* (Edward Elgar 2017)

Batiffol H, 'Le pluralisme des méthodes en droit international privé' (1973) 139 Recueil des Cours 75

Beaumont P, 'Hague Choice of Court Agreements Convention 2005: Background, Negotiations, Analysis and Current Status' (2009) 5 Journal of Private International Law 125

——'The Revived Judgments Project in The Hague' [2014] Nederlands Internationaal Privaatrecht (NIPR) 532

——'Respecting Reverse Subsidiarity is an Excellent Strategy for the European Union at The Hague Conference on Private International Law: Currently being Well Deployed in the Judgments Project' (2016) 2 Centre for Private International Law Aberdeen Working Paper Series, Working Paper No 2016/3, <www.abdn.ac.uk/law/documents/CPIL_Working_paper_2016_3_revised.pdf> accessed 31 August 2021

——'Forum Non Conveniens and the EU Rules on Conflicts of Jurisdiction: A Possible Global Solution' [2018] Revue critique de droit international privé 447

——'Some Reflections on the Way Ahead for UK Private International Law after Brexit' (2021) 17 Journal of Private International Law 1

——and McEleavy PE, *Anton's Private International Law* (3rd edn, SULI/W Green 2011)

Bell A, 'The Natural Forum Revisited' in A Dickinson and E Peel (eds), *A Conflict of Laws Companion: Essays in Honour of Adrian Briggs* (OUP 2021) ch 1

Bergson I, 'The Death of the Torpedo Action?' (2015) 11 Journal of Private International Law 1

Bingham T, *The Rule of Law* (Allen Lane 2010)

Blackaby N and Partasides C with Redfern A and Hunter M, *Redfern and Hunter on International Arbitration* (5th edn, OUP 2009)

Blom-Cooper L QC, '1966 and All That: The Story of the Practice Statement 1' in L Blom-Cooper QC, B Dickson, and G Drewry (eds), *The Judicial House of Lords: 1876–2009* (OUP 2009) 128

——Dickson B, and Drewry G (eds), *The Judicial House of Lords: 1876–2009* (OUP 2009)

Bogdan M, *Private International Law as Component of the Law of the Forum* (Martinus Nijhoff 2012)

Borchers PJ, 'Categorical Exceptions to Party Autonomy in Private International Law' (2008) 82 Tulane Law Review 1645

Brand RA, 'Comparative Forum Non Conveniens and the Hague Convention on Jurisdiction and Judgments' (2002) 37 Texas International Law Journal 467

——and Jablonski SR, *Forum Non Conveniens: History, Global Practice, and Future Under the Hague Convention on Choice of Court Agreements* (OUP 2007)

——and Herrup PM, *The 2005 Hague Convention on Choice of Court Agreements* (Cambridge University Press 2008)

Briggs A, 'Foreign Judgments and Res Judicata' (1997) 68 British Yearbook of International Law 355

——'The Unrestrained Reach of an Anti-Suit Injunction: A Pause for Thought' [1997] Lloyd's Maritime and Commercial Law Quarterly 90

——'The Impact of Recent Judgments of the European Court on English Procedural Law and Practice' (2005) II (124) Zeitschrift fur Schweizerisches Recht 231

——*The Conflict of Laws* (2nd edn, OUP 2008)

——*Agreements on Jurisdiction and Choice of Law* (OUP 2008)

——'What Should Be Done about Jurisdiction Agreements' (2010) 12 Yearbook of Private International Law 311
——'The Brussels I bis Regulation Appears on the Horizon' [2011] Lloyd's Maritime and Commercial Law Quarterly 157
——'The Principle of Comity in Private International Law' (2012) 354 Recueil des Cours 65
——'Service out in a shrinking world' [2013] Lloyd's Maritime and Commercial Law Quarterly 415
——*The Conflict of Laws* (3rd edn, OUP 2013)
——*Private International Law in English Courts* (OUP 2014)
——*Civil Jurisdiction and Judgments* (6th edn, Informa Law from Routledge 2015)
——'The Hidden Depths of the Law of Jurisdiction' [2016] Lloyd's Maritime and Commercial Law Quarterly 236
——'Secession from the European Union and Private International Law: The Cloud with a Silver Lining' Commercial Bar Association Brexit Lecture, 24 January 2017 <adrian_briggs_brexit_lecture.pdf (ox.ac.uk)> accessed 31 August 2021
——*The Conflict of Laws* (4th edn, OUP 2019)
——*Civil Jurisdiction and Judgments* (7th edn, Informa Law from Routledge 2021)
——'Four Decades of Private International Law' Oxford Law Faculty Website accessed 31 August 2021
Bucher A, La dimension sociale du droit international privé (Cours general) (2009) Recueil des Cours 341
Camilleri SP, 'Recital 12 of the Recast Regulation: A New Hope?' (2013) 62 International and Comparative Law Quarterly 899
Chan FWH, 'Anti-suit Injunctions and the Doctrine of Comity' (2016) 79 Modern Law Review 341
Cheshire GC, *Private International Law* (OUP 1935)
Chong A and Yip M, 'Singapore as a Centre for International Commercial Litigation: Party Autonomy to the Fore' (2019) 15 Journal of Private International Law 97
Coke E, *The First Part of the Institutes of the Laws of England, or, A Commentary on Littleton* (first published 1628, F Hargrave and C Butler eds, 19th edn, London 1832)
Collins L, *The Civil Jurisdiction and Judgments Act 1982* (Butterworths 1983)
——'Comity in Modern Private International Law' in J Fawcett (ed), *Reform and Development of Private International Law: Essays in Honour of Sir Peter North* (OUP 2002) 89
——and others (eds), *Dicey Morris & Collins The Conflict of Laws* (14th edn, Sweet & Maxwell 2006)
——*Dicey, Morris & Collins The Conflict of Laws* (15th edn, Sweet & Maxwell 2012)
Craig P, 'Miller: Alternative Syllogisms' (23 November 2016, Oxford Human Rights Hub), <http://ohrh.law.ox.ac.uk/miller-alternative-syllogisms/> accessed 31 August 2021
——and De Burca G, *EU Law: Text, Cases and Materials* (5th edn, OUP 2011)
Crawford EB and Carruthers JM, 'Connection and Coherence Between and among European Instruments in the Private International Law of Obligations' (2014) 63 International and Comparative Law Quarterly 1
Cross R and Harris JW, *Precedent in English Law* (4th edn, Clarendon Press 1991)
——Bell J, and Engle G, *Cross: Statutory Interpretation* (3rd edn, OUP 1995)
Cuniberti G, *Conflict of Laws: A Comparative Approach* (Edward Elgar 2017)
——'Ex Officio Application of EU Choice of Law Rules: Should the Interests of the Parties Matter?' (EAPIL Blog, 9 August 2021) <Ex Officio Application of EU Choice of Law Rules: Should the Interests of the Parties Matter? – EAPIL> accessed 31 August 2021

Davies M, '*Forum Non Conveniens*: Now We Are Much More Than Ten' in A Dickinson and E Peel (eds), *A Conflict of Laws Companion: Essays in Honour of Adrian Briggs* (OUP 2021) ch 2, 31–51

De Verneuil Smith P, Lasserson B, and Rymkiewicz R, 'Reflections on Owusu: The Radical Decision in Ferrexpo' (2012) 8 Journal of Private International Law 389

Dicey AV, *Digest of the Law of England with Reference to the Conflict of Laws* (Stevens & Sons, 1896)

Dickinson A, 'A Charter for Tactical Litigation in Europe?' [2004] Lloyd's Maritime and Commercial Law Quarterly 273

——'Resurgence of the Anti-Suit Injunction: The Brussels I Regulation as a Source of Civil Obligations?' (2008) 57 International and Comparative Law Quarterly 465

——*The Rome II Regulation* (OUP 2008)

——'Surveying the Proposed Brussels I bis Regulation—Solid Foundations but Renovation Needed' (2010) 12 Yearbook of Private International Law 247

——'Back to the Future: The UK' s EU Exit and the Conflict of Laws' (2016) 12 Journal of Private International Law 195

——'Faulty Powers: One-Star Service in the English Courts' [2018] Lloyd's Maritime and Commercial Law Quarterly 189

——'The Interference Paradox' (2020) 136 Law Quarterly Review 569

——'Walking Solo—A New Path for the Conflict of Laws in England' (Conflictoflaws.net, 4 January 2021) <Walking Solo—A New Path for the Conflict of Laws in England—Conflict of Laws> accessed 31 August 2021

——'Realignment of the Planets—Brexit and European Private International Law' [2021] Praxis des Internationalen Privat- und Verfahrensrechts 213

——'Taming Anti-suit Injunctions' in A Dickinson and E Peel (eds), *A Conflict of Laws Companion: Essays in Honour of Adrian Briggs* (OUP 2021) ch 4, 77–110

——'No Coming Back?' (EAPIL Blog, 19 February 2021) <https://eapil.org/2021/02/19/dickinson-on-the-fate-of-the-1968-brussels-convention-no-coming-back/> accessed 31 August 2021

——and Lein E (eds), *The Brussels I Regulation Recast* (OUP 2015)

——and Peel E (eds), *A Conflict of Laws Companion: Essays in Honour of Adrian Briggs* (OUP 2021)

Droz G, *Compétence judiciaire et effets des jugements dans le marché commun* (Dalloz 1972)

Duhs E and Rao I, *Retained EU Law: A Practical Guide* (The Law Society 2021)

Dworkin R, *Taking Rights Seriously* (Harvard University Press 1977)

Dworkin R, *Taking Rights Seriously* (Duckworth 1978)

Fawcett JJ and Carruthers JM, *Cheshire, North & Fawcett: Private International Law* (14th edn, OUP 2008)

Fellmeth AX and Horwitz M, *Guide to Latin in International Law* (OUP 2011)

Fentiman R, 'Comity and Antisuit Injunctions' (1998) 57 Cambridge Law Journal 467

——*Foreign Law in English Courts* (OUP 1998)

——*International Commercial Litigation* (2nd edn, OUP 2015)

Fiorini A, 'The Codification of Private International Law in Europe—Could the Community Learn from the Experience of Mixed Jurisdictions' (2008) 23 Tulane European and Civil Law Forum 89

Fitchen J, *The Private International Law of Authentic Instruments* (Hart Publishing 2020)

Forner-Delaygua Q, 'Changes to Jurisdiction Based on Exclusive Jurisdiction Agreements under the Brussels I Regulation Recast' (2015) 11 Journal of Private International Law 379

Franzina P (ed), *The External Action of the EU in the Field of Private International Law after Opinion 1/13* (Intersentia 2016)

Franzosi M, 'Worldwide Patent Litigation and the Italian Torpedo' [1997] European Intellectual Property Review 382

Fried C, *Contract as Promise: A Theory of Contractual Obligation* (Harvard University Press 1981)

Garcimartin F, 'Chapter 9—Article 25' in A Dickinson and E Lein (eds), *The Brussels I Regulation Recast* (OUP 2015) 338

——and Saumier G, 'Explanatory Report on the Convention of 2 July 2019 on the Recognition and Enforcement of Foreign Judgments in Civil or Commercial Matters' (Permanent Bureau of the Hague Conference on Private International Law 2020) <a1b0b0fc-95b1-4544-935b-b842534a120f.pdf (hcch.net)> accessed 31 August 2021

Gardella A and Radicati Di Brozolo LG, 'Civil Law, Common Law and Market Integration: The EC Approach to Conflicts of Jurisdiction' (2003) 51 American Journal of Comparative Law 611

Garnett R, 'Stay of Proceedings in Australia: A 'Clearly Inappropriate' Test?' (1999) 23 Melbourne University Law Review 30

——'The Hague Choice of Court Convention: Magnum Opus or Much Ado about Nothing?' (2009) 5 Journal of Private International Law 161

——*Substance and Procedure in Private International Law* (OUP 2012)

Geeroms S, *Foreign Law in Civil Litigation* (OUP 2004)

Gonzalez SA, 'The Spanish Tribunal Supremo Grants Damages for Breach of a Choice of Court Agreement' [2009] Praxis des Internationalen Privat- und Verfahrensrechts 529

Gottschalk E and others (eds), *Conflict of Laws in a Globalized World* (Cambridge University Press 2007)

Grusic U, *The European Private International Law of Employment* (Cambridge University Press 2015)

——'International Environmental Litigation in EU Courts: A Regulatory Perspective' (2016) 35 Yearbook of European Law 180

Harris J, 'Anti-Suit Injunctions—A Home Comfort' [1997] Lloyd's Maritime and Commercial Law Quarterly 413

——'Understanding the English Response to the Europeanisation of Private International Law' (2008) 4 Journal of Private International Law 347

——'Agreements on Jurisdiction and Choice of Law: Where Next?' [2009] Lloyd's Maritime and Commercial Law Quarterly 537

——'Brexit & Cross-Border Dispute Resolution' New Law Journal (2016) <Brexit & cross-border dispute resolution | New Law Journal | The leading weekly legal magazine> accessed 31 August 2021

Harris JW, *Legal Philosophies* (2nd edn, Butterworths 1997)

Hart HLA, 'Positivism and the Separation of Law and Morals' (1958) 71 Harvard Law Review 593

——*The Concept of Law* (2nd edn, OUP 1994)

Hartley TC, *Civil Jurisdiction and Judgments: The Application in England of the Convention on Jurisdiction and the Enforcement of Judgments in Civil and Commercial Matters under the Civil Jurisdiction and Judgments Act 1982* (Sweet & Maxwell 1984)

——'The European Union and the Systematic Dismantling of the Common Law of Conflict of Laws' (2005) 54 International and Comparative Law Quarterly 813

——'Jurisdiction in Conflict of Laws—Disclosure, Third-party Debt and Freezing Orders' (2010) *126* Law Quarterly Review 194

——*The Foundations of European Union Law* (8th edn, OUP 2010)
——'Choice-of-Court Agreements and the New Brussels I Regulation' (2013) 129 Law Quarterly Review 309
——*Choice of Court Agreements under the European and International Instruments* (OUP 2013)
——'The Brussels I Regulation and Arbitration' (2014) International and Comparative Law Quarterly 843
——*Civil Jurisdiction and Judgments in Europe* (OUP 2017)
——'Jurisdiction in Tort Claims for Non-Physical Harm under Brussels 2012, Article 7(2)' (2018) 67 International and Comparative Law Quarterly 987
——and M Dogauchi, 'Explanatory Report on the Preliminary Draft Convention on Exclusive Choice of Court Agreements' (Preliminary Document No 26 of December 2004) in *Proceedings of the Twentieth Session of the Hague Conference on Private International Law* (Permanent Bureau of the Conference, Intersentia 2010)
——'Explanatory Report on the Preliminary Draft Convention on Choice of Court Agreements' (Preliminary Document No 25 of March 2004) <www.hcch.net/upload/wop/jdgm_pd25e.pdf> accessed 31 August 2021
Hartley T, 'Arbitration and the Brussels I Regulation—Before and After Brexit' (2021) 17 Journal of Private International Law 53
——'Is the 2005 Hague Choice-of-Court Convention Really a Threat to Justice and Fair Play? A Reply to Gary Born' (EAPIL Blog, 30 June 2021) <Is the 2005 Hague Choice-of-Court Convention Really a Threat to Justice and Fair Play? A Reply to Gary Born – EAPIL>accessed 31 August 2021
Hay P, 'Notes on the European Union's Brussels-I "Recast" Regulation' (2013) 13 *The European Legal Forum* 1
Heinze C and Steinrotter B, 'The Revised Lis Pendens Rules in the Brussels Ibis Regulation' in V Lazic and S Stuij (eds), *Brussels Ibis Regulation: Changes and Challenges of the Renewed Procedural Scheme* (TMC Asser Press/Springer 2017) 1
Herrup P and Brand RA, 'A Hague Convention on Parallel Proceedings' (2021) University of Pittsburgh School of Law Working Paper No 23
Hess B, 'The Draft Hague Convention on Choice of Court Agreements, External Competencies of the European Union and Recent Case Law of the European Court of Justice' in A Nuyts and N Watté (eds), *International Civil Litigation in Europe and Relations with Third States* (Bruylant 2005) 263
——Pfeiffer T, and Schlosser P, *The Brussels I Regulation 44/2001: Application and Enforcement in the EU* (Verlag CH Beck 2008) (Study JLS/C4/2005/03, September 2007)
Hess B, 'The Brussels I Regulation: Recent Case Law of the Court of Justice and the Commission's Proposed Recast' (2012) 49 Common Market Law Review 1075
——'Back to the Past: BREXIT und das europäische internationale Privat- und Verfahrensrecht' (2016) 36 Praxis des Internationalen Privat- und Verfahrensrechts (IPRax) 409
——'The Unsuitability of the Lugano Convention (2007) to Serve as a Bridge between the UK and the EU after Brexit' (2018) Max Planck Institute Luxemburg for Procedural Law Research Paper Series No 2018 (2)
——'Reforming the Brussels Ibis Regulation: Perspectives and Prospects' (2021) MPILux Research Paper Series 2021 (4) <MPILux Research Paper Series> accessed 31 August 2021
Hill J, *Cross-Border Consumer Contracts* (OUP 2008)
——and Chong A, *International Commercial Disputes* (4th revised edn, Hart Publishing 2010)

——and Ní Shúilleabháin M, *Clarkson & Hill's Conflict of Laws* (5th edn, OUP 2016)
Hohfeld WN, 'Some Fundamental Legal Conceptions as Applied in Judicial Reasoning' (1913) 23 Yale Law Journal 16
Holmes OW, *The Common Law* (Macmillan 1882)
Illmer M, 'Neutrality Matters—Some Thoughts About the Rome Regulations and the so called Dichotomy of Substance and Procedure in European Private International Law' (2009) 28 Civil Justice Quarterly 237
Johnson A, 'Morrison v National Australia Bank: Foreign Securities and the Jurisdiction to Prescribe' in D Fairgrieve and E Lein (eds), *Extraterritoriality and Collective Redress* (OUP 2012) 379
Jones RE and MacCormack G, 'Obligations' in E Metzger (ed), *A Companion to Justinian's Institutions* (Duckworth 1998) 127
Joseph QC D, *Jurisdiction and Arbitration Agreements and their Enforcement* (Sweet & Maxwell 2010)
Keyes M (ed), *Optional Choice of Court Agreements in Private International Law* (Ius Comparatum, Global Studies in Comparative Law, Springer 2019)
Kramer X and Sorabji J, 'International Business Courts in Europe and Beyond: A Global Competition for Justice?' [2019] Erasmus Law Review 1
Kruger T, *Civil Jurisdiction Rules of the EU and their Impact on Third States* (OUP 2008)
Lambrecht P and Peetermans E, 'The Brussels International Business Court: Initial Overview and Analysis' [2019] Erasmus Law Review 42
Landbrecht J, 'The Concepts of "Injustice" and "Public Policy" in Article 6(c) of the Hague Choice of Court Convention' (2019) 15 Journal of Private International Law 339
Law J and Martin EA (eds), *Oxford Dictionary of Law* (7th edn, OUP 2009)
Layton A, 'The Brussels I Regulation in the International Legal Order: Some Reflections on Reflectiveness' in E Lein (ed), *The Brussels I Review Proposal Uncovered* (BIICL 2012) 75
Layton A, 'Shadows and Illusions in European Private International Law: Reflections on Reflexive Effect' in G Barrett and others (eds), *The Future of Legal Europe: Will We Trust in It?* (Springer 2021)
Lehmann M, 'Regulation, Global Governance and Private International Law: Squaring the Triangle' (2020) 16 Journal of Private International Law 1
Lein E and others, 'Factors Influencing International Litigants' Decisions to Bring Commercial Claims to the London Based Courts' Ministry of Justice Analytical Series 2015 <Ministry of Justice Analytical Series 2015 - Factors Influencing International Litigants' Decisions to Bring Commercial Claims to the London Based Courts (publishing.service.gov.uk)> accessed 31 August 2021
MacCormick N, *Legal Reasoning and Legal Theory* (Clarendon Press 1978)
Magnus U and Mankowski P, *Brussels Ibis Regulation* (2nd edn, Sellier European Law Publishers 2012)
Mailhé F, 'France: A Game of Asymmetries, Optional and Asymmetrical Choice of Court Agreements Under French Case Law' in M Keyes (ed), *Optional Choice of Court Agreements in Private International Law* (Ius Comparatum, Global Studies in Comparative Law, Springer 2019) 197. <https://doi.org/10.1007/978-3-030-23914-5_8> accessed 31 August 2021
Mance J, 'Exclusive Jurisdiction Agreements and European Ideals' (2004) 120 Law Quarterly Review 357
Mance Lord, 'The Future of Private International Law' (2005) 1 Journal of Private International Law 185

——'Should the law be certain?' The Oxford Shrieval Lecture given in the University Church of St Mary The Virgin, Oxford on 11 October 2011
Marshall BA, 'Reconsidering the Proper Law of the Contract' (2012) 13 Melbourne Journal of International Law 1
McLachlan C, *Lis Pendens in International Litigation* (Martinus Nijhoff 2009)
McClean D and Abou-Nigm VR, *Morris: The Conflict of Laws* (9th edn, Sweet and Maxwell 2016)
McParland M, *The Rome I Regulation on the Law Applicable to Contractual Obligations* (OUP 2015)
Merrett L, *Employment Contracts in Private International Law* (OUP 2011)
——'The Future Enforcement of Asymmetric Jurisdiction Agreements' (2018) 67 International and Comparative Law Quarterly 37.
——'International Employment Cases Post-Brexit: Choice of Law, Territorial Scope, Jurisdiction and Enforcement' (2021) 50 Industrial Law Journal 343
Michaels R, 'Two Paradigms of Jurisdiction' [2006] Michigan Journal of International Law 1003
——'The Functional Method of Comparative Law' in M Reimann and R Zimmermann (eds), *The Oxford Handbook of Comparative Law* (OUP 2006) 339
——'Some Fundamental Jurisdictional Conceptions as Applied in Judgment Conventions' in E Gottschalk and others (eds), *Conflict of Laws in a Globalized World* (Cambridge University Press 2007) 29
——'Post-critical Private International Law: From Politics to Technique' in H Muir Watt and D P Fernandez Arroyo (eds), *Private International Law and Global Governance* (OUP 2014) 54
——'Comparative Law and Private International Law' in J Basedow and others (eds), *Elgar Encyclopedia of Private International Law* (Edward Elgar 2017)
Mills A, 'Variable Geometry, Peer Governance, and the Public International Perspective on Private International Law' in H Muir Watt and DP Fernandez Arroyo (eds), *Private International Law and Global Governance* (OUP 2014) 245
——*Party Autonomy in Private International Law* (Cambridge University Press 2018)
Mortensen R, 'Brexit and Private International Law in the Commonwealth' (2021) 17 Journal of Private International Law 18
Moses M, *The Principles and Practice of International Commercial Arbitration* (3rd edn, Cambridge University Press 2017)
Muir Watt H, 'Party Autonomy in International Contracts: From the Makings of a Myth to the Requirements of Global Governance' (2010) 3 European Review of Contract Law 1
——and Fernandez Arroyo DP (eds), *Private International Law and Global Governance* (OUP 2014)
Niboyet ML, 'Le Principe de Confiance Mutuelle et Les Injonctions Anti-Suit' in P de Vareilles-Sommieres (ed), *Forum Shopping in the European Judicial Area* (Hart Publishing 2007) 77
Nietzsche F, *Nietzsche: Human, All Too Human: A Book for Free Spirits* (RJ Hollingdale ed, Cambridge University Press 1996)
Nygh P, 'The Preliminary Draft Hague Convention on Jurisdiction and Foreign Judgments in Civil and Commercial Matters' in P Borchers and J Zekoll (eds), *International Conflict of Laws for the Third Millennium: Essays in Honor of Friedrich K Juenger* (Transnational Publishers 2001) 264
——and Pocar F, 'Report on the Preliminary Draft Convention on Jurisdiction and Foreign Judgments in Civil and Commercial Matters,' Prel Doc 11, August 2000 <FAX MESSAGE (1 page) (hcch.net)> accessed 31 August 2021

Nygh PE, *Autonomy in International Contracts* (OUP 1999)
Ooi M, 'Choice of Law in the Shifting Sands of Securities Trading' in A Dickinson and E Peel (eds), *A Conflict of Laws Companion: Essays in Honour of Adrian Briggs* (OUP 2021) ch 8
Peel E, 'Exclusive Jurisdiction Agreements: Purity and Pragmatism in the Conflict of Laws' [1998] Lloyd's Maritime and Commercial Law Quarterly 182
Permanent Bureau of the Conference, *Convention of 30 June 2005 on Choice of Court Agreements: Text and Explanatory Report by Trevor Hartley and Masato Dogauchi* (HCCH Publications 2013) <Tome III off print.indb (hcch.net)> accessed 31 August 2021
Pitel SGA, 'A Modern Approach to Enforcing Foreign Judgments' [2004] Lloyd's Maritime and Commercial Law Quarterly 289
Plender R and Wilderspin M, *The European Private International Law of Obligations* (4th edn, Sweet & Maxwell 2015)
——*The European Private International Law of Obligations* (5th edn, Sweet & Maxwell 2020)
Pocar F, 'The New Lugano Convention on Jurisdiction and the Recognition and Enforcement of Judgments in Civil and Commercial Matters' (2008) 10 Yearbook of Private International Law 1
Portland's annual Commercial Courts Report for 2021. <Commercial Courts Report 2021 - Portland (portland-communications.com)> accessed 31 August 2021
Prince P, 'Bhopal, Bougainville and Ok Tedi: Why Australia's Forum Non Conveniens Approach is Better' (1998) 47 International and Comparative Law Quarterly 573
Raphael T, 'Do as You Would Be Done by? System-transcendent Justification and Anti-Suit Injunctions' [2016] Lloyd's Maritime and Commercial Law Quarterly 256
Raphael QC T, *The Anti-Suit Injunction* (2nd edn, OUP 2019)
Ratković T and Zgrabljić Rotar D, 'Choice-of-Court Agreements under the Brussels I Regulation (Recast)' (2013) 9 Journal of Private International Law 245
Reed A, 'To Be Or Not To Be: The Forum Non Conveniens Performance Acted out on Anglo-American Courtroom Stages' (2000) 29 Georgia Journal of International and Comparative Law 31
Reimann M, 'Comparative Law and Private International Law' in M Reimann and R Zimmermann (eds), *The Oxford Handbook of Comparative Law* (OUP 2006) 1363
——and Zimmermann R (eds), *The Oxford Handbook of Comparative Law* (OUP 2006)
Reuters T, 'The Impact of Brexit on Dispute Resolution Clauses', 23 July 2018
Rogerson P, *Collier's Conflict of Laws* (4th edn, Cambridge University Press 2013)
——'Chapter 11—Arts 29–30' in A Dickinson and E Lein, *The Brussels I Regulation Recast* (OUP 2015) 321
——'After BREXIT: Is International Commercial Litigation in London Doomed?' New Law Journal (2016) <https://www.newlawjournal.co.uk/content/litigation-post-brexit-0> accessed 31 August 2021
Roodt C, 'Reflections on Theory, Doctrine and Method in Choice of Law' (2007) 40 Comparative and International Law Journal of Southern Africa 76
Rühl G, 'The Protection of Weaker Parties in the Private International Law of the European Union: A Portrait of Inconsistency and Conceptual Truancy' (2014) 10 Journal of Private International Law 335
——'Human Rights in Global Supply Chains: Do We Need to Amend the Rome II-Regulation?' (Conflictoflaws.net, 9 October 2020) <https://conflictoflaws.net/2020/human-rights-in-global-supply-chains-do-we-need-to-amend-the-rome-ii-regulation/> accessed 31 August 2021
Schulz A, 'Reflection Paper to Assist in the Preparation of a Convention on Jurisdiction and Recognition and Enforcement of Foreign Judgments in Civil and Commercial Matters'

(Preliminary Document No 19 of August 2002) in *Proceedings of the Twentieth Session of the Hague Conference on Private International Law* (Permanent Bureau of the Conference, Intersentia 2010).

Sim C, 'Choice of Law and Anti-Suit Injunctions: Relocating Comity' (2013) 62 International and Comparative Law Quarterly 703

Symeonides SC, *The American Choice-of-Law Revolution: Past, Present and Future* (Martinus Nijhoff 2006)

——*Codifying Choice of Law Around the World* (OUP 2014)

Tetley W, 'Mixed Jurisdictions: Common Law v. Civil Law (Codified and Uncodified)' (2000) 60 Louisiana Law Review 677

Torremans P (ed), *Cheshire, North & Fawcett: Private International Law* (15th edn, OUP 2017)

van Calster G, *European Private International Law* (3rd edn, Hart Publishing 2021)

von Hein J, 'Back to the Future—(Re-)Introducing the Principle of Ubiquity for Business-related Human Rights Claims' (Conflictoflaws.net, 12 October 2020) <https://conflictoflaws.net/2020/back-to-the-future-re-introducing-the-principle-of-ubiquity-for-business-related-human-rights-claims/> accessed 31 August 2021

von Mehren AT and Gottschalk E, *Adjudicatory Authority in Private International Law* (Martinus Nijhoff 2007)

Vos G, 'A View from the Business and Property Courts in London' [2019] Erasmus Law Review 10

Walker J, 'The Great Canadian Comity Experiment Continues' (2004) 120 Law Quarterly Review 365

——'The Distant Shore: Discretion and the Extent of Judicial Jurisdiction' in A Dickinson and E Peel (eds), *A Conflict of Laws Companion: Essays in Honour of Adrian Briggs* (OUP 2021) ch 3, 53–75

Walker N, 'Brexit Timeline: Events Leading to the UK's Exit from the European Union' (6 January 2021) House of Commons Library Research Briefing <Brexit timeline: events leading to the UK's exit from the European Union - House of Commons Library (parliament.uk)> accessed 31 August 2021

Weller M, 'Choice of Court Agreements under Brussels Ia and under the Hague Convention: Coherences and Clashes' (2017) 13 Journal of Private International Law 91

Wittgenstein L, *Philosophical Investigations* (Blackwell 1953)

Index

For the benefit of digital users, indexed terms that span two pages (e.g., 52–53) may, on occasion, appear on only one of those pages.

www.ingramcontent.com/pod-product-compliance
Ingram Content Group UK Ltd.
Pitfield, Milton Keynes, MK11 3LW, UK
UKHW020810290926
15470UKWH00003B/1078

9 780192 848116